Founding Factions

Founding Factions

How Majorities Shifted and Aligned to Shape the U.S. Constitution

Jeremy C. Pope and Shawn Treier

University of Michigan Press
Ann Arbor

For questions or permissions, please contact um.press.perms@umich.edu

Published in the United States of America by the
University of Michigan Press

Printed and bound by CPI Group (UK) Ltd, Croydon, CR0 4YY

First published December 2020

A CIP catalog record for this book is available from the British Library.

ISBN 978-0-472-13222-5 (hardcover: alk. paper)
ISBN 978-0-472-12732-0 (ebook)

Contents

Digital materials related to this title can be found on the Fulcrum platform via the following citable URL: https://doi.org/10.3998/mpub.11388330

Preface

As this book was put to bed, the Senate voted in the impeachment trial of Donald Trump. Though it is far too early to say what history will make of that episode, it is not too early to remind ourselves that America's political fights—whether they be an impeachment or simply an appropriations bill—are carried out in the shadow of the Constitutional Convention. The influence of the delegates looms large, all of the time. As both sides quote from the *Federalist Papers* and debate the aims of the Founders, we are constantly reminded of their influence, and when we consider that they exerted that influence over two and a quarter centuries ago, their efforts are all the more impressive.

The argument of this book is not that their influence is always positive (or negative). Rather, the argument is, in essence, that we cannot understand our own political fights without understanding what happened in Philadelphia during the summer of 1787. It is not that America's political fights are an extension of theirs, rather that our fights are guided by a complex dance of coalitions that came out of that summer. We never escape them, and so we must understand them. The problem is that we have often simplified that fight a bit too much. It is not that there was no structure or a simple bundle of compromises. There is an underlying structure, but it is not ideological and unidimensional the way that American politics is today. Instead, we find multiple cross-cutting coalitions. The traditional group of five "small" states is there in our findings (CT, NY, NJ, DE, MD), but the other states divide into two categories. The most ardent reformers make up the core of the reforms (MA, PA, VA) and the Deep South (NC, SC, GA), who worked so hard to defend slavery. How those three factions interacted to create a previously unimagined government is the story we tell herein.

Often, we attribute grand historical events to monumental forces, nefarious conspiracies, or indisputable ideas, the outcomes of which were inevitable. These stories are, of course, simplest when they are about good vs. evil or left vs. right. Human beings tend to like stark, binary polar distinctions, delineating a clear matchup between a winner and a loser. In reality, the course of events is much more fractured and complicated, without clear winners or losers.

When we do create these historical poles—reformers vs. conservatives, revolutionaries vs. reactionaries, or, in the case of the Convention, the large states and the small states—we are left with an impoverished picture of the past. Such models or simplifications of the Convention are not necessarily wrong, they are just incomplete. It is not that there were dozens of factions, as some might suggest (Forrest McDonald, for instance). It is that there was a complicated dance of those three factions at the Convention (Small states, Core Reform states, and the Deep South) and no one faction ever completely dominated because each faction always needed a partner to accomplish anything.

The government we have today is an uneasy, untidy collection of the compromises that came out of that three-coalition dance. One coalition formed the Congress and the more powerful national government (Core Reform states with the Deep South). A different coalition (Core Reform states with Small-state defectors) formed an independent executive—an executive so independent that it turns out to be very hard to remove him.[1] That conflict of coalitions at the Convention set up our own fights now and does so, in large measure, through the two key institutions they created: the Congress and the presidency. From the very beginning of the republic, those two institutions have been the battlefield of our political fights. Whether it was during the Jacksonian period fights over the spoils system, the post-Civil War disagreements over reconstruction, Wilson's conception of the presidency vs. the new "normalcy" of the 1920s, or more recent fights over war powers, executive orders, and the limits of the imperial presidency, Americans fight innumerable political battles over the relationship between these two branches of government.

Knowing how those institutions came into being is an essential part of any American politics scholar's toolkit. It is our aim in this book to tell that story.

So, what is it we can learn from the Convention? Why did we write this book? In a nutshell, it is because we want people to better understand the coalitions that created the different features of the American political system. There was no single alignment that created this system; instead, it was a series of overlapping alliances and arrangements that created a government of competing institutions—a much more powerful Congress, but one that faced an independent chief executive. How the various coalitions formed to create different constitutional majorities in favor of each part of the national government is the key.

The most prominent issue up for debate at the Convention was representation, an argument that continues today and is especially vexing to progressives who believe that a more equitable distribution of representatives would not include a Senate that favors Republicans. They argue for one person, one vote, while the right defends the representation of states as political entities. At least that is true in the current configuration, but it is subject to change because these "ideological" positions also align well with the office-seeking interests of the left- and right-leaning parties. At least for now, Democratic votes are concentrated in a relatively smaller number of urban areas concentrated in fewer states, and the American form of government continues to represent states as distinct polities in the form of the Senate because the Convention and the Constitution's ratification solidified that practice.

While these divisions fall upon partisan lines that the Framers could not have anticipated, the principles at stake actually are echoes of the divisions at the Convention. James Madison certainly was not in favor of the resulting compromise. Like many of the Reform coalition, he cared a great deal about the inherent unfairness of a single state having a single vote and believed the basis of a national government should be its people (albeit without any modern ideas of universal rights). Reformers like James Madison, Gouverneur Morris, and Alexander Hamilton wanted to see a more representative body that would help lead to a much stronger national government. This much is well known and understood. What we often forget, however, is that these reformist ideas had to be embodied in a particular coalition of state votes because (as seen below) the states were still the relevant voting units. Madison and Morris were from states sympathetic to these changes (Virginia and Pennsylvania). Hamilton was less able to affect the debates because his own state (New York) was not sympathetic.

As it turned out, the states in agreement with representation reforms were the slaveholding states. They anticipated gaining more representation in the future with much greater population growth (an incorrect belief, as it happened). The Carolinas and Georgia were apparently content with a more proportional scheme of representation in the government and to make that government more powerful, at least in part, we will argue, because of slavery.

Today, when the left argues for more representative bodies, they ironically pay their respects to the arguments championed by the slaveholders of the past. Indeed, one might say that the principle of one person, one vote is a legacy, in part, of slavery (see also Rakove, 1996, particularly chapter 4). This is not to say that the arguments of modern progressives are rooted in the same calculation of the slaveholders, merely to note that the institutional change that the slaveholders achieved is one that helped lead to the doctrine of one person, one vote. Facts like this lead the careful student of the Convention to see just how complicated the past can be and how straight-line projections of our own categories and arguments onto the past (or vice versa) are often problematic.

Of course, this also should force us to realize that the cleavage of slaveholding was one of the most important distinctions across state delegations, and the legacy of race and slavery deeply remains with us still in ways that are difficult to predict, and sometimes even understand. James Madison, in a desperate hour, as his plans for government reform appeared to be disappearing, pointed out the importance of the distinction between slaveholding and non-slaveholding states (or, as he put it, northern and southern states, see chapter 1, p. 5). He was right to point to this cleavage because American history often turned on the question of how slaves and slaveholders would be treated in government.

The issues of representation and national power are often conflated, but one of our contributions is to show that they constitute distinct concerns and, accordingly, are decided upon separately. While the coalitions that increased the power of the national government are the same (reform and slave states), the Core Reform states are much more enthusiastic about a strong national government. In contrast, the Deep South struggled with balancing the necessity of a strong national government against the possibility that it could turn against its own interests (e.g., slavery). Though the southern slaveholders could not know the future, the strong central power created by the national government would one day doom their peculiar institution.

We should note that the government created by these complex coalitions was not merely concerned with representation and increased federal power. The new executive was one commensurate to this newly arranged national government. After a great deal of debate, they decided to make this executive very independent of Congress—in contrast to the earlier plan in which they had originally decided to make him a creature of the legislature, dependent on their ideas and interests. This conflict between presidency and Congress helped not only to define much of American political history, but also, in ways we are only coming to grips with today, to create the need for two parties in American political life. A central feature of the American government is that the parties must coordinate across multiple, independent branches. It is an historical irony that the strong, independent executive was created by a completely different set of interests—the Core Reform states allied with the willing members of the Small-state faction. This incongruity is now one of the defining characteristics of the U.S. Government.

The implication is that it was not simply the "reformers" who created these changes and this ultimate outcome, particularly with regard to the presidency. The slaveholding states were not part of the coalition to form this new independent executive; indeed, they were broadly not in favor of it. The new executive came about because of an alliance of Small-state delegates allying themselves with the reformers, meaning that no one majority faction controlled the outcome. It was, instead, an emergent agenda that led to a completely unanticipated form of government.

It is common to say that the framers of the Constitution did not anticipate parties. This is accurate, in most ways, but what this formulation misses is the deep truth that the Constitution incentivizes the kind of parties necessary to capture such an unwieldy form of government with multiple centers of power. Perhaps this is not by design, but the need is no less true for the lack of a purposeful design. America's partisan fights over the presidency and the Congress—and the relative status of those institutions—have helped define much of political history, but these fights remain difficult because of the structure created in 1787. Even today, often the best the parties are able to do is to emphasize the easier branch to control—the presidency—rather than to truly coordinate across the institutions (let alone the courts). At the beginning of the twenty-first century, members of Congress defer to the president of their own party (and oppose presidents of the other party) but do not truly try to control the Congress because the institutional design is so difficult to fully master. Executive deference is the most that the parties have been able to come up with so far.

That is the deepest lesson of this book. The Convention produced a terribly complicated institutional design that had both positive and negative features. This is not a book about the institutional design per se, but rather where that complex government came from. The central finding is that the underlying structure came from a fight among three coalitions trying to find a compromise position of some reform. In the end, the design ended up being no one group's clear intention or strategy. It took all of them to create this unplanned final product.

We have many people to thank. First, we deeply appreciate the excellent data collection skills of Josephine Borich, Tatiana Flexman, Audrey Hayes, Mallory Rush, Alissa Wilkinson, and Morgan Williamson. Morgan was especially helpful in administering some of the data collection and in helping Jeremy Pope organize some of this material. Jack Vassau helped us both put together the index and find many of the final corrections and problems in the manuscript. Errors are our own, but we are grateful to all of these students.

The manuscript benefited from many conferences over the years. The members of the research lab in the Center for the Study of Elections and Democracy at BYU commented on multiple sections on multiple occasions. And the Center (under the leadership of our friend, J. Quin Monson) helped give funding for a book conference that helped us formulate our ideas. We are particularly indebted to Robert McGuire, Alan Gibson, and Keith Dougherty who attended that conference, as well as student assistance from Alejandra Gimenez Aldridge and several BYU faculty who attended, including Clayne L. Pope, Richard Kimball, and especially Chris Karpowitz, who commented on multiple chapters of that iteration of the book. Keith Dougherty was particularly helpful in the way he helped us conceive of the contributions the book could make and both what was good and bad about that iteration.

This work benefitted from many presentations, including at such places as the "James Madison and the Founding Scholar Conference, Robert H. Smith Center for the Constitution" at Madison's home in Montpelier; a University of Georgia department seminar, as well as "The American

Constitution: 225th Anniversary of the Ratification," also held at the University of Georgia; the Behavior and Institutions Seminar, Department of Political Science, Duke University; the Inter-university United States Studies Conference at Monash University, Melbourne, Victoria, Australia; a Liberty Fund Colloquium on the founding in Park City, Utah; the Conference of the Australian and New Zealand American Studies Association (ANZASA), as well as multiple presentations at the Midwest Political Science Association, American Political Science Association, and Southern Political Science Association meetings.

Jeremy C. Pope has long had the good fortune to teach a class on this subject at Brigham Young University and has benefitted enormously from discussions with excellent students—too many to name here, though Alejandra Gimenez Aldridge, James Lee, and Soren Schmidt stand out.

The data collection was funded from the BYU Political Science Department's Constitution Fund, and multiple drafts of chapters were given to members of that department in seminars.

At the University of Michigan Press, two anonymous reviewers went above and beyond the call of duty providing many comments that dramatically improved the draft. We thank Elizabeth Demers, as well as the entire team of editors at Michigan for their work on the book.

Jeremy wants to personally thank his family, daughters Grace, Carly, and Delaney, for their patience with being dragged to every Constitution-related site their father could think of, and his wife, Kori, for her endless patience with the process of book drafting—and academia generally. She is a wonder. Jeremy's parents, Clayne L. and Carolyn M. Pope, deserve much of the thanks for his interest in this subject, beginning with childhood. The fingerprints of Clayne L. Pope's thinking on how to think through social science are all over Jeremy's contributions.

Shawn thanks the United States Studies Centre at the University of Sydney, where he held a postdoctoral fellowship from September 2011 to August 2012 to work on this project and related articles. The time spent at the Centre was critical to the development and refinement of the statistical methods in this book, and we received valuable feedback through discussions at Centre-hosted events. The Centre's support has continued throughout the book project, hosting Shawn as a visiting fellow since June 2013 and providing research support.

Finally, Shawn would like to thank his parents, Dale and Deborah, along with his sister, Jen, and her family, for their steadfast support from beginning to end. As a consequence, Jeremy has seen all of their homes through Skype. Most of all, Shawn would like to thank his partner, Katrine, for her support and understanding through the final push to publication. Not surprisingly, her elevator summary of the book is also much better than Shawn's or Jeremy's. Errors are, of course, our own.

CHAPTER I

Understanding a Secretive Convention

> Early in the sessions, one of the delegates dropped a copy of the propositions which were before the Convention for consideration, and it was picked up by another of the delegates and handed to General Washington. After the debates of the day were over, just before putting the question of adjournment, Washington arose from his seat and reprimanded the member for his carelessness. "I must entreat gentlemen to be more careful, lest our transactions get into the newspapers, and disturb the public repose by premature speculations. I know not whose paper it is, but there it is (throwing it down on the table), let him who owns it take it." At the same time, he bowed, picked up his hat, and quitted the room with a dignity so severe that every person seemed alarmed. It is something remarkable that no person ever owned the paper.
>
> —William Pierce (Farrand 1966, vol. III, 86–87)

> If you think of the past as a landscape, then history is the way we represent it, and it's that act of representation that lifts us above the familiar to let us experience vicariously what we can't experience directly: a wider view.
>
> —John Lewis Gaddis, *The Landscape of History*, 5

After the fact, we can only represent history, we cannot really reexperience it. When it comes to the Federal Convention of 1787—popularly known as the Constitutional Convention—part of the reason for that fact is the veil of secrecy the delegates cast over their deliberations. Early on, they decided that the rules would include

> That no copy be taken of any entry on the journal during the sitting of the House without the leave of the House.

and

> That nothing spoken in the House be printed, or otherwise published, or communicated without leave.

To enforce these rules, they made sure that "members only be permitted to inspect the journal" (Farrand 1966, vol. I, 15–16). Further, they rejected the idea that a member of their House could call for a recorded division of the individual votes,[1] on the grounds that it was "unnecessary" or that such a roll call might "be an obstacle to a change [of opinions] on conviction" (Farrand 1966, vol. I, 10). These decisions mean that we know far less than we otherwise might about the events of the Convention. If our goal as students of the Convention is to find the best possible representation of that event, in order to achieve that wider view suggested in the above quotation, we are faced with several problems.

First, what we do know about the Convention comes from a biased lens, as Madison (and the other notetakers) did not simply record the debates; rather, they selected and probably interpreted some of the speakers and their motivations (Bilder 2015). The notetakers were hardly recording devices. In fact, the Convention never even tried to keep complete records.

Second, and even worse, the delegates themselves had little interest in creating clear records—especially of individual votes and opinions. Rufus King of Massachusetts argued that clear records of individual votes were unnecessary because "the acts of the Convention were not to bind the Constituents" (10), implying that delegates to this convention—not yet the Constitutional Convention[2]—may have had the power to produce a proposal for a new government, but they lacked the power to make any citizens support that proposal.

Though these decisions for secrecy and lack of clear records only took them a few minutes, this confidentiality leaves the modern student of the Convention with a serious lack of knowledge, and the need (or at least the strong desire) to fill in those gaps. Scholars have largely tried to remedy this situation by analyzing the notes of the Convention collected by Farrand (1966) and then Hutson (1987). A massive enterprise of textual analysis has followed in their wake, judging the speeches, the motions, and the notes of the Convention—largely those taken by James Madison. What scholars have not done as well is analyze the voting at the Convention—which is very difficult because of the structure of voting—in which individuals cast ballots that were aggregated into state votes (discussed more below).

When we interpret the Constitution as relying largely (or solely) on the written record of the interpreted speeches, we are required to fill in the gaps—sometimes with our best guesses, sometimes with our own preferences about the way the Constitution should look, and sometimes only with what we have heard might be true about the Convention. In this way, the decision for secrecy has had far-reaching consequences. Because the event was not rigorously documented at its inception, because the voting was not exhaustively recorded, and because so many different interpretations seem possible, people can employ many different interpretations of this event—and they have.

With notable exceptions, like Jillson (1988), McGuire (2003), and Heckelman and Dougherty (2013), among others, the bulk of Convention analysis focuses on the text of the speeches and debate as the guide to the debates in Philadelphia. While words and speeches have their own distinct and important value, they are not a substitute for the actual votes and positions taken. The votes—part of an unfolding agenda of the Convention—provide the real, deep structure around which speeches were offered. It is this deep structure that can be obscured without a direct focus on voting. While the speeches and text have received lavish attention from multiple perspectives—all of it fairly systematic and clear, if sometimes controversial—the voting has been sprinkled into most analyses but rarely in a systematic way. It is not an exaggeration to say that, with a few of the exceptions cited above, the scholarship on the Convention sets aside systematic analysis of the most fundamental element of the Convention: voting.

In some respects, this focus on speeches is a reasonable approach. As noted above, we do not have most of the individual votes. Moreover, text can convey nuance and meaning that mere votes cannot. It can sometimes shed light on interests and philosophies that motivated the voting. Textual analysis lends itself well to narrative accounts of the Convention and provides a way of connecting statements in the Convention to the broader historical context. So textual analysis has many virtues. However, it is not the only way to represent the Convention and, in some respects, may not even be the best way to represent the deep structure of coalitions and alliances at the Convention. The problem with speeches is that they are essentially reflections on what is being discussed at any given time. Delegates did not speak about the president in the abstract. They spoke about the president because the length of term, the mode of election, or some other aspect of that office was under discussion. It was the proposals and the voting that created the coalitions and alliances—and it is to this deep structure of voting that speeches responded.

The voting record of the Convention provides an unambiguous record of delegation positions (with some information about individual delegates). It is the record of what they actually decided, and it is less ambiguous than are many speeches—though it obviously requires careful analysis as well. Despite these virtues, the technology to analyze the roll call record is not a standard part of the toolkit of historians, so this aspect of the Convention has not been given the attention it deserves. However, the tools of roll call analysis, common in political science, allow us to build full multidimensional maps that represent a crucial, wider view of the Convention. This book employs just that strategy to map the positions of the delegations, many delegates, and most of the proposals at the Convention, all in service to offering a better understanding of what happened in Philadelphia. With this wider view in hand, we can say confidently that some important "facts" about the Convention are either incomplete, or plain wrong.

A key change in our thinking needs to be about the coalitions. Though it is common to speak of the nationalists who inhabited the "large states" debating the conservatives who came from "small states," this is an incomplete picture of the Convention. Indeed, even as the debates were proceeding, the nature of the coalitions at the Convention were part of the debate and under dispute. James Madison's famous allusion to the real interests of the different coalitions illustrates just how fluid the coalitions could be.

This necessitates both a new understanding of the Convention and what it meant to be a "nationalist," because it was more complicated than simply favoring reform—we have to distinguish different types of reform in our map of the Convention.

1.1 A New Map of the Convention

By July 13, the delegates had grown weary of an unending discussion of representation. They had already appointed a "grand" committee of one member from each state to draft a compromise that would satisfy enough delegates to win a majority, a proposal that was still being debated—much to James Madison's chagrin. He wanted to move past this debate and finish structuring the government they were aiming to design. In fact, he believed the Convention had already reached agreement on making representation proportional to state population size, though he must have known that this victory was still tenuous and subject to debate. On Friday, July 13 the delegates were still going back and forth about how many representatives each state should have. It was at this moment that James Madison made a somewhat odd statement:

> having always conceived that the difference of interest in the U. States lay not between the large & small, but the N. & Southn. States, and finding that the number of members allotted to the N. States was greatly superior, that should have preferred, an addition of two members to the S. States, to wit one to N & 1 to S. Carla. rather than of one member to Virga. He liked the present motion, because it tended to moderate the views of both of the opponents & advocates for rating very high, the negroes.[3]

This was really just a continuation of a theme that Madison had broached two weeks earlier on June 30 when he said, "the states were divided into different interests not by their difference of size but by other circumstances . . . [which] did not lie between the large and small States: it lay between the Northern and Southern, and if any defensive power were necessary, it ought to be mutually given to these two interests" (Farrand 1966, 486–87).

Madison's speeches can be interpreted in many ways, and they have been by historians and other students of the Convention. Both Beard (1913) and Farrand (1913), though they rely heavily on the speeches as a whole, tend to ignore speeches related to slavery, perhaps because both generally downplay slavery as being crucial to the Convention. Carl Van Doren (1948, 103) mentions Madison's thinking as possible grounds for a compromise that would balance representation in one chamber against that of another. McDonald (1965), in his treatise on the power of economics at the Convention, mentions slavery with respect to navigation acts, but because he ignores its implications for representation, he also makes little of Madison's speeches. Catherine Drinker Bowen (1966), though she does reference these speeches, focuses not on the question of slavery per se, but on how Madison was also impugning small states like Connecticut that had not paid their fair share to the treasury of the young government (129). Writing at the same time, Rossiter (1966) ignores this aspect of the debate.

Rakove (1996) makes, by far, the most of Madison's speeches. He claimed that the earlier speech had "injected a new argument, broaching a subject so far left unexplored" (68). He also notes that immediately after Madison's failed attempt to raise slavery as an issue on July 2, the Convention elected a Grand Committee that would eventually produce the Great Compromise. Throughout, Rakove implies that Madison's speeches were an attempt to produce a legislative victory on representation. And while Richard Beeman (2010) calls Madison's claims "profound," he, like Bowen, goes on to emphasize the "cheap shot" at Connecticut without placing much emphasis on how Madison's "profound" claim may have altered the debate. His analysis generally suggests this speech about North and South was not terribly important. And, of course, perhaps it was not, but it is difficult to say from the text alone.

Many authors (and we could multiply this list substantially, but it would not alter the conclusion) interpret Madison's speeches in different ways, some placing great weight on the speech, others ignoring it, and still others arguing that the speech itself was important, but not the specific claim about slavery. Which is the correct interpretation? And what does it mean for slavery or the mode of representation at the Convention? Rakove's interpretation—that Madison is injecting a new dimension into the debates—is certainly possible, but does the idea that slavery was separate from questions of representation match up to the record of voting? Furthermore, how are we to know which interpretation is correct? There is no obvious method of textual interpretation that can settle this question. And, in fact, the list above is not really exhaustive.

From our perspective, the key point in Madison's speech was that he knew the coalitions were in flux. On some issues, the conventional "large" vs. "small" state divide was paramount. But, clearly, Madison could sense that other coalitions were possible because he was worried about them. Consider the possibility that Madison references the obvious sectional divide because it reinforces an existing division within the Convention. Though Madison's speech could reference many possible sectional differences, the most obvious possibility is slavery. Madison's speech was made in the context of a series of votes leading up to the Great Compromise—something Madison regarded as such a great failure that, on the day after this vote, he described a special meeting "before the hour of the Convention" where the allies of reform met and debated responses to this turn of events, but without reaching any firm conclusions (Farrand 1966, vol. II, 20). He made clear that withdrawing from the Convention was a real possibility. At the time Madison made his slavery remarks, he was working very hard to stop the eventual outcome—a compromise that gutted the idea of proportional representation. He was trying to keep all of the southern states in line (and he would eventually lose both North Carolina and Massachusetts from his coalition).

The maps of the agenda and the voting displayed below thus suggest an alternative interpretation of Madison's speech. Instead of raising a novel issue, Madison was trying to reinforce the coalition that supported representational reform with an appeal to those states that favored it (Massachusetts, Pennsylvania, and Virginia) united with the three southernmost states (the Carolinas and Georgia). This was the group that Madison felt could create the government he envisioned. In the end, of course, Madison lost, and the coalition fell apart when North Carolina defected and Massachusetts divided its vote, and on that turn of events the Great Compromise passed, despite Madison's best efforts.

A typical story about the Convention that pits nationalist (large states) against localist (small states) misses a key element of the debate: this coalition only makes sense on certain dimensions. While Madison may have wanted to align the Deep South with the reform-minded states on this vote, on other questions the coalition would shift, and Madison sometimes would join other coalitions.

We argue that, without a map of the deep structure of voting at the Convention, it is difficult—if not impossible—to know how to interpret these events. Even if the reader ultimately questions some of our choices about this map, the rest of this book will prove the importance of having a map of voting for interpreting the Convention. Many of our current arguments about interpretation of the Constitution turn—at least partially—on questions that were debated in Philadelphia. How much power should the executive have? How would legislators be appointed or elected? And, of course, the overarching question facing political contestants related to the power of government—and in the context of the Convention, the power for which level of government, the national or state governments? Each of these questions benefits from some clarity about the structure of voting. What were delegate and delegation positions on the key questions of reform? How did the agenda impact the ultimate outcomes of the Convention? None of these questions can be answered without a full understanding of the structure of the coalitions at the Convention.

Our main and most important contribution in this book is to argue that there are *three key coalitions*, not two, as is often described in the literature. Most of our other points flow from this insight. It was the alliance of the core reformers with the slave interests that helped change representation and make a stronger national government. But when it came time to create a strong executive, it was a group of small-state delegates who provided the crucial votes to create a strong president. Traditional accounts gloss over the complicated coalition politics that produced these important compromises. Our contribution is to show the specific voting alignments that created these compromises. It is true that the delegates came with common purposes, but they were divided by both interests and ideas into three cross-cutting factions. There was no persistent dominant coalition of reformers or nationalists; rather, there was a series of minority factions that allied with one another on the major issues to fashion the compromise. In this sense, the Constitutional Convention is like a Supreme Court opinion where a small number of justices (conceivably only one) controls the balance, with blocs of justices on opposite sides of the question. In the case of the Convention, the small group that dominated came from the Core Reform states: Massachusetts, Pennsylvania, and Virginia. This group had to work for their reforms by convincing members of the other factions to support them.

Traditionally, the literature (especially the historical literature) explains the compromises by emphasizing how two groups—the nationalist reformers and their small-state opponents—argued about the defining issues. To the degree that coalitions are described, they are often just explained in terms of the size of groups related to representation. The "large states" favored reforms against the "small states" who opposed such reforms. Our contention is that there were two separate coalitions that created the ultimate "nationalist" position, and these coalitions diverged because different factions favored the two major institutions created at the Convention: the Congress and the presidency.

Table 1.1 provides a representation of our explanation of the coalitions and how the different factions interacted on the major issues. The Core Reform states—Massachusetts, Pennsylvania, and Virginia—worked with the Deep South states—the Carolinas and Georgia—to enact a powerful but limited legislature with a defined list of powers. This nationalist vision of a stronger government was in conflict with a different vision of a strong, independent executive. The Small states—Connecticut, Delaware, Maryland, New Jersey, and New York—though fixated on preserving state sovereignty (a goal they pushed with the creation of the Senate), also contained many delegates who wanted to reform the executive power in the new government and create a strong executive.

The Convention thus created a Constitution that was not quite the vision of any particular majority. Not only did no single person envision the resulting set of institutions, no one majority coalition supported the complete vision. The resulting Constitution was the result of three different coalitions often working at cross-purposes, so detecting a coherent

Table 1.1 A Visual Representation of Coalition Goals and Actions

Coalition	**Deep South States**		**Core Reform States**		**Small States**
Key motivations	Slavery and representation		Madison's reform proposal		Fixing the executive and state sovereignty
Key outcomes		<u>*Enacts:*</u> A more representative legislature A strong legislature with new powers Origination of revenue bills A more powerful national government		<u>*Enacts:*</u> An independently elected executive A potentially powerful presidency	
What they did not get	Permanent legislative supremacy A complete guarantee for slavery as an institution				True state sovereignty

vision will in some cases prove impossible. Scholars have noted two separate visions of a powerful (but limited) Congress or a powerful (and far less clearly limited) presidency. The former vision fits the ideas of the Deep South and the Core Reform states, but the latter was the project pushed by the reformers and certain key Small-state delegates. In our view, there is no principled reason to pick one of these sides over the other, and the combination was not the aim of any single, coherent majority. But scholars of the Convention must recognize that it was the amalgamation of these competing visions that created a much more powerful national government than either coalition ever envisioned on its own.

In modern politics, conservatives and liberals fight endlessly about the meaning of the Constitution. Conservatives tend to invoke a vision of the Constitution where government is quite limited. They argue that the views of the founders serve as a guide to what government should look like. Liberals tend to be relatively skeptical of these claims—though they also often invoke the founders to push their own political agenda, typically mining the debates in Philadelphia and during ratification for support for modern agendas. No one can settle these claims definitively (and we will not try to do so here), but the entire debate would benefit from some empirical grounding that comes from this altered view of the debates. What claims can we make about voting at the Convention? What "facts" about the Constitution are wrong, or exaggerated, or incomplete?

Two Separate Nationalist Coalitions: Our proposed three-faction structure for the Convention is the key to each of these lessons. They all hinge on the perspective we will offer in chapter 3—that the Convention is not easily divided into groups of nationalist reformers and localist conservatives. If we can demonstrate that the nationalist coalition was complicated, several lessons will flow from that insight. The key point that divided types of nationalists is slavery. While it is well-known that slaveholders were important, our own approach illuminates the fact that slavery divided the types of nationalists: southern nationalists favored congressional power, while other types of nationalists favored a strong executive.

Big Government: While it may be true that the founders were concerned about the proper design of government, limiting government was obviously not everyone's first concern. Certainly Madison and other reformers wanted a much more powerful government (though not everyone agreed; see Robertson 2005). What is less well-understood is how the three complicated factions each played a distinct role in bringing about a larger, stronger national government with both a potentially powerful president and an immediately empowered legislature. Deep South slaveholders, relatively confident in their future power within the legislature, were quite ready to create a much stronger national government. But, wary of too much executive power, they dropped out of the emerging coalition that produced the strong executive and were replaced by the sympathetic smaller states of Delaware and Maryland. In the end, an even more powerful government was created than anyone anticipated.

Compromises: It is common to separate the famous Convention compromises into "good" compromises (over representation) and "bad" ones (over slavery). However, once we understand the shifting majorities and the importance of the Deep South faction's preferences and motivations, the implied separation between these two compromises shrinks (Rakove 1996). Instead of two separate items on the Convention's broader agenda, we begin to see how intimately the Connecticut Compromise was linked to slavery and satisfied both parts of the Deep South–Core Reform state coalition. There was no "Great" compromise without a dismaying "three-fifths" compromise.

Madison's Agenda: Though there is debate over how influential Madison was during the Convention, our maps reveal that Madison's influence at the outset—expressed in the Virginia Plan—is difficult to overstate. However, he won most of his battles at the beginning of the meetings while in alliance with the Deep South. After a few weeks of debate, the Convention had already found the middle ground on each of the key questions, and the range of possible outcomes diminished. At that point, no one could alter the outcome very much, but Madison's work had already been done.[4] Also, Madison's own position was not quite what the literature sometimes describes. While it is true that he was in the vanguard of reform, his actual position comes somewhat closer to the position of the Deep South faction than it does those in the Core Reform states. He may have set the agenda at the beginning, but once the Convention moved on from his key issues of representation and national power, the majority shifted to an alliance between Core Reform states and some of the Small states. By this point, Madison was less central to the outcome.

Delegation Divisions: Madison is also emblematic of a broader theme that receives less attention in the literature than it should—delegations were not consistently unified. Our method is the perfect system for illuminating how delegations differed on key issues. While some delegations were fairly unified (see South Carolina), others were far less so. Virginia may have been for reform, but Madison was quite different from many of his fellow delegates. Even though the states voted as units, the true coalitions were made up of men who disagreed on the outcomes.

Interests: There is a strain of thought among historians that dismisses Charles Beard completely. In some respects, this is deserved. Beard's theory of the Convention was far too simplistic. Complete dismissal of Beard, however, is an overstatement—as has already been shown conclusively by McGuire (2003). Our maps suggest that interests—especially in the form of slavery and proximity to trade—were a powerful influence in Philadelphia. If anything, we fail to appreciate just how important slavery was to the deep structure of voting because it helped define and separate the three key factions.

Originalism: The settled document is the work of many different groups of individuals, all of whom had complicated and contradictory hopes, beliefs, and intentions. While it is true to say that this settlement is a bundle of compromises, to say only that is incomplete. The compromises are the fruit of a particular constellation of factions that aligned in specific ways over the course of the Convention. An originalism that takes into consideration more than just the meanings of words in clauses accepts that the key structures set up by the Constitution came from different (and in some ways contradictory) coalitions. The modern presidency—increasingly powerful over foreign affairs—was created by a coalition of reformers from core states allied with the small-state delegates from the mid-Atlantic who were sympathetic to a strong executive. But the representative structure that defines legislation and the electoral votes was brought into being by an alliance of reformers and slaveholders. Any originalist account of the Convention must take this deep structure of voting into consideration.

This last point about originalism really highlights the need for models and maps of voting at the Convention. Originalism and textualism as modes of historical thinking suggest that the text alone can give us the answers about the meaning of the Constitution. Oddly, this line of reasoning ends up removing much of the politics from a highly political event. After all, if the meanings were clear and understood by the participants, we would need only look up the meanings of the words. The actual debates themselves would become a bit irrelevant, except as ammunition for contending views about what the meanings were. Once one acknowledges the complicated, multidimensional politics of the debates, it becomes difficult to support tidy views of the Convention. For instance, if there are two reform coalitions that created different pieces of the government, how are we to view executive power? Given the disparate views of the framing coalitions, it is impossible to believe that we would not get different answers to that question depending on which coalition we consulted.

Because so many delegates disagreed, and because the final proposals were complicated compromises that did not easily fit within any single perspective on the Constitution, we believe that scholars should aim for a kind of humble originalism where the events of the past are of vital importance but are not necessarily straightforward or easy to understand. The maps we will draw below allow us to show the aims of the different coalitions and how successful or unsuccessful they were in achieving various goals of reform. The text and speeches, by themselves, have difficulty settling these debates, given that they can be interpreted in so many different ways. With so many complex issues and diverging interpretations on the table, it is fruitless to think this can simply be settled by an appeal to the text. It is a text of multiple speakers addressing multiple questions, all on a complicated agenda. In fact, it is so complicated that no single book can really settle all of it, and any book that sheds light on these questions is forced to simplify dramatically, whether that is stated explicitly or not. Simplification is a feature of a narrative account of the debates, a broad historical interpretation of the social and cultural forces on the Convention or anything else.

It is true that none of these views is utterly absent from the literature. For instance, McDonald (1958) certainly talked about the many coalitions in play during the period (he came up with more than 30, applied to the question of ratification), and Waldstreicher (2009) has eloquently written about the role of slavery at the Convention. Our aim is to show which claims hold water when held up against the map of the deep structure of voting at the Convention.

We have no illusions about being able to settle everything, but we do believe that such a model can help reveal what happened. By employing a model and maps like this, we will also be simplifying things greatly, although we hope that our simplifications are relatively transparent and helpful to understanding the deep structure of the debate. Once we know where to place Madison relative to Sherman, or the Great Compromise relative to the Articles of Confederation, it becomes much easier to understand and interpret the key conflicts in the debates. It allows us to fit together the speeches with the overall politics of the Convention. If Madison was reminding southern, slave-owning states (North Carolina, in particular) that proportional representation was vital to their interests, that is very different than if Madison was simply tweaking the Connecticut delegation.

Three things—the issues, the agenda, and the positions of the delegates—make up the politics of the Convention and help explain the massive institutional change that took place in Philadelphia and during the ratification debates. They literally redesigned the Articles of Confederation government out of existence (Jillson and Wilson 1994). Though we cannot answer every question, we will use the tools of political science to analyze the voting record and explain these three components. This perspective on the Convention is certainly not the only one, but it is a vital one and is, so far, not really represented in the literature. Gaddis's point at the beginning of this chapter about finding ways to represent history is one that all students of the past should take seriously. And, though we suspect Gaddis would be annoyed by the quantitative nature of this study, we aspire to create maps that show just what he wants to see: a wider view that systematically takes into consideration the politics, voting, and coalitions.

1.2 The Plan of this Book

To get this wider view, we ask three key questions:

- First, what issues did they agree and disagree about? (chapters 2 and 3)
- Second, how did those agreements and disagreements unfold within the agenda of the debates? (chapters 4, 5, and 6)
- Finally, what does the deep structure of voting at the Convention tell us about the government we have inherited? (chapter 7)

Chapter 2 begins with a brief summary of the previous literature from history, political science, and economics emphasizing current ideas about the dimensions of conflict at the Convention. What issues were primary? When were they discussed? And can the issues be summarized by a limited number of dimensions? Drawing on the literature, our theory suggests that three dimensions were paramount at the Convention: representation, federalism, and national institutional design.

The first set of maps appears in chapter 3, which is devoted to showing the positions of the delegations and delegates at the Convention. The tools of spatial analysis are uniquely helpful here as it allows us to array all of the delegates in an ideological map relative to one another. Everyone knows that Alexander Hamilton favored a strong national government; the advantage of a spatial model is that a reader can immediately see Hamilton in connection with Gouverneur Morris, John Rutledge, or his colleague, Robert Yates. With this map in mind, it is easy to see where delegates agreed and where they disagreed.

Chapters 4, 5, and 6 trace the unfolding issues and votes in Philadelphia. What happened on each of the key dimensions—representation, federalism, and executive power? Here, the maps will address the proposals and questions debated by the delegates. The aim is to show just how far reform succeeded on each of our key dimensions, and where it stalled and when. The picture that emerges is one of a fast-moving agenda that immediately reveals the delegates are prepared to make major changes to the proposed form of government, but eventually realize that there is only so far they can go. Madison wins the early rounds but eventually falls short of his goals. Still, the resulting movement, relative to the status quo of the Articles of Confederation, is substantial and it highlights Madison's achievements.

Chapter 7 finally turns to the implications of our model and the question of Originalism. Our main point has been to show that the Constitutional Convention was not simply a contest between two consistently opposed coalitions, and it was not a myriad of tiny ad hoc coalitions that came together on individual separate issues. Rather, it is best thought of as three consistent state coalitions, two of which could form a majority. The Core Reform states—Massachusetts, Pennsylvania, and Virginia—worked with the Deep South states—North and South Carolina and Georgia—to enact a powerful but limited legislature with a defined list of powers. This vision of a stronger government was in conflict with a different vision of a strong, independent president. The Small states, though fixated on preserving state sovereignty (a goal they pushed with the creation of the Senate), also wanted to fix the executive power in the new government and create a strong executive.

The Convention created a Constitution that was never the vision of any particular group. Not only did no one person envision the resulting set of institutions, no single majority coalition supported the complete vision. What does this mean for Originalism as a philosophy about the Constitution? For one thing, it makes it difficult to proceed with certain forms of originalism. Since the resulting Constitution was the result of three different coalitions often working at cross-purposes, detecting a coherent vision will in some cases prove impossible. Scholars have seen two separate visions of a powerful (but limited) Congress or a powerful (and not clearly limited) presidency. The former vision fit the ideas of the Deep South and the Core Reform states, but the latter was the project pushed by the reformers and certain key Small-state delegates. In our view, there is no principled reason to pick one of these views over the other, and the combination was not the aim of any single, coherent majority. But scholars of the Convention must recognize that it was the amalgamation of these competing visions that created a much more powerful national government than either coalition ever envisioned on its own.

All events, no matter how hallowed or impressive, involve some degree of politicking—the Constitutional Convention was not an exception. Modern accounts of the delegates that ignore the origins of American institutions do so at their peril. We live in a time of rising interest in the Constitution as activists on both the right and the left argue that their proposals inherit the favor and sometimes the endorsement of the framers. This book serves as a corrective to any simplistic view of the debate that suggests that the founders' views are simple and easy to understand. In contrast, we argue that the intense politics of the Convention show just how subtle and impressive their debates were. The deep structure of voting at the Convention shows that they argued over timeless issues of governance and managed to do so in a way that provided lasting, but not simple, answers.

CHAPTER 2

The Dimensions of Conflict

> Resolved that in the opinion of Congress it is expedient that on the second Monday in May next a Convention of delegates who shall have been appointed by the several states be held at Philadelphia for the sole and express purpose of revising the Articles of Confederation and reporting to Congress and the several legislatures such alterations and provisions therein as shall when agreed to in Congress and confirmed by the states render the federal constitution adequate to the exigencies of Government & the preservation of the Union.
>
> —Resolution of the Articles of Confederation Congress authorizing the Federal Convention of 1787

This was the grant of authority to the Constitutional Convention. It is only a single (long) sentence. After the Convention had ended (in November 1787), Luther Martin, speaking against the Constitution in the Maryland state legislature, argued that the delegates had clearly exceeded their authority, going beyond the "sole and express purpose" of revising the Articles—a difficult charge to rebut in many respects. The Convention had changed the entire basis of representation, enlarged the powers of the national government relative to the states, and had completely redesigned the function of that national government, creating an independent executive along the way. This story is told in later chapters, but before we can get there, we need to explain the model that serves as the basis for those chapters. What issues should we model, and how were those issues organized? The answer turns out to be just what we have already mentioned: representation, federalism, and the independent executive, an answer apparent in the writings of both Madison and—the first person to chronicle Madison's thinking in a critical way—Charles Beard. Besides them, many other historians and social scientists have suggested these dimensions.

Though Martin had a point about the grant of authority, the resolution does say that the changes would need to "render the federal constitution adequate to the exigencies of Government & the preservation of the Union" (Farrand 1966, vol. III, 14). A reasonable person might conclude that little short of the changes we just described could have accomplished that goal. Indeed, given later ratification, it seems likely that many—perhaps most—people agreed that at least some changes were necessary (even if some people might not have liked the specific Constitution on offer). Delegates arrived at the Convention with varying answers to the question of what to reform. John Dickinson of Delaware had been at the earlier Annapolis Convention and was clearly disposed toward making changes in the government. However, he wanted to avoid too many changes. "Dickinson and his colleague George Read had bolstered their position in the Convention by having the Delaware assembly instruct them to oppose any change in the existing rule of voting" (Rakove 1996, 60). They were willing to talk about strengthening the national government, but they were leery of changing anything relative to how states were represented in that government. They were hardly the only delegates willing to make some changes. Pauline Maier (2010) notes in her discussion of the ratification period that even eventual dissenters like Edmund Randolph and George Mason were prepared for massive changes. She specifically describes Mason as a man who "did not question the need for fundamental change" (47), though Beeman (2010, 44) describes Mason's attitude as one of a willingness to entertain major changes out of deference to his neighbor George Washington. The Pennsylvania delegation certainly contained delegates hungry for changes, but not all of the same sort. Gouverneur Morris was a thorough elitist, but his colleague, James Wilson, argued for direct election of the president. What united all of these delegates was not a clear view of how the government should be constructed, but a desire to see some kind of changes that would institute a national government strong enough to govern.

Given this (somewhat inchoate) desire for a stronger national government, one could imagine that the problem was a straightforward one with a single dimension of conflict: how much stronger a government should they have? The dimension of conflict would simply range between a much "more powerful government" vs. a relatively "less powerful government." Delegates could be arrayed on a continuum of how much change they preferred. This would be a very simple map needing only a line to describe the differences between delegates on each side of the reform issue. Indeed, there are models (discussed below) that either explicitly, or sometimes implicitly, assume this form of conflict. The problem with this formulation of the debates is that it ignores several key questions that come up as soon as one makes a decision to make the government stronger. Which part of government would be strengthened? Legislative power? Executive power? Of course, the question of representation hung over everything.

Perhaps some delegates came expecting a relatively straightforward debate. However, some, like John Dickinson, realized that representation was an issue that could not be ignored. This was not simply because the issue was potent; it was also because the most important instigator of the agenda—James Madison—would not let that issue be ignored. In the end, the complexity of the problem requires us to draw a map that would include multiple dimensions of conflict.

Before turning to those dimensions, we need to make sure the reader understands a key point: the dimensions of conflict must be kept separate from the motivations of the delegates. This is, often, easier said than done. When Charles Beard first wrote about the Constitution, he was not completely successful at keeping these concepts separate (or perhaps he was not successful at communicating his concepts clearly). His aim was to explain how the framers were self-interested and motivated to protect their upper-class interests. As such, Beard's (1913) substantive views—though they certainly imply dimensions—are more about the motivations and economic interests that he believes affected voting. His claim that "our fundamental law was not the product of an abstraction known as 'the whole people,' but of a group of economic interests which must have expected beneficial results from its adoption" (17), conveys the idea that economics was at the heart of things, but also illustrates that economics was not directly the issue being debated. Rather, economic class served as the motivation for positions within the debate over the "fundamental law." Well, what were the issues in that fundamental law?

When we look carefully to see what dimensions Beard believed were at issue, we find more complexity than scholars have previously recognized in his work. In fact, as we shall see below, Beard's ideas about the dimensions of conflict follow Madison's own ideas relatively closely, in some ways elucidating them. When we compare their ideas to the literature explaining the Convention, some clarity about the issues that divided the delegates begins to emerge.

2.1 Madison's Preparations and Beard's Analysis

In the mid-1780s, Madison and others began to call for a national convention to correct the Articles of Confederation. Originally planned for Annapolis, the meeting location eventually moved to Philadelphia after the initial effort foundered. Madison wanted a large, strong central government that more equitably represented the people. This position was not one that he had arrived at lightly or without study. Madison famously closeted himself in his study for much of the winter of 1786 and 1787, poring over 200 volumes of books sent from Thomas Jefferson in Europe. The topics included everything from modern political theory to histories of the ancient republics. Madison digested all of it and distilled it into a set of lessons that he would apply to the American republic.

The most famous fruit of this analysis is Madison's memo on the "Vices of the Political System" (Rakove 1999, 69). This comprehensive analysis represented his intellectual preparations for the Philadelphia debates.[1] The memo is a series of propositions describing the state of the American union, and it is rather pessimistic. Madison's view of government led him to believe that the relationships both among the states and between the states and the national government do not serve the people well at all; this culminated in a position that representation must be changed, a view that was perhaps Madison's core driving belief during the early days of the Convention.

Some of Madison's thinking runs along commonplace lines: the national government was powerless to deal with the current problems. In point seven of the memo, Madison described a "want of sanction to the laws, and of coercion in the Government of the Confederacy." However, he quickly moved beyond that to castigate the states. In the same point he asked if legislative acts are "merely recommendatory . . . or if they were to be rejudged by County authorities . . . what probability would exist . . . that they would be carried into execution?" He was well aware of the fact that the national government was not sufficient to the exigencies of the situation, but saw that part of the problem was the ability of states to "rejudge" the question. Point nine of the memorandum is scathing: "In developing the evils which viciate the political system of the U.S. it is proper to include those which are found within the States individually, as well as those which affect the States collectively, since the former class have an indirect influence on the general malady and must not be overlooked in forming a compleat remedy" (Rakove 1999, 72–73).

He goes on to use descriptions like "injustice" and "vicious" to describe the states. Madison laid most of the problems of the young nation squarely at their feet, but even this did not seem to go quite far enough for him. At the end of the memo, he wrote that all of this "brings into question the fundamental principle of republican Governments, that the majority who rule in such Governments, are the safest guardians of both the public Good and of private rights" (75).

It is possible to read the Vices memo and miss Madison's focus on representation. Indeed, it is only in point 11 (the final point he fully composed) that he gets to direct questions of representation. Even there, Madison steps around the question without ever directly mentioning representation under the articles. However, he does say that "[t]he great desideratum in Government is such a modification of the Sovereignty as will render it sufficiently neutral between the different interests and factions, to controul one part of the Society from invading the rights of another" (75).

Madison realized that if the legislators did not represent the actual interests in society, but instead represented the intermediate units of states, the legislature would never be "sufficiently neutral" (75). Rakove (1996)[2] describes Madison's preparations and his influence on the Convention as "the Madisonian Moment."[3] Of Madison's realization, he writes that "states *as such* were not real interests deserving of representation. States processed interests, but these were rooted in the attributes of individuals" (55, emphasis in original), which are the units deserving of representation. For Madison, any questions about representation would have been largely about the question of how people should be represented in their government. The Vices memo implies that only in a large republic where people were represented equitably—in proportion to their numbers in each state—could good government be possible. Of course, representation implicated more than that. The inherent complexity of these debates meant that representation was not simply about the mathematical question of counting people, but affected other areas as well. How would slaves be counted? Who would pay the representatives? Would that system of representation be more about protecting state power by sending ambassadors from each state (something close to the confederation model), or would it be more like creating a true legislature?

Madison's memo is hardly the only place to find his ideas and his commitment to changing the form of government. Citing several letters,[4] Keith Dougherty (2001) writes that Madison had recognized representation as being at the heart of "the collective action problem and was ready to propose a solution" (145). He goes on to note that Madison was "not alone" (145) in this view (something we will see definitively in chapter 3). Like his fellow reformers, Madison's preparations led him to see opportunities to make the debates about more than simply the powers of the national government. Once Madison began talking about how people should be represented in this strong government, the debates could not simply be about making a longer list of powers. We cannot know how much other delegates initially wanted to discuss representation. Certainly, many of them must have thought about it. "Nevertheless it was Madison's insistence on solving the problem of representation first that set the course of debate" (Rakove 1996, 60).

Madison did think about more than simply representation as a means to creating a stronger central government. However, his thoughts on the nature of that central government were never quite as concrete. Creating a new government necessarily involved creating new national institutions, and the key innovation would clearly be some kind of national executive power. Here, Madison was far less clear in his thinking than with respect to representation. Beeman (2010) describes his ideas as "hazily formed notions" and goes on to quote Madison as admitting just prior to the Convention that he had "scarcely ventured as yet to form my own opinion either of the manner in which [the executive] ought to be constituted or of the authorities with which it ought to be clothed" (55–56). If James Madison had not clearly considered these ideas, we can be certain that few, if any, of the other delegates had clearly formed any views on the division of powers within that national government.

The clear implication of Madison's preparations for the Convention suggest three key dimensions: representation, federalism, and the balance of powers within the federal government. Charles Beard drew on these issues for his own scholarship. Being the first scholar to suggest an "economic" model of the Convention, it is natural for people to believe that the dimension of interest was economics. Beard's thesis—about class differences—certainly encouraged that idea. However, Beard clearly understood that the dimensions of actual debate and conflict at the Convention were not about economics, but how to design a government. In chapter 6, "The Constitution as an Economic Document," Beard lays out the case for how economic motivations affected preferences on different dimensions of the new government. After clearing his throat with a few comments on how *The Federalist* explains the document, Beard divides the balance of the chapter with the following headings.

- The Underlying Political Science of the Constitution
- The Structure of Government or the Balance of Powers
- The Powers Conferred Upon the Federal Government
- Restrictions Laid Upon State Legislatures

Despite the fact that there are four headings, there are really only three dimensions that come out of this discussion: representation (Beard references Madison's thoughts on representation throughout the first section on the underlying political science); national institutional design, or the balance of powers within the government; and federalism, or the division between the federal government and the state governments—Beard separates this dimension into two categories, one about the powers of the federal government and one about the restrictions on states. Certainly, Beard's thesis about economic motivations is the most revolutionary part of his claims, and he did little in the text to distinguish how different economic motivations might play out differently on various dimensions.[5] However, while he was not as clear about it as we might wish, Beard does see separate dimensions of conflict in the debates.

A great problem with any analysis of the Convention is that discussion of dimensions tends to focus only on how that dimension's debates unfolded. What happened on the question of representation? or how did their thinking on the presidency evolve? These are important questions (and, indeed, will be the focus of later chapters), but to really understand the entire constitution we must focus on how different coalitions came together on different dimensions. One of the virtues of focusing on ideological differences reflected in the vote records is that it forces us to consider how the ideas relate and how they structure the Convention debates. As the first in a long line of scholars to analyze the Convention (rather than merely describe it), Beard's influence looms large. But in the next section we turn to see whether or not Beard's dimensions of conflict—not necessarily his economic thesis, but the dimensions suggested by Madison and copied by Beard—are prominent in the literature. And how the coalitions might have interacted with each other on those key dimensions.

2.2 Existing Hypothetical Dimensions

What is a dimension of conflict? If Beard identified—in Madison—several important dimensions of conflict, what do those dimensions mean? It is vital to understand that a dimension is not simply a particular issue, for example, how should representatives be paid? How long should a senator's term be? Rather, it is a latent difference of opinion that exists across multiple discrete issues and explains as much as possible about each group of issues. The use of dimensions is explicit in the social science literature, but only implicit in the historical literature. This does not mean that historians do not discuss dimensions of conflict in their narrative accounts; instead, it simply means that, because the methods used by historians do not measure policy preferences or locate specific issues on dimensions, they need not be so categorical or precise. Nevertheless, many scholars who write about the Convention simplify their discussion by collapsing the issues in question into such categories—often the Madisonian dimensions suggested by Beard.

It is difficult to completely analyze all discussion of dimensions of conflict at the Convention—especially across disparate literatures. The total sum of such speculation vastly outweighs the amount of direct information we have about the Convention. Another very real problem is being systematic. Conventional narrative histories of the debates discuss dimensions of conflict constantly, but not systematically. Exhaustively reviewing the entire literature on the Convention is far beyond the scope of a single book. While we make no claims that we have even selected a random sample of the literature, when immersed in the literature on the Convention, certain themes do emerge. Table 2.1 lists just a few of the key historical works and displays, in only a phrase or two, the dimensions of debate suggested by these historians.[6] This table is meant to be purely illustrative about dimensions of conflict and not a full account of the rich scholarship in each of these works.

The typical story told about Beard's scholarship is that he thinks the debates over the Constitution were about economics. In a sense that is true, but it deeply shortchanges Beard's view of the dimensions of conflict, and it helps illustrate the need to keep dimensions and motivations separate. Beard believed that delegates to the Convention were trying to protect the wealth of the upper class.[7] While that may have been their motivation, a careful reading of Beard's chapter 6—his explanation of the content of the Constitution—displays that the dimensions on which they were debating were representation, the structure of the national government, federalism,

Table 2.1 Selected Accounts and Dimensions of Conflict at the Federal Convention—Historians

Scholar	Major Dimensions	Lesser Dimensions
Beard (1913)[a]	Representation Structure of national government Federalism Restrictions on state legislatures	International economics
McDonald (1958)		No real key dimensions but many coalitions
McDonald (1965)	Nationalism	Representation as an impediment
Bowen (1966)	Representation	Many small, subsequent issues
Wood (1969)	Democracy vs. aristocracy	
Lynd (1962), Main (1965), and Beck (1972)	Centralized government power	
Banning (1995)	Representation	Definition of central government Other complicated issues
Rakove (1996)	Representation Federalism The Presidency Ratification	
Maier (2010)	Strengthening the national government	Very many lesser issues
Beeman (2010)	Multiple major issues emphasizing federalism and representation	

[a]*Note*: Beard's dimensions, as discussed above, were not about economics, but his explanation of the motivations for action on those dimensions decidedly was about economics. This table reflects the contents of the dimensions, not the motivations.

and the specific restrictions on state legislatures (these last two subjects are intimately related).

Beard's most famous critic, Forrest McDonald, is far less clear on the dimensions of conflict (in part, because McDonald sees an enormous number of coalitions at the Convention, implying far more dimensions than he actually references; for our purposes, the coalitions will be discussed in more detail in the next chapter). In his 1958 book, *We the People*, McDonald spends a significant amount of time cataloging the different coalitions (more than 30 such factions, by his count). However, an appreciation of this book requires remembering that it was a response to Beard in ways that few other books have been. McDonald (1958) explicitly claims that his purpose is to "examine Beard's thesis as history" (xxiii). He closes the book by noting that a purely economic interpretation is perhaps beyond any analyst. However, in the final section of the book, he does hold out hope for a more pluralist account of the Convention (see 415–17).

In McDonald's later book, *E Pluribus Unum*, he argues that the key question in front of the Convention was not what kind of national government would be created, "but whether a national government would be created at all" (1965, 309). In essence, despite the large number of coalitions and alliances, he boils things down to only a couple of dimensions. His narrative account of the Convention suggests the key questions of centralizing power and how states and people would be represented in the young nation, making his key dimensions nationalism and representation. On several occasions, McDonald muddies the difference between representation and centralized government power. He notes that Madison "saw six states as being committed on one side and five on the other. The majority were what he viewed as the 'large states' and the 'nationalist' bloc, the minority were the 'small states' and the 'states-rights' bloc" (273).

But McDonald claims that this was a completely erroneous view of the Convention and that a true view of the debate would reveal that several small-state delegates were "willing, even eager, to abolish the states entirely and place all power in the hands of a national government" (281). In this way, McDonald brings the focus of debate back to the question of nationalism and the strength of that national government. Would the central government be given the scope and power it needed to forge a nation? According to McDonald, the question of representation that Madison erroneously focused on was merely an impediment to finally resolving the question of national government power. It might even be accurate to say that he saw only a single dimension, which really does not fit his claims about a large number of coalitions and alliances, but suggests there were two sides locked in conflict.

For historians taking a more narrative approach, McDonald's sidelining of questions of representation is not typical. Instead, such work that attempts a blow-by-blow account of the Convention usually gives pride of place to the question of representation that "was to take up half the summer" (Bowen 1966, 44). Bowen (1966) is emblematic in that she specifically argues that the Convention would not have been able to move any further without resolving the question of representation on July 16 (185–87). She is far from alone in this. Many narrative accounts give representation a special place in the lore of the Convention (Garver 1944; Roche 1961; Rossiter 1966; Collier and Collier 1986; Peters 1987; Wirls and Wirls 2004).

However, taking a narrative approach to explaining the Founding is hardly the only way to examine the question of representation. For instance, Gordon Wood (1969) identifies his own conception of the American founding's key dimensions as aristocracy vs. democracy (515–18). Wood's position is not one of an author trying to explain the day-to-day voting or coalition structure of the Convention. Instead, Wood is interested in a grand explanation of the culture and ideas of the period (despite the fact that he might not use the term dimension to describe that theory). Wood—and others like him, such as Bailyn (1967) and Pocock (1975)—pay enormous attention to the details of the ideas proffered during the period. Alan Gibson (2010) refers to this cohort as the "Linguistic Contextualists." As a group, their goal is not to offer a complete account of the Convention but to suggest a method for understanding the past, with particular focus on the founding. Without disputing this characterization, Wood does more than this. In his book, *The Creation of the American Republic*, he argues for a set of ideas that motivated debates, ideas that protected elite power but, perhaps unwittingly, permitted the emergence of true democratic politics. For Wood, the level of democracy (as opposed to aristocracy) in the new nation was the real dimension of conflict.[8] Similar to McDonald, Wood's proposed theory implies the existence of only two coalitions (those favoring aristocracy opposed to those favoring democracy).

Alan Gibson (2010), in summarizing a section of the literature on the economic questions at the Convention, points out that a number of authors like Staughton Lynd (1966), Jackson Turner Main (1961), and Van Beck Hall (1972) have reconstructed some dimensions of Beard's thesis, typically with a focus on centralized government power. According to Gibson, these historians "argue that the formation and ratification of the Constitution are best understood as a series of contests over governance . . . [between] a popular faction that represented the interests of ordinary debtors and yeoman, and a conservative faction made up of elite leaders" (36–37). Their work implicitly provides some support to the idea that the key dimension was the question of centralized government power to protect elites against an excessively democratic populace, again suggesting only two coalitions.

At this point, a theme has clearly emerged. Despite the differences across these authors, they consistently identify similar ideas—representation and the centralization of power—and it is no accident that most scholars treat the Convention in this way. The first few weeks of the Convention were dedicated to feeling out delegate positions on two key questions: can the central government be strengthened (essentially at the expense of the states)? And, if that is to be done, how will the people and the states be represented in this new form of government the delegates will suggest? Lance Banning's (1995) biography of Madison—which pays special attention to the consistency of Madison's thoughts and his preparations for the Convention—explicitly notes these two issues: "[Madison] had come to Philadelphia convinced that clearer definition of the central government's responsibilities, though needed, was not the most important task" (143). Representation was the greater issue. That general pattern does not mean the authors ignore questions about other issues, such as slavery, trade and commerce, and especially issues surrounding how presidents will be elected and how power will be divided within the national government. Indeed, Banning notes that the subsequent conflict over representation "cannot entirely account for developments" on that issue (145). Though it is impossible to be sure exactly how Banning saw the debates, he certainly saw more complexity than most, and he would, no doubt, suggest a model of the Convention with many different dimensions of debate.

Jack Rakove (1996) spends more than half of his narrative account of the politics of the Convention discussing the debate over representation, indicating he sees it as of paramount importance. However, he also devotes entire chapters to other elements, including federalism, the presidency, and ratification, giving each one a thorough treatment. Indeed, Rakove's view is the closest to a truly multidimensional perspective available among historians in that he avoids treating every issue as separate by grouping key issues under specific headings. At the same time, he also does not fall back on the simplicity of the nationalists vs. localists dichotomy. If he emphasizes one dimension over the others, it is representation, and in the years since his work was published, the emphasis on representation has not ceased. Richard Beeman (2010) similarly gives a very convincing account of how the delegates began on a "disquieting" note as Delaware made clear that it would "protect its interests at all costs" (72). The implication was that the real work of the Convention could not go forward until this question of representation was resolved. Pauline Maier's (2010) book on ratification opens with some discussion of Washington's correspondence on how to strengthen the national government. She frames that section by saying that, on September 18 (the day after the instrument was signed), Washington no longer thought of the Constitution "as a first step toward the development of a strong national government sometime in the future" (39). Rather, he saw it as having accomplished at least some of that. Maier summarizes all of the other questions earlier in the chapter by listing the many key decisions that were made, but she does not attempt an empirical analysis of the dimensions of conflict.

The approach of historians is to explain key events, and any dimensionality that they find or explain is a by-product of that goal. Richard Beeman's work is emblematic. Beeman (2010) occasionally discusses the "moral dimension" of slavery, but otherwise avoids the idea of a dimension of conflict that could summarize the complexity of the Convention. *Plain, Honest Men* serves as a guide to all of the conflicts, debates, and questions posed at the Convention. He certainly mentions representation, separation of powers, and the power of the central government, but he does so in a way that treats them all relatively separately. Despite this, one can read the book and get a sense that the most important issues—the issues to which the delegates returned again and again—were representation, the power of the central government, and the design of that government.

In reviewing table 2.1, it is clear that most of the historians offer a large number of dimensions, but without much rigorous definition or measurement. There are a couple of exceptions—Beard and Rakove—both of whom have stronger connections to the social sciences.[9] Nevertheless, it is probably true that these two authors are simply more willing to be explicit about their views of the dimensions than are authors of other accounts—often more narrative-oriented accounts—who saw so much complexity that it is difficult to sort out the dimensions or find the need to explain them. In our view, the entries in the table describe the overarching and most important questions touched on during the Convention. Although many historians understand different issues as being separate from one another and not really as part of any dimension, there are still lessons to be learned from these observations: no historian ignores representation or the size and scope of the new government, and few of them mention institutional design as a theme (with Rakove and Beard as exceptions).

Do social scientists view these questions differently than do historians? Yes, in subtle ways. Though we have no wish to completely recreate the literature review of the past few pages, table 2.2 lays out the views presented in some of the key social science literature. We include the table for the sake of completeness, noting mostly that the dimensions here parallel many of those laid out in the previous table. A few quick points do deserve attention, however, as a prelude to our own theory of the Convention.

First, while our own work focuses on social science scaling methods, this is not true of all of the social science literature. Roche (1961) identified implicit dimensions, claiming, for instance, that the Convention was a "*nationalist* reform caucus which had to operate with great delicacy and skill in a political cosmos full of enemies to achieve the one definitive goal— popular approbation" (799, emphasis in original). Though he does not use the word dimension, he does speak of specific problems that they encountered and had to solve: centralization of power, representation of the states, and then, as lesser problems, the design of the executive and slavery. McGuire (2003) is similar in that he provides another account of the Convention that explicitly attempts to refurbish Beard's emphasis on economics, but it is not really an effort to model any dimensions the way that some of the other scholars on this list do. With that said, he does talk about a "general" dimension of conflict related to the strength of the national government (109).

Table 2.2 Selected Accounts and Dimensions of Conflict at the Federal Convention—Social Scientists

Scholar	Major Dimensions	Lesser Dimensions
Roche (1961)	Central government Representation of the states	The executive Slavery
Londregan (1999)	Scope and power of government Proportional representation	
Jillson (1988)	Control of the legislature Scope of national government State integrity and federalism Control of executive and Senate	Extended vs. small republic
McGuire (2003)	General issue of strengthening the national government	Many specific clauses
Dougherty and Heckelman (2006)	Representation Centralization	
Slez and Martin (2007)	The rise of the New Jersey Plan Toward the Connecticut Compromise The breakdown of Madison's coalition The slave trade compromise The solidification of positions	
Heckelman and Dougherty (2013)	Localism to nationalism	

Second, our own method of scaling differs from that of others, quite a bit in the case of Slez and Martin (2007) and Jillson (1988), both of whom use a scaling technique that separates the Convention not by issue but by period. Slez and Martin's work emphasizes the importance of rigorous thinking about timing and the Convention's agenda. Both their work—and that of Jillson—underscores how important it is to realize that different dimensions were important at different stages of the Convention—in other words, the agenda mattered. In their work, however, the agenda matters because of their choice to divide the Convention into periods, not because of the content of the dimensions.[10] Modeling all of the dimensions simultaneously permits us to analyze how different dimensions mattered at different times, but also keeps the number of estimated dimensions relatively parsimonious.

Our approach is closer to that of Londregan (1999) and Dougherty and Heckelman (2006). John Londregan was the first political scientist to really attempt to measure all of the delegation positions as points on a graph where the dimensions are defined by the fundamental issues of the Convention.[11] His unpublished work assumed a pair of dimensions: the scope and power of the national government and the nature of representation—specifically, whether it would be proportional or not. Dougherty and Heckelman's work employed an optimal classification model using roll call vote data. They argued that the estimated dimensions corresponded to representation and centralization of government (an interpretation that is in accord with both Roche and Londregan). Dougherty and Heckelman noted that the dimensions of the conflict were in some doubt, and that it was possible that the "appropriate number of dimensions is greater than two" (298). However, they also noted that the addition of the third and fourth dimensions did not substantially alter their story about the centrality of the Connecticut delegation (and of Roger Sherman within that delegation)—a claim consistent with keeping the number of dimensions small.

To sum up both the historical and the social science literature, we see that there is a consistent emphasis on a group of issues, most commonly representation and centralization of power. Other issues are mentioned, but once we get beyond these two issues, the uniformity disappears. The lesson of this discussion is that these two issues are strong contenders for the key dimensions of conflict at the Convention.

Social scientists, true to their reputation for parsimony, tend to be a bit more explicit about their dimensions of study. Historians tend to analyze the Convention by describing what they perceive as the most significant dimension of debate between (typically two) camps. They focus on the most significant questions—with, typically, at least two dimensions—but then also mention many smaller areas that are treated *sui generis*. Conventional historical accounts of the Convention typically make one of two choices. They either focus on a relatively clear single dimension, like Beard's centralization of government power or Wood's aristocracy vs. democracy, as the key dimension of conflict. The typical alternative to this—Beeman is an example—is to deliver a narrative account that may highlight some of the biggest issues but also to discuss a large number of smaller issues as implied dimensions (e.g., the power to regulate trade, the presidential veto, whether or not North Carolina would get extra representation in the Congress, etc.).

Social scientists tend to have as much discussion of smaller dimensions or lesser questions but, even more than historians, emphasize the most important dimensions in their scholarship. Examining the work of social scientists, the number of possible conflict dimensions ranges from one (in the case of McGuire) to five or more. The nature of those dimensions is sometimes defined by the topic (in Londregan and Dougherty and Heckelman), while at other times the dimensions are temporally defined (in Jillson and Slez and Martin). We strongly prefer the former because it focuses attention on the conflict and not simply the time period. With a great deal of literature summarized quickly, we turn to a discussion of our specific dimensions and their justification.

2.3 Our Dimensions

Our short (and necessarily incomplete) tour of the literature reveals two key lessons. First, despite the disagreements, there are two dimensions that appear over and over again: representation and centralization of power. This is true regardless of whether or not one looks at the historical literature or the social science literature. Sometimes these two sets of issues are combined (or perhaps conflated) as "nationalism," but they are always present. The second lesson is that both historians and social scientists—each in their own way—seek a small number of dimensions, despite the deep complexity of the set of issues in front of them. Historians do this by describing what they see as the largest themes in the pattern of voting and then treating most items that do not fit this theme as individual and separate issues. There are relatively few historians who are willing to describe large numbers of dimensions without simply resorting to treating issues as *sui generis*—Beard and Rakove are the only exceptions we found and are highlighted here.

Being social scientists, we want to explain as much of the voting as possible, but, respecting the work of historians, we do not want to create dimensions that are too distant from what the delegates discussed. Balancing both of these considerations suggests that our model must examine representation and centralization of power. The question is, should we go any further than that or not? History gives us little guidance here, since beyond those two baskets of ideas—representation and centralization of power—historians were not able to agree on what else merited discussion as a dimension. Social scientists have employed several different dimensions, but they, similarly, have not settled the question.

Elsewhere, we have argued that using either three or four dimensions does a reasonably good job of explaining the Convention because, while a "one-dimensional model may illuminate the central conflict of the Convention . . . there is significant improvement with a three-dimensional model" (Pope and Treier 2012, 163).[12] Too many dimensions makes the problem both less tractable for estimation and less helpful as an explanation of the Convention. Still, this does suggest that a two-dimensional model may not be enough—as does the fact that much previous work draws out other themes.

For our purposes here, a dimension must have a relatively large number of votes. Certain questions no doubt have great significance, but if there are few votes on the issue, then it cannot qualify as a dimension—otherwise, the historical solution of simply describing issues would probably be best. For instance, slavery is obviously an issue of great importance at the Convention.[13] However, slavery as a specific issue comprises a relatively small number of votes—depending on one's definition, perhaps as few as five or six, but certainly fewer than ten. Slavery affects a much larger number of votes on other dimensions, but we do not treat it here as being a separate, single dimension. Which issue—that is not covered by representation or federalism (or centralization of power)—does have a large number of votes and was a key question at the Convention?

In order to finally answer this question, we found ourselves returning to Beard's work—not his arguments about "personalty" and "realty"—but his claims about the "underlying political science" of the Convention, which he attributes to Madison. We remind the reader of his discussion of Madison's three dimensions—representation, the independence of the executive,[14] and federalism—in chapter 6 of Beard's book (see section 2.1 above). Beard believed that the "personalty" would assume the same positions on all of these questions: change the basis of representation to protect property rights; strengthen the national government's power; but also make sure property interests are powerful within that government by limiting the ability of a majority in the legislature to seize property.

Returning to the tables again for a moment, we see that Rakove did something similar where he explicitly discussed the presidency, and that among the social scientists, both Roche and Jillson also emphasized the executive.[15] Though one can never settle questions like this forever (we have no doubt some will disagree with our choices), the fact that scholars as diverse as Madison, Beard, Rakove, and others all point to the importance of the executive—particularly to the question of the president's power relative to the legislature—we begin to see three key questions emerge among the issues that motivated the delegates to the Convention. This foundation, combined with our own close analysis of the available votes, suggests that this should be our starting point for estimating dimensions of debate.

Accordingly, we settled on the three most prominent dimensions in the literature. First, we consider a *representation* dimension. How will institutions count people in the new republic? Madison, and others, chose to place great weight on the question of representation, and it became the focal point of the key first six weeks of the Convention. The important question was never simply whether or not people will be represented. The issue was whether states would receive equally weighted votes in the legislature, or whether the votes would be weighted by some criteria like population or wealth. By early July, it was clear that the Convention was at a full stop and that nothing could be decided until this question had been resolved. This makes it the first and most important dimension at the Convention, one that virtually every scholar describes in some way—no matter the methodology.

Second, we identify a *federalism* dimension. How much power would the national government have relative to the states? This question often frames how people discuss the Convention's debates. Beeman (2010) says that they believed the "continental government's lack of 'energy' posed [a] formidable threat to liberty" (21). This issue is obviously different from the question of representation, but they are related. For instance, a delegate could hold the view that state power should be dramatically trimmed, but within a system where states are given equal representation in the national government. Alternatively, a delegate might hold the position that the states should be well represented in the national government but relatively autonomous, with only a weak central core. How much energy could be tolerated?

Finally, we examine an *executive power* dimension. How will power be distributed within that government? If the delegates had decided to simply change representation slightly, leaving the central government weak, or if they had found that their preferences would not let them make reforms, there would probably be no need for a third dimension. However, once they chose to create a strong national government, concerns like how much power a president would have, how to elect him, and how Congress and the president could check one another became inevitable. Delegates were dealing with the most complex issues imaginable, and they had relatively little constituent feedback to guide them.

It is important to be careful in the interpretation of these dimensions. The most important tendency to avoid is interpreting conflicts not as the delegates would have understood them, but through modern lenses. Bernard Bailyn (1967) offers a correction to this point of view. He argues that it is important to see the past not merely as a prologue to the present. Rather, according to Bailyn, the goal is to understand "that world not as it anticipated the future but as it was experienced by those who live[d] in it" (v). It is vital to try to interpret these dimensions without looking to plunder or ransack the historical record in order to help us understand our own world (Pocock 1975). Avoiding this temptation is much harder than it seems. Our search for the deep structure of voting at the Convention is directly in this spirit. We aim to avoid imposing our own standards of reasoning and consistency on our subjects, while looking for ways in which their arguments are recognizably strung together. This is a difficult task, and we do not pretend that it can be done easily.

The representation dimension—focused most on the question of proportional representation—is a good example of the care we need to take. Today's arguments about representation are virtually always discussed in terms of representing people: one person, one vote is both a slogan and a standard. However, these sorts of questions are very different from the ones the delegates faced in 1787. On one side were the small states that clearly favored retaining the status quo—equal state representation. On the other side were the larger states that favored representation in proportion to each state's population, or at least some other metric that afforded them greater representation. One of the issues intimately connected to representation was slavery. However we interpret this dimension, we should not think of it as being about modern issues, and we must remember that it is not the only topic that defined a "nationalist" position. There were other dimensions where preferences differed.

A critic might raise the cogent objection that, even if we do take care in our interpretations, delegates would have never recognized this model of the Convention. Of course, that is superficially true. They were not arguing about their positions on the representation dimension, they were arguing over the question of how to represent people and states in the new government. Similar points could be made about the other dimensions.

The value of the model is not that it accurately describes the thought processes of delegates in 1787. Indeed, the value will be found in the ability of the model to describe and accurately simplify the actions taken by the delegates. Does our map illuminate what happened at the Convention? Can we use the model to better understand why they made the decisions that they did? If we grant that no human being can simply understand all of the complexities of hundreds of roll call votes, we are going to need some kind of model to simplify the situation and gain the "wider view" we discussed above.

Roll call analysis is an opportunity to produce just such a picture of the past. The roll call model estimates delegate positions using their votes, not just our interpretation of their votes. True, we will need to make some identifying assumptions (like identifying the dimensions). But in doing so, we hope not to have destroyed the original relationships between the votes. Instead, we aim to find new knowledge about the deep structure of voting at the Convention. This is the real test of the model. If the model can be validated and reveal new information, it will have accomplished something. In the next chapter, we present the results of the model by displaying the positions of the delegates and delegations. The results suggest that the traditional thinking of large vs. small states, or "nationalists" and their opponents, is a bit limited, and that it is better to think in terms of three coalitions: the Small states, the Deep South states, and the Core Reform states. Thus, "nationalism" was a complicated concept not easily pinned down to a single camp. The next chapter illustrates the reason for that conclusion.

CHAPTER 3

Delegations and Delegates

The central claim of this book is that scholars of the Constitutional Convention should reappraise the Convention story that tells of two coalitions at the Convention: nationalist reformers against parochial conservatives, with the overlapping monikers of "large states" that worked against "small states." These stories are true as far as they go, but they do not fully capture the key dynamics of the Convention in multiple dimensions. Our approach is to look at the deep structure of the shifting majorities at the Convention. This chapter maps that deep structure, using the conventional tools of roll call analysis—the results are graphs (or maps) of the Convention coalitions that display visually the deep structure of overlapping majorities that created the document. The maps illustrate that there was a group of Core Reform states—Virginia, Pennsylvania, and Massachusetts—that allied with the slaveholding Deep South states of the Carolinas and Georgia to vastly strengthen the national government and change the basis of representation. It was this coalition that led to the Great Compromise and the expanded role of the national government. On a different set of issues, namely the independence of the executive, the majorities shifted. The Core Reform states allied with the Small states most sympathetic to reform of the executive—Delaware and Maryland—to create a much stronger presidency than the one preferred by those in the Deep South who favored locating national power within the legislature, but not in the newly created executive.

This is a large claim, and the key way we illustrate it in this chapter is through the maps of the positions and the coalitions. However, before we can substantiate that claim, we need to establish why this kind of model is not only useful but also necessary to understanding the Convention. To do that, we must observe how the delegates voted and why the system of voting mattered.

3.1 The Voting Rules

The Constitution was debated and voted upon by 12 state delegations (all of the former colonies except for Rhode Island, a state that declined to send delegates). As a result, the key votes that shaped the Constitution were the products of delegates voting *within* delegations. If the majority of a delegation was in favor of a proposal, that delegation cast an "aye" vote. That majority might be a thin one, as was often the case with, for example, Virginia, where a pair of dissenters (Mason and Randolph) frequently voted against the body of the delegation. Figure 3.1 displays patterns of votes by type of vote. In each of the bars—which are grouped by delegation—the dark portion of the bar indicates an opposition vote on the proposal, while the lightest section of the bar indicates an affirmative vote on the proposal. The middle shading of gray indicates a divided vote, such as when an even-numbered delegation deadlocked. The bars are of uneven length because, for most individuals whose votes were only recorded sporadically and inconsistently, the modal case is missing data. For some states, like New York, missing data are quite common because multiple delegation members did not attend past early July. We note that we are analyzing a subset of the votes at the Convention. The best way to describe this subset is the set of non-unanimous, non-procedural votes found in Farrand's notes.[1] We drop unanimous votes because they show no divisions of opinion at the Convention and, thus, are not useful in this process. We drop procedural votes because it is not clear what they are about: Delay of the proposal? Substance? Or simply a change in schedule? It is difficult, if not impossible, to say, so we have omitted them from the sample.

Due to this data structure, we know far more about the state delegation votes than we do about those cast by individual delegates, as can be seen in figure 3.1. In the case of the delegations, most of the data are available, but the length of the bars for individuals is much shorter because of attendance and inconsistent vote recording. Delegations either voted "Aye" or "Nay" or, in the event of a tie, the delegation was "divided," and the vote did not

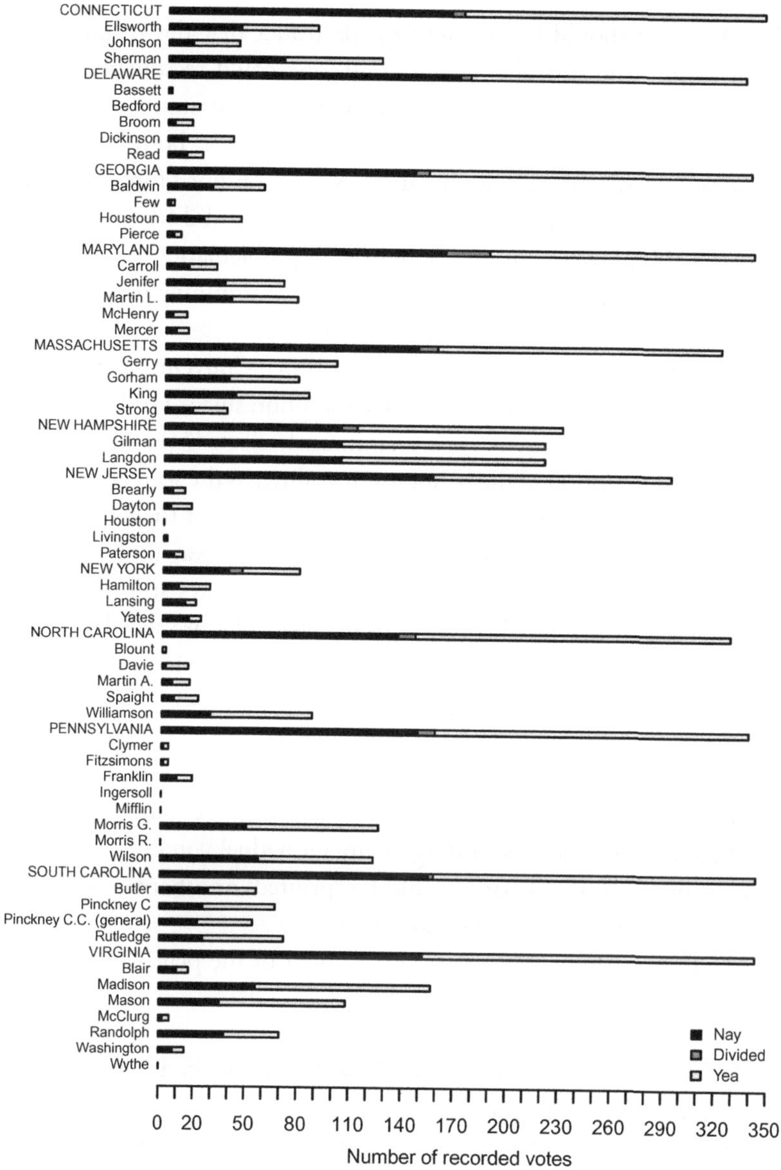

Fig. 3.1.

Note: The figure displays the number of votes by type. The dark portion of the bar indicates an opposition vote on the proposal, while the lightest section of the bar indicates an affirmative vote on the proposal. The middle shading of gray indicates a divided vote. Delegates such as Wythe and Houston, who attended so infrequently that they cannot be estimated, are omitted from the figure and the estimation.

count. Already it should be apparent to the reader that the voting rules were not simple and not obvious (after all, one could reasonably count "divided" votes as a negative or as a preference for the status quo). The method for counting votes was a subject of some debate, both before the Convention and as it was just getting underway. It was not a foregone conclusion that voting would take place in the way that it did (though, as we will see, the alternatives would have been very problematic). Because the rules of debate played such an important role in determining outcomes, it is crucial to understand those rules in context.

The first mention of voting at the Constitutional Convention comes on May 25. The ballot was not a question of contention since "His Excellency George Washington Esquire . . . was unanimously elected" (Farrand 1966, vol. I, 2). The description of the ballot was revealing, as the secretary's notes say that "Members then proceeded to ballot on behalf of their respective States" (2). With the election of a president out of the way (and the election was an obvious one, given his stature), the delegates still needed to draw up a set of rules for the Convention. Five rules are worth further comment here because some were explicit and some were implicit.

- Each state delegation would have a single vote.
- To pass any proposal required only a majority of the states voting in a particular roll call—and divided states did not count.
- There was no official recording of any individual votes.
- Nothing from the debates would be "printed, or otherwise published or communicated without leave."
- The Convention could revise any element of the plan whenever they decided to do so.

Though some of these rules were explicit, well-considered decisions of the Convention, others were simply assumed regularities or artifacts of the status quo procedures, inherited from practices applied during the writing of the Articles of Confederation.[2]

Although equal state voting—where Virginia's vote counted the same as Delaware's, despite the population difference—had been the explicit rule since the first Continental Congress in 1774 (Jillson and Wilson 1994)[3] there was no guarantee that it would be the rule at this Convention. When the Virginia and Pennsylvania delegations began consultations before other delegations arrived, there was at least some support for changing that traditional voting rule. Madison records that both Robert Morris and Gouverneur Morris of Pennsylvania (no relation to one another) believed the "large States should unite in firmly refusing to the small States an equal vote, as unreasonable, and as enabling the small States to negative every good system of Government" (Farrand 1966, vol. I, 11). This sounds like the germ of a plan to insist—even before the Convention began—on weighting state votes by population.[4] Madison records that the Virginia delegates opposed this plan and felt that it could create "fatal altercations" (11) between the delegates. For whatever reason, the Pennsylvania and Virginia delegates never pressed this point, so the status quo rule was entered into the Convention rules on May 28: *each state delegation would have a single vote.*[5] Equal state votes had been the rule for years, so this was not a surprise, but it was an important point, as it determined which votes would matter at the Convention.

Despite this decision that fixed the potential number of votes available to be cast for each vote, the particular rules of voting were such that equal state voting did not actually result in a consistent denominator for counting votes. This is because of a second rule: *to pass any proposal required only a majority of the states voting in a particular roll call—and divided states did not count.* This was a crucial point that was never explicitly discussed by the delegates, a fact that we find something of a mystery. Under the Articles of Confederation, the practice was that all major legislation must be approved by at least nine states. Minor legislation and simple rules votes could be passed by 7 of the 13 states—the denominator was fixed. At the Convention, the rule became simply "more aye votes than nay votes," a much easier threshold. This was a key departure from the rules of the Confederation Congress.

At the opening of the Convention, there were 11 delegations present (New Hampshire would arrive later, and Rhode Island would never attend). Thus, if every state voted, six state votes were required to pass a proposal. However, because some states were made up of an even number of delegates, or because a specific delegate might be absent for any number of reasons, the possibility existed for a "divided" vote, which really meant that the delegation was internally conflicted and tied. In practice, proposals sometimes passed with fewer than six favorable state votes. For instance, on the ninth roll call, five states voted in favor of a proposal for a seven-year term for president. Four states voted against the proposal, and one state (Massachusetts) was divided. The vote passed because a majority of those states voting preferred it (five votes to four). So, at that moment, the president's term was considered to be seven years.

This rule about the denominator of votes is worth additional comment because it was a major deviation from the voting rules of the Articles of Confederation, which required nine states to accomplish anything of special significance. As Jillson and Wilson (1994) point out about the Confederation Congress, this set of rules "contributed to the inability of the delegates [to the Continental Congress] to coordinate their diverse interests in a way that would allow congressional business to be accomplished expeditiously" (67). It is astounding that the rules were slightly loosened, allowing for such small majorities when the stakes were so high. Furthermore, because some states could effectively abstain by having an even division of delegates, a tie vote among the states was also a possibility, and this too had ramifications. In the 79th roll call, for instance, the vote was four states in favor, four states against, and three states divided. The proposal did not pass, which meant that the Convention decided to permit former officeholders to immediately seek new offices upon leaving government (instead of waiting a year).

The implications of these first two rules[6] should not be understated. The delegates—consciously or not—built a powerful status quo bias into their deliberations (though, of course, a majority could always revisit anything). No vote could be passed without a majority of states voting in a particular roll call (or at least without those states being counted as voting). Ties were a defeat. Because abstentions were dropped from the counting of the majority, a vote could theoretically pass with a relatively small number of votes, given enough divided or absent states. This was rare but far from unheard of. Several votes passed with only five votes in favor, rather than six—including some dramatically important votes, like the acceptance of the Great Compromise on July 16 when Massachusetts was divided and the Senate was created. On any number of occasions, the Convention deadlocked five to five and a proposal was dropped (or sometimes amended). Thus, five votes could mean either passage or defeat, depending upon the circumstances.

When the voting rules were debated and accepted, three other amendments to the basic rules were added. First, *there would be no official recording of any individual votes.* But this was not the original idea. In the original rules proposed,[7] any member of the Convention could call for the yeas and nays of all individuals on any vote. However, Mason of Virginia and King of Massachusetts both objected. Mason was opposed on the grounds that "such a record of the opinions of members would be an obstacle to a change of them on conviction; and in the case of its being hereafter promulged must furnish handles to the adversaries of the Result of the Meeting" (Farrand 1966, vol. I, 10). King's comment on the rule was that, "as the acts of the Convention were not to bind the Constituents it was unnecessary to exhibit the evidence of the votes" (10). After hearing those two comments, the Convention decided against recording individual votes (though Madison occasionally recorded such votes in his notes on the Convention). Only delegation votes would be added to the official record.[8] This means that, for purposes of inferring individual votes, we must rely on speeches, motions, and the logic of the delegation's vote, given who was in attendance and other factors that are known.

Another amendment to the rules came on May 29: that *"nothing spoken in the House be printed, or otherwise published or communicated without leave"* (17). The debates would be in secret. Oddly, the Convention did not consider this in the first batch of rules on May 28. Instead it was proposed by Pierce Butler of South Carolina when he moved that the "House provide . . . against licentious publication of their proceedings" (10). The implications of this rule are potentially profound. Delegates could offer unpopular opinions, test their arguments, and not fear that their words would be printed in the local newspapers (or further abroad). It helped permit consideration of truly fundamental and thoroughgoing reforms to the government. It also bolsters the claim that votes were "sincere" and not strategically conditioned on a carefully crafted agenda.[9] The field was wide open for change. Luckily, this secrecy did not mean the events of the Convention would go unrecorded.

The final addendum was raised by Spaight of North Carolina: that *"the house, may not be precluded, by a vote upon any question, from revising the subject matter of it, when they see cause"* (9–10). There would be no final votes without a durable majority still supporting that position. This meant that delegates could never be sure that a question was finally resolved, unless they could tell that their fellow delegates were unwilling to revisit the question. It also helped produce a type of unstructured agenda. Because anyone could raise a vote at any time, and there was no legislative leadership constraining the agenda, the votes at the Convention became a long string of votes on a single plan. Though competing plans existed, almost all votes were about a single plan under discussion at all times in the Convention.

These rules matter a great deal at the Convention, and behavior was obviously contingent on those rules. Though the rules have many implications, three are important for our purposes of mapping the delegations and then showing the unfolding, emergent agenda.

First, these rules meant that proposals had to be crafted to win, not a majority of the delegates, but a majority of the states. The compromises that helped limit national power and give authority to individual states are foreshadowed by these rules. Without them, it is possible that the national government would have been much stronger—though it is also possible that no satisfactory agreement would have been reached. Because proposals were crafted to win a majority of the states, not the individual delegates, in studying the key coalitions at the Convention, we must put the states first.

Second, these rules also required broad support across many delegations—though not as broad as under the Articles. There are exceptions. The Connecticut Compromise passed on a vote of five states in favor, four against, and one abstaining (Massachusetts). However, most proposals that actually passed did so by more than a single vote because the delegates could generally not afford to push proposals that were only marginally popular.

The other reason proposals had to be popular is that they were constantly vulnerable to an unstructured agenda that permitted the delegates to reconsider all decisions. In practice, as they neared the end of the summer, there were decisions that could not be reconsidered because of time constraints, but over most of the debates, the situation could change at any moment. To take a single example (discussed in more detail below), the mode of election for the presidency was completely revised at least three times, from selection by the legislature, to selection via a state mechanism, to the relatively familiar Electoral College arrangement of today. This happened, at least in part, because as the plan of the new government was revised, individual proposals raised new considerations and opened up new possible amendments and offerings. The delegates were never quite done until the very end.

Finally, this unstructured agenda, along with the powerful status quo bias of the rules, gave enormous power to those who moved quickly.

James Madison has long been lauded for his agenda-setting role at the Convention, earning him the appellation "Father of the Constitution" (Banning 1995; Rakove 1996; Sheehan 2004; Larson and Winship 2005; Robertson 2005). Certainly, Madison's preparations before the Convention equipped him to play this important role. However, it must also be acknowledged that the rules created a situation ripe to be exploited, and that without them Madison might never have been as successful.

Once the Convention had selected a particular path or plan, the preference for the status quo—as expressed by the need for a majority of delegations voting—meant that as long as that proposal could remain reasonably popular with the delegates it could not easily be overturned, despite the fact that the rules admitted a reconsideration. Only when a point in the plan became deeply unpopular could it be changed. The formal term for this is *win-set*, or the possible outcomes likely to be accepted. Early on, there were a large number of plausible outcomes. Once voting adjusted the plan, the number of possible results shrunk dramatically because delegations accepted a proposal that was reasonably popular.

Today, legislators are clearly and unambiguously organized into political parties that approach debate under a highly structured set of rules. It would be unthinkable in a modern setting to have political engagement without institutional constraints. Calendars, for instance, are often agreed upon weeks in advance of a vote. Legislators know what will be debated that day, and for how long it will be debated, before they have consumed their morning coffee. Sometimes they have known for several days. Party leaders are the guarantors of this regular system. The House of Representatives best characterizes this modern pattern. The Speaker of the House and the Rules Committee plan out debate in great detail, deciding such matters as which amendments will be in order, the sequence in which they will be considered, and the time allotted to each moment of debate. This debate is always structured around a majority party and a minority party (and this is even true in the Senate, where the system is far less regimented).

Describing modern legislatures, Cox and McCubbins (2004) argue that leaders in the legislature have negative agenda power. Leaders of the party cartel determine what comes to a vote on the floor. This prevents members from taking unwelcome votes. It also means that issues that will divide a majority coalition are never placed on the agenda. There is a great deal of scholarly debate about the role of parties in the United States and elsewhere; however, there can be little debate that the agenda at the Federal Convention of 1787 was nothing like this at all.

There was no legislative leader to organize and control debate. The rule in legislatures of this period was equality between the members. When the legislature elected George Washington as President of the Convention and then elected Nathaniel Gorham as Chair of the Committee of the Whole, they were endowing them with no special powers to shape the agenda. Indeed, a careful reading of the notes in this first period reveals that neither of those men spoke much at all (Washington spoke very little throughout the Convention). Instead, their role was to simply recognize a delegate with a proposal. Any delegate could offer a proposal, and debate would proceed until the Convention had concluded the business.

To modern political science ears, this sounds like a recipe for endless cycles,[10] as debate could get stuck on a long series of proposals that ended in deadlock. Though some scholars have pointed out that such cycles may well have existed at the Convention (Riker 1986), in general the debate proceeded without absolute deadlock. Even on the question of representation, which generated most of the heat for the first six weeks of the Convention, the delegates never stopped debating and offering proposals (even if they sometimes deferred to committees).

Instead of having a schedule dominated by agenda-setters and party leaders, the debate in Philadelphia was set by an unstructured agenda where men offered proposals on the problems facing the Convention at any given moment. Influence over the agenda could only be maintained by a popular proposal. What changes were possible given the configuration of preferences?

This unstructured agenda reminds us both of Madison's brilliance and his limitations. Knowing the type of legislature he was about to enter, Madison arrived with a fully formed plan and somehow persuaded his colleagues to begin with his plan (ignoring Charles Pinckney's competing proposal). What Madison realized was that the beginning of debate was his only opportunity to truly shape it. Once the Convention had been together for a few weeks, any chance to move debate would disappear. There was no way to prevent unwelcome amendments or problematic proposals. Once the course had been set in the early days, the only thing that would limit debate and subsequent decisions was the set of delegate preferences. Thus, if Madison or any other delegate was to have influence, it had to come early.

We should expect to see, therefore, that any bold moves came very quickly. Madison seized control of the moment and offered bold reforms. In the early days, Madison's role was to shepherd this plan by making motions and speeches to push the Convention toward approval of the resolutions. There was no more that could be done in this environment. The agenda simply had to emerge as it would. Although, once the shape of debate had emerged, any chance to control the agenda would disappear because of the nature of the schedule. Bold strokes at the beginning could be overwhelmed by a sea of amendments and counterproposals later on. As we shall see below, this is exactly what happened.

Because the agenda was slowly unfolding and decisions piled on top of one another, it is easy to see the Convention as an undifferentiated mass of proposals. In truth, there are certain distinct stages, such as the Committee of the Whole (May 25–June 19), revisions on the floor (June 20–July 26), and the final push after a brief break where the Convention revised the Committee of Detail's Draft (August 6–September 17). All three of our dimensions are in play across each of these periods, though some periods emphasize certain issues more than others (e.g., representation is largely decided during the first two periods, etc.). Though we believe the periods mattered, our underlying assumption is relative consistency in opinion across the periods. We now turn to estimates of those opinions.

3.2 The Estimates

Scholars writing about the Convention typically use two frames of reference: the "founders"[11] or the "states." In the latter case, people typically divide the states into the "large" and "small" states. Individual delegates are most often described either as "nationalists" who preferred a stronger central government, or "localists" who favored state power. Neither frame is wrong; in fact, one must understand both levels to describe voting in Philadelphia because the Convention was made up of individual delegates assembled *within* state delegations to debate an agenda of governmental reform.

Understanding this arrangement is a prerequisite for understanding the Convention because we need to take into account this odd voting structure.

It was not the case that James Madison cast a personal vote. Instead, his vote counted within the Virginia delegation. Typically, Virginia's vote went as Madison's did, but sometimes it did not. Virginia's delegation depended on the collection of Virginia delegates. Our solution is to model individual delegates as part of a particular delegation.

Specifically, our model posits that without any additional information, our best guess to a delegate's ideological position is that it is identical to his state's position. On the other hand, any indications of difference—such as a position taken during debate that is contrary to the state's final vote—would lead us to believe that the position of the delegate was more distinct.[12] This choice of model has two key advantages. First, it is realistic because of the way that it groups delegates within delegations hierarchically. While no model can ever produce the realism of an actual event (nor should a model try to do that), this model comes much closer to the actual event than others with which we are familiar. Second, this model allows us to capture ideal points for delegates who did not speak very often. By leveraging the information available about the state, we can at least say something about most delegates;[13] in turn, the information from the delegates enhances the estimation of state positions because we use information from the former to estimate the positions of the latter. While we believe this is the best available model of voting at the Convention, we emphasize that it is largely a model of states with limited information about individual delegates.

The purpose of this chapter is to display the model estimates of the delegations and delegates at the Convention. Importantly, these estimates help validate the model. If the model uncovers estimates that make no sense, this would suggest that the model is not performing well. However, we will show that the estimates broadly conform to the conventional wisdom about the Convention. However, the estimates serve another function as well. This three-dimensional model allows us to go beyond identifying the one-dimensional groupings of large or small states, nationalists or localists. Instead, we see a picture of three relatively distinct coalitions: the Small states, the Deep South states, and the Core Reform states. Only the Core Reform states were enthusiastic about reform on each of the dimensions described in the previous chapter. The Deep South favored reform on representation and federalism but opposed a strong executive. The Small states opposed reform on representation and federalism but were more open to changes regarding the executive power.

We will turn to a discussion of the coalitions later, but first we begin by clarifying the estimates of the state delegations. We then turn to estimates of some individual delegates, mostly comparing within each delegation.

3.3 Results

Below we plot estimates for each of the delegations and as many individual delegates as possible, we begin by discussing the key delegation coalitions.[14]

3.3.1 The State Delegations

Some states came to the Convention determined to keep the status quo—or something very much like it. Connecticut, New York, New Jersey, Delaware, Maryland, and New Hampshire (though this last state did not arrive until deep into the Convention in late July) all generally favored varying degrees of reforms but wanted to avoid dramatic changes.[15] This group has come to be known in the literature on the Convention as the "*small states*." In most accounts, their opponents are described as either the "large states" or the "nationalists." So far as it goes, there is nothing particularly wrong with this description, but it hides a truth about the coalitional structure of the Convention: there were really three key groups.

One such group was the *Deep South* states: North and South Carolina and Georgia. These delegations certainly favored reform to the basis of representation—especially in ways that advantaged slaveholding states. They also favored a strong federal government, but the Deep South opposed the idea of a strong executive, wanting to leave power with the legislature rather than a single national leader. The Deep South favored significant reform on multiple dimensions, but not the reforms that would create a strong executive branch.

The other group of states that most vigorously pushed for reform—Massachusetts, Pennsylvania and Virginia—we call the *Core Reform* states. It was this set of delegations that favored reform on all dimensions under discussion at the Convention. Without this core group of states that favored most reforms under discussion, the Constitution would have looked very different. Perhaps there would have been no Constitution at all. George Washington greatly feared this outcome. Writing to the

Marquis de Lafayette, he spoke of his duty to resist the anarchy that might result from a Convention failure.

> I could not resist the call to a convention of the States which is to determine whether we are to have a Government of respectability under which life, liberty, and property will be secured to us, or are to submit to one which may be the result of chance or the moment, springing perhaps from anarchy and Confusion, and dictated perhaps by some aspiring demagogue who will not consult the interest of his Country so much as his own ambitious views.
>
> (Washington 1787)

Washington spoke of his fear of a demagogue, but he must have known that the immediate outcome of the Convention would hinge on the collective decisions of the delegates in Philadelphia.

The broad delegation patterns are plotted in figures 3.2, 3.3, and 3.4.[16] Each figure plots the individual delegates grouped within their delegations by dimension. For each plot, higher values on the scale suggest a preference for reform over the status quo, which is assumed to be -1.5 for each dimension. This means a delegation with a position at -1.5—on any of the graphics—essentially favored no changes whatsoever, for that particular dimension. A delegation like Virginia, with consistently positive values, favored reform on all of the dimensions.[17] Relatively few states held the position of favoring no reform—New York and New Jersey are alone in this on the representation dimension. In this sense, the state delegations generally agreed on some level of reform; the questions were what kind and how much?

In figure 3.2 the dimension on the x-axis is representation. Would the Convention approve of a system of proportional representation, or would it resist that reform and stick with equal state representation in the legislature? Though there were other issues on the table, this was the central concern for this dimension. Delegations to the left favored equal state representation, while those on the right preferred proportional representation. Toward the top of the plot, we can see the cluster of states that most strongly opposed change: Connecticut, Delaware, Maryland, New Jersey, and New York, or what we call the Small states. The last two states

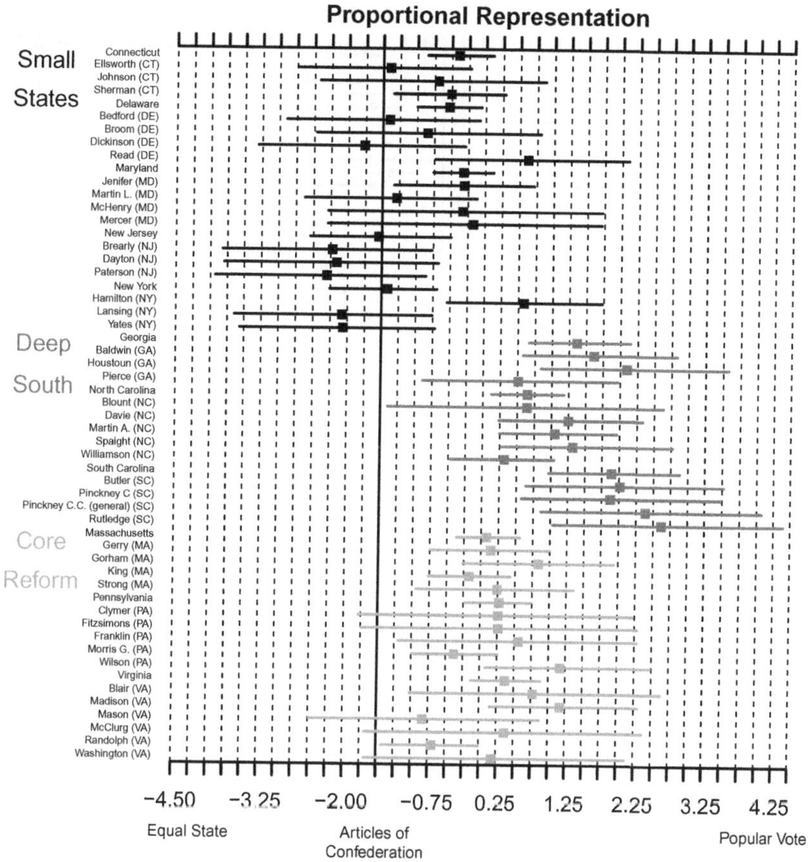

Fig. 3.2.

Note: The figure displays each delegation's position on the proportional representation dimension, along with 95% HPD intervals for each estimate. Within each grouping, the top dot displays the overall delegation's position (note that this is typically estimated with the smallest amount of error), and below that are all other delegate estimates. Lower estimates indicate a preference for the status quo of equal state representation, while higher estimates indicate a preference for changing the basis of representation in substantial ways.

of New Jersey and New York held the strongest anti-reform positions on representation, while the other states were more open to some form of compromise.[18]

In contrast, the middle section of the plot displays the states most consistently in favor of reform on representation: Georgia, North Carolina, and South Carolina—or the Deep South states. These delegations and

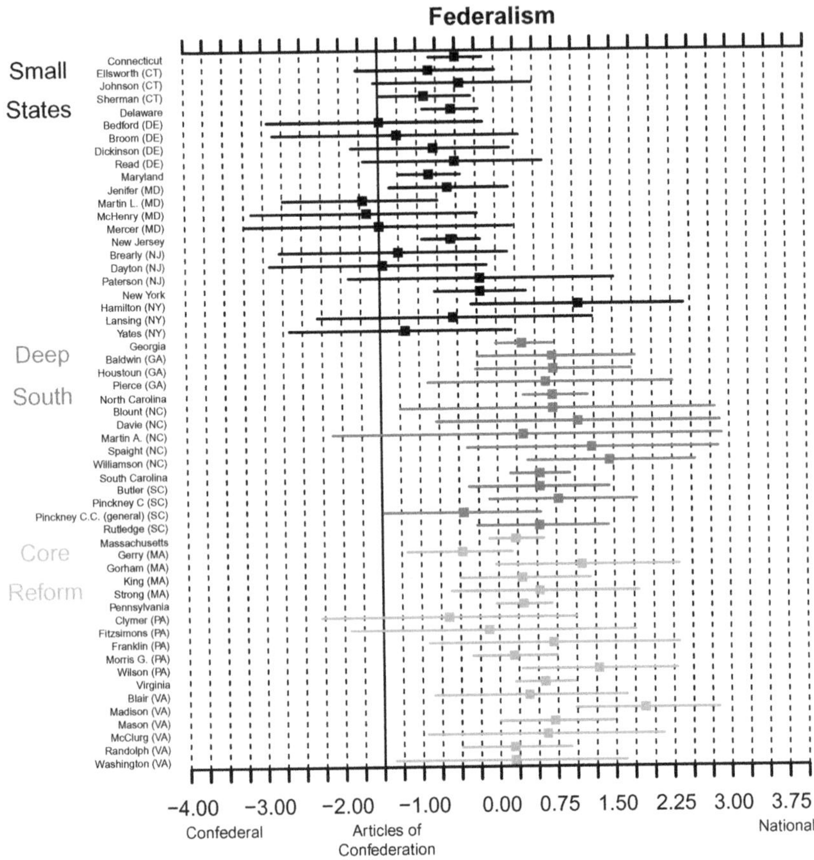

Fig. 3.3.

Note: The figure displays each delegation's position on the federalism dimension, along with 95% HPD intervals for each estimate. Within each grouping, the top dot displays the overall delegation's position (note that this is typically estimated with the smallest amount of error), and underneath that are all other delegate estimates. Lower estimates indicate a preference for the status quo of strong state power, while higher estimates indicate a preference for creating a stronger national government.

delegates strongly favored change, as did the Core Reform states at the bottom of the graph: Massachusetts, Pennsylvania, and Virginia. On this dimension, the states most strongly in favor of changes were the slaveholding states from the South (although Maryland and, especially, Virginia, also had many slaves). As we have argued elsewhere (Pope and Treier

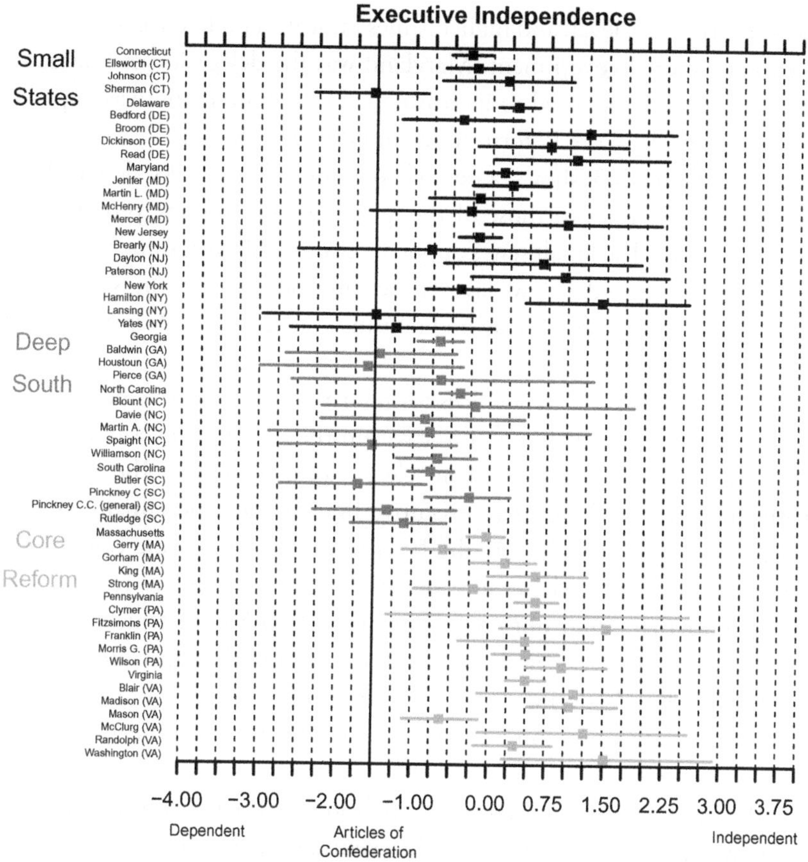

Fig. 3.4.

Note: The figure displays each delegation's position on the executive independence dimension, along with 95% HPD intervals for each estimate. Within each grouping the top dot displays the overall delegation's position (note that this is typically estimated with the smallest amount of error) and underneath that are all other delegate estimates. Lower estimates indicate a preference for the status quo of a relatively strong Congress while higher estimates indicate a preference for reform and the creation of a more independent executive.

2011, 2012), the pernicious institution of slavery was intrinsically linked with the debate over proportional representation.

The second dimension of debate is plotted in figure 3.3, and it was about federalism. How much power would the central government have relative to the states? Again, lower values indicate a preference for leaving power at the state level, and higher values indicate a preference for creating a strong national government. Maryland was the delegation estimated to be most strongly opposed to increasing national power, and was opposed by the rest of the Core Reform states and the Deep South.

Thus, figure 3.3 shows a set of coalitions that breaks down along roughly similar lines to those of the questions surrounding proportional representation. The Small states opposed reform and, with some individual exceptions discussed below, favored keeping power with the states. The collection of delegates who favored reform came from the Deep South and the Core Reform states.

Figure 3.4 displays preferences for reform of the executive power. This dimension is about dividing power within the national government. The Articles of Confederation had no clear executive power. The proposed Constitution would create an executive branch and a potentially powerful president (eventually). At the bottom of the figure, one can see the Core Reform states, where most delegates favored executive reform. The delegations that stand out come from the Deep South, which opposed giving power to the executive, favoring placing it in the legislature instead. Pennsylvania and Virginia most strongly favored a strong executive, but their allies on the question were more likely to come from the Small states than from the Deep South.

The debate between these three coalitions at the Convention defined what was possible and what would eventually pass. The eventual document's outline can almost be seen in these figures. The Convention passed a change to proportional representation that moved representation dramatically in the direction of the pro-reform states. This was, at least partially, to placate the slave-owning interests. Ironically, a fairer system of representation was motivated in no small part by the fact that slave-state delegations required it. They did so not to move closer to an ideal of "one person, one vote," but to maximize the representation guaranteed to the Deep South. On the federalism dimension, the Convention broke down along similar lines. The national government would be given much more power. Again, this was the desire of the Core Reform states and the Deep South. The Small states were able to maintain some controls on the new government but were not in a position to stop all change.

If the Deep South held a position similar to the Core Reform states on all dimensions, there would be no need to consider the separate issues. Indeed, the formulation of pro-reform and anti-reform states would make sense and we could simply describe the Convention by alluding to Small states and the Nationalists. However, the Core Reform states were not joined by the Deep South in their desire for a strong national executive. For reasons we elaborate below, the Deep South favored legislative power over executive power. They did not want a strong president.

It is worth noting that George Washington was at the center of the Core Reform states on most issues. He is estimated to have been a strong proponent of a powerful executive—among the most strident on this question at the Convention—which brings us to the discussion of individual delegates. So far, we have only discussed the results by delegation. In many respects, this makes sense. But the figures do hold interesting findings about what went on within the individual delegations, including some that split and some that were united, and how the overall delegation dynamics may have played a role at the Convention.

3.3.2 The Individual Delegates

Our model places individual delegates in context—as part of a delegation. Despite the fact that all of the delegates are tied to a specific context, we do observe some significant variation within delegations. Some are quite unified, others are much more divided, and of course, sometimes these patterns vary by dimension. Other books focus attention on the biographies of the delegates, but our focus is on the model described above (and in the appendix). Our purpose in this section is not to provide a full background on each delegation, but to demonstrate how the model reveals patterns within each delegation. Were there splits in the delegation? Were they relatively unified? What were the individual delegation dynamics?

The Small State Delegates

Connecticut lends its name to the Great Compromise of the Convention, and the deal is sometimes referred to as the Connecticut Compromise. As can be seen in figure 3.4, Connecticut was clearly more moderate than some other Small-state delegations like New Jersey or New York, but it was not much different than Delaware or Maryland. It was, in general, a relatively unified delegation, with one key exception: Sherman was much more opposed to executive power than were his two colleagues (Johnson and Ellsworth).[19]

On the question of presidential power, Sherman actually fits best with the delegations from the Deep South. He is clearly skeptical of the idea of an independent executive. Robertson (2005) argues that Sherman "played a pivotal role in spoiling Madison's agenda and altering his substantive plans for Constitutional design." He helped create "a Constitution that nationalized only enumerated public goods and imposed potentially high transaction costs on any further nationalization of policy authority" (225). These estimates suggest that Sherman was relatively out of step with most colleagues on federalism, though he was closer to a moderate position on representation. Dougherty and Heckelman (2006) point out that Sherman's success may have had more to do with his moderate position than with any special rhetorical talents. Our model concurs, although only on the representation dimension. In other respects, Sherman was against reform.

Delaware, similar to Connecticut, was relatively unified, but not quite a united front. Overall, the delegation opposed proportional representation and was clearly not warm to the prospect of strengthening the national government too much. However, all of the delegates except for Bedford were generally in favor of a strong executive relative to the Congress.

John Dickinson was the Delaware delegate who spoke most often at the Convention. His position on most dimensions can be found near the delegation's center, with the exception being a relatively anti-reform stance on representation—very much in line with the typical portrait of Dickinson. On June 7, John Dickinson entered the debate initially by (successfully) arguing that state legislatures should elect the second branch of the national legislature, but his vision for the Senate was clearly less pro-reform than was Madison's, who argued on the same day that proportional representation was essential. Madison was so perturbed by Dickinson's argument of June 7 that he later added into his notes a footnote remarking that "an election by the State Legislatures involved a surrender of the principle insisted on by the large States & dreaded by the small ones, namely that of a proportional representation in the Senate. Such a rule would make the body too numerous. As the smallest State must elect one member at least" (Farrand 1966, vol. I, 150). On that day of debate, Madison did not yet grasp that his cherished principle of proportional representation would founder on the preferences of the Small-state delegates that would firmly oppose him—men like Dickinson who had gone so far as to ask his state legislature to instruct him to insist upon representation in the upper chamber of the Congress.

George Read is the other outlier on representation. He argued that it was completely insufficient to simply amend the articles, comparing that to "simply putting old cloth on a new garment." He wanted stronger national power, but the dimension where Read really stood out is representation. It is true that he worried about the small states becoming "ciphers" in the new government (and worked with Dickinson to get instructions to vote for an equal state vote). However, he also took the position that the small states had little to fear from the form of government then being proposed (Farrand 1966, vol. I, 463). And he actually went so far as to propose that the states be abolished, though perhaps only as a rhetorical gesture. Read is thus very difficult to pin down ideologically (as seen by the significant uncertainty of his estimate).

Gunning Bedford, though he was clearly anti-reform, does not look that different from Dickinson and the other Delaware delegates on representation and federalism. Bedford is, of course, well-known for his rhetoric, going so far as to argue that "the small [states] would find some foreign ally of more honor and good faith, who will take them by the hand and do them justice" (Farrand 1966, vol. I, 481). His opinion on that point may have been unpopular, but historians cite it as an example of the small states proving their credibility on the point of insisting on a "compromise." From the model, it appears that Bedford's voting record was more out of step with the other delegates on executive power than anything else.

Maryland delegates, though close in physical proximity to the Philadelphia Convention site, did not arrive quickly and were not a cohesive group for much of the Convention. James McHenry arrived first on May 28, but did not have a partner—for his short stay of a few days—until June 1.[20] After McHenry left, Daniel of St. Thomas Jenifer arrived, followed by Luther Martin one week later. Daniel Carroll would not arrive until July 9, and John Francis Mercer would join the delegation for less than two weeks in August. McHenry finally returned on August 6 and remained to sign the Constitution along with some of the delegation—though not Martin. Maryland's delegation was definitely not temporally unified. Moreover, though the differences were not as stark as those of

New York, this delegation was relatively more divided than some of the other Small states. Jenifer, McHenry, and Mercer made up the relatively moderate core of the delegation, while Luther Martin was often in dissent and certainly opposed to reform on both the proportional representation and federalism dimensions.

At age 64, Jenifer was one of the older members of the delegation. William Pierce, in his famous sketches of the delegates, described him as a man "who sits silent" (Farrand 1966, vol. III, 87) at the Convention. Whether this was because of Jenifer's age or because he was simply less gregarious is unknown, though some biographers note that he was a long-time friend or acquaintance of George Washington, based on a mutual interest in horses (Morton 2006, 150). Regrettably, Jenifer's silence leaves far less room to find out his own views. However, it is possible he exerted significant influence on the delegation votes, especially on the federalism dimension (see, in particular, figure 3.3). Note that the position of Maryland on that dimension is far more moderate and pro-reform than it would be if Martin and McHenry, the two other long-serving delegates, had been the key actors. This delegation was divided 14 percent of the time, a greater number than all but Massachusetts.

McHenry is also often described in terms that suggest him as a moderate. Steiner (1907) says that "McHenry took a middle ground, though his own views were not strongly in favor of much centralization of power" (97). It is probably the latter phrase that describes McHenry best. As the figures suggest, McHenry was against reform on most dimensions, though he was possibly more moderate on the question of representation.

The anti-reform position in the delegation was truly anchored by Luther Martin. As is obvious in the figures, Martin strikes a stridently state-oriented, anti-proportional representation position. His own biographers describe him as "ignored," noting that "his grave is unmarked and unknown today" because of his like of fame which

> lies in the principles—largely undervalued and misrepresented in his own day—which Luther Martin espoused and in the unpopular persons and causes which he represented so successfully. . . . [H]e antagonized the delegates to the Constitutional Convention of 1787 from the large states by exposing, denouncing, and ultimately defeating their plan to push through the convention a form

> of government which would have put all state and local offices and legislation under the thumb and all citizens under the heel of an omnipotent national government.
>
> (Clarkson and Jett 1970, 2)

Martin's aim was to keep the Constitution from being passed, and he was one of the few delegates to vigorously campaign against the document in his home state.

When it came to representation, New Jersey was a delegation on the fringe. They were uniformly against reforming representation. Yet, when we examine the individual estimates, an interesting pattern emerges; Paterson, the very author of the New Jersey Plan, appears to have been relatively open to reform. Virtually all textbook accounts of Paterson place him as the anti-reformer. Without disagreeing with any of that, it is also clear that William Paterson was much more open to reform on federalism and the executive than were many other delegates; indeed, he was a proponent of the Electoral College and giving the president significant independence (Farrand 1966, vol. II, 50–59). Perhaps this is because, as Richard Beeman (2010) puts it, Paterson had an "abiding fear of disorder. . . . He fervently believed that 'obedience to the law is the first political maxim and duty in a republican government.'" And Paterson did agree that the government "should have new powers, including that of coercing state governments to bow to the superior will of the central government" (148–49). He was opposed to reform of representation but wanted the new central government to be able to succeed.

New Jersey is best seen as a relatively unified delegation, but its neighbor New York, is perhaps better thought of as two delegations. No other set of delegations displays the divide seen in the figures above. Alexander Hamilton was not a member of the dominant faction in New York politics that was led by Governor George Clinton, but he was selected anyway because of his prominence and previous work calling for such a convention. This made him the third-wheel of the delegation, and he clearly found himself out of step with the other two delegates, Robert Yates and John Lansing. The model's estimate of the position of the delegation puts New York at the far left on the representation dimension and particularly hostile to proportional representation and to enhancing executive power.

This estimate is obviously justified by the fact that both Lansing and Yates were strongly against any kind of reforms. Their participation in the early portion of the Convention (both would be gone by July 10, a week before agreement on the Great Compromise) was largely limited to opposing a strong central government and insisting that the states should be represented equally in the state legislature. They left because they could sense where the Convention was heading, and they returned home to prepare to fight the outcome. Ironically, their departure hurt the cause of the Small states by eliminating a state vote in their coalition. However, Hamilton was not able to cast New York's vote in their absence. The rules of the delegation required two voting delegates for New York to cast a vote, giving Yates and Lansing tremendous power over the delegation's decision. When they left, Hamilton (who was already gone, but would later return) was unable to cast any kind of vote for New York.

Hamilton has been criticized by biographers who portray him as being out of step with American ideals (Knott 2002). Whether or not that characterization is true, at least at the Convention, Hamilton was the delegate from New York most likely to be in step with the sentiment for reform. His positions were closer to the overall final product than were those of either Lansing or Yates. Some biographers describe him as playing little direct role at the Convention. Beeman (2010) wrote that Hamilton's own plan of government had "little influence on the subsequent proceedings of the Convention" (164). However, seen in the context of voting between alternatives, Hamilton probably played a much larger role than people realize. We will return to the influence of his relatively extreme alternative plan in chapter 4.

As a group, the Small-state delegates were more unified than the other delegates, but within each delegation there were interesting differences and compromises that reflected the individual delegation vote—though no delegation was as divided as New York. Had these delegations alone been making the decisions, they would have reformed relatively little. The one exception is that they appear open to a strong executive power. This is in contrast to the Deep South delegates who favored reform in other ways, but not for a strong president.

Deep South Delegates

The Deep South states are commonly classed as part of the large-state coalition in favor of reform. Our model broadly agrees with this simplification on the dimensions of representation and federalism where the Deep South favored reform. However, on the question of a strong national executive, the Deep South opposed reform and favored congressional power over executive power.

The Georgia delegation is emblematic of this pattern, and no delegate stands out too much from the group. Abraham Baldwin, originally from Connecticut, was the son of a blacksmith and grew up to become a lawyer after serving in the Continental Army as a chaplain. Biographers, relying on Yates's notes, have generally argued that Baldwin favored representation in the Senate based on property, rather than population or statehood (Coulter 1987, see chapter 6). As the Convention came to an impasse over representation, Baldwin cast a very interesting vote. On July 2, the states voted on equal state representation in the upper chamber. Up to this point in the Convention, Georgia had voted against such proposals. But on this day, biographers speculate that Baldwin voted for the proposal, leaving the representation of the Senate in limbo. Because Georgia's vote was not counted in the totals—recall that for a vote to pass decisively, it required a majority of states voting on that specific roll call—the vote stood at five votes to five (with Georgia divided).[21]

One biographer describes this as an act that "saves the convention" by giving the delegates "time to work out a solution" (Coulter 1987, 96–97). It is a generous interpretation of Baldwin's actions and may have some validity. There are, however, problems with it that can be seen in the estimates. Baldwin's position on the representation dimension appears slightly more moderate than Houstoun's, but he was more extreme than Pierce, who voted more consistently with the small-state coalition. Because Baldwin—to our knowledge—never publicly commented on this vote at the Convention, it is difficult to know what could have motivated it. Luther Martin argued that it could have been due to a conviction that the Convention might dissolve. However, that is mere conjecture.[22]

William L. Pierce, also a transplant (born in Virginia) and also a veteran of the war and an aide to General Nathanael Greene, is famous mostly for drawing several character sketches of Convention delegates. This is probably because he only attended the first month of debates, leaving by July to represent Georgia in the Confederation Congress. Of his own character, Pierce said "I shall not attempt to draw [it], but leave those who may choose to speculate on it, to consider it in any light that their fancy of imagination may depict" (Farrand 1966, vol. III, 97). Because of his relatively small number of votes, Pierce's positions are estimated with less precision than his colleagues', but it is clear that on questions of representation and executive power he was more moderate than his other Georgia colleagues, rarely saying much of consequence and generally voting with the delegation.

Houstoun, though London-educated in the law and a very successful politician, appears to have played very little role at the Convention (other than his supposed vote against Baldwin), merely serving on one of the representation committees. In general, it was a unified delegation, but perhaps not quite as unified as North Carolina.

North Carolina fits the general pattern of the Deep South. William Blount, Richard Dobbs Spaight, Hugh Williamson, William R. Davie, and Alexander Martin made up one of the single most homogenous delegations. Only Williamson stands out slightly on representation for his moderation and probably helped bring about the Connecticut Compromise. Speaking of Alexander Martin, one biographer classifies him as a "mild" states' rights advocate (Morton 2006, 191), but Martin was only a hair more skeptical than the other delegates. He voted much more consistently in favor of national power than did most others. Though the entire delegation was against an independent executive, Spaight took the strongest stance in this direction. Though he appears to have attended virtually every session, Spaight's most consequential speech came early in the process when he moved to allow the Convention to reconsider all proposals (not a small point, as we discuss in the next section). On the whole, the North Carolina delegation had very little division or difference. One oddity, despite their pro-reform position on representation, is that they eventually voted for the Connecticut Compromise, probably because of the concessions made with respect to slavery (we take up this story in the next chapter).

Finally, the South Carolina delegation—filled with Pinckneys—also fits the southern pattern. John Rutledge and Pierce Butler were joined by Charles Pinckney and General Charles Cotesworth Pinckney in as firmly a pro-reform delegation as any on representation and federalism. Charles Pinckney introduced his own plan of the Convention, though it never received any serious attention. He was clearly willing to grant powers to the national government—even more enthusiastic about that than were many of the other southern delegates. In opposition to this position was General Charles Cotesworth Pinckney, who was more skeptical of national power than were any of the other southern delegates. General Pinckney could certainly be classified as a nationalist, just not one as committed to the cause as others, like Madison or Hamilton, were. For instance, on June 6 he argued that he "wished to have a good national Govt. & at the same time to leave a considerable share of power in the States" (Farrand 1966, vol. I, 137). Like the other delegates from his state, he was a distinct advocate for slavery; though he argued that the national government should someday be able to stop the importation of slaves, he introduced the amendment that prevented such a proposal from being considered until 1808. Despite these small intra-delegation distinctions, South Carolina, as a delegation, can accurately be described as one of the more extreme states at the entire Convention. As a group, they were as strongly for proportional representation (never wavering, as did North Carolina) and against an independent executive as any delegation.

Thus, the picture that emerges of the Deep South is one of unity and clarity—probably even more so than among the Small states. Most every delegate wanted to reform representation (so that their slaves could be counted in their favor). They uniformly favored a stronger national government (General Pinckney being the lone, minor exception). But they wanted this stronger national government to be dominated by the legislature. This makes these delegations, in many respects, pivotal for the reform agenda (Dougherty and Heckelman 2008). Despite their support, this reform agenda never would have passed in the form it eventually did without the pivotal group of delegations: the Core Reform states.

The Core Reform States

This group of delegations was the key to the changes that were made. Collectively, they favored reform on every dimension. They wanted to make representation fairer for states with large populations. They wanted to centralize power in a stronger national government. They wanted a strong executive to check the Congress. And yet, though such descriptions are collectively true of the delegations, not every delegate can be described that way. Indeed, perhaps more than the other groups, these delegations display some surprising intra-delegation differences.

The best way to think of Massachusetts is as the Core Reform state that was the most open to compromise. The best known example of this is Massachusetts's divided vote that sealed the "Great Compromise" on representation.[23] In general, the Massachusetts delegates favored reform. This was especially true of Gorham who took a strong reform position, particularly on representation and federalism.[24]

The delegates who were closest to the overall delegation's mean position were Caleb Strong and Rufus King. Strong, a Massachusetts lawyer, was a fairly moderate delegate on many dimensions. He voted with the small states some of the time on representation. He was for a stronger national government, but not to the degree of other delegates. He favored a stronger national executive than did many of the southern delegates, but he was hardly leading that charge. Rufus King was known as a great orator and attended virtually every session of the Convention. Sometimes described as a "nationalist" (Rossiter 1966), the model suggests that King was actually fairly moderate and a man near the center of his state's politics.

The final delegate from the group was Elbridge Gerry. A very vocal delegate, Gerry must have been frustrating because he often appears in the notes to take contradictory positions. An eventual opponent of the constitution, he worked hard in the Massachusetts Convention to defeat the proposal. At the Convention, he claimed as his justification that the Constitution lacked a bill of rights and was a threat to republican government. Without disputing the importance of that claim to his thinking, it is also clear that Gerry opposed too much centralization of power and feared a strong executive. On both of those dimensions, Gerry fits better with the opponents of reform than with his own delegation. This is ironic given his later career as a federalist, but perhaps it fits with the view of Gerry as an iconoclast.

Pennsylvania is similar to Massachusetts in that the delegation has some divisions but was clearly in favor of reform. The Pennsylvania delegation had few if any travel needs (they were all from Philadelphia or nearby, many of them serving in the state legislature). Thus, it was easy to caucus with the Virginia delegates before the Convention and form a correspondence of views. However, a glance at the estimates for Pennsylvania reveals that a meeting of the minds would have been easy not merely as a result of time spent in conversation, but also because the two delegations were quite near one another ideologically. Both delegations favored proportional representation and a stronger central government, and when it came time to discuss a strong presidency, the bulk of the Pennsylvania delegation would have sided with true nationalists like Madison and Washington.

The core of the delegation included Benjamin Franklin, Thomas Fitzsimons, Robert Morris, and George Clymer. Each of them took a reform position on all dimensions: strongly in favor of proportional representation, a stronger national government, and a powerful, independent executive. The two delegates that lie slightly apart from this core are Gouverneur Morris and James Wilson.

Gouverneur Morris, though absent for much of June and July, was a force at the Convention, and his estimated position—clearly pro-centralized government but more moderate when it came to representation—fits his aristocratic tendencies very well (he helped establish the first Bank of North America). Morris's negative view of the mass public permeated his opinions: "Give the votes to the people who have no property, and they will sell them to the rich who will be able to buy them" (Farrand 1966, vol. I, 533). Morris was against counting slaves, at least if they could not vote, and argued sharply against the Deep South on this point. His position on slavery made him no friend of proportional representation with the entangled three-fifths compromise, an important reminder that proportional representation—at least as it was expressed at the Convention—was bound up with the view that slaves should be counted, at least for something. This benefit to the South was of paramount importance to them.

James Wilson wanted as strong a national government as could be obtained. One biographer describes him as "impatient" with "the misgivings of the state sovereignty" arguments. He opposed "Randolph's plan whereby members of the upper house would be nominated by the state legislatures and elected by the House" (Smith 1956, 222). Wilson felt that gave too much power to the states. More than just about anyone at the Convention, he wanted sovereignty to rest at the higher level of government—almost to the point that he did not recognize a lower level of government.

Finally, it is worth pointing out that although Thomas Fitzsimons was not a frequent speaker at the Convention, the model estimates him to be among the firmest proponents of a strong national executive (along with Alexander Hamilton). For instance, he seconded the motion to change the restrictions on presidential electors and prevent any non-property holders from serving in this capacity (Farrand 1913, 201, Vote 241). He also spoke often about regulating trade. Morton (2006) describes him as a friend of "mercantile and banking interests" (92). He is an example of a case where the model permits us to see things that might otherwise go unnoticed.

Fitzsimons spoke so little that he is widely considered in a lesser light, but in a model of voting, his views on a strong executive are easier to see.

Finally, we turn to the most important delegation of all: Virginia. These delegates were unquestionably the leaders of the Convention—without Madison's agenda-setting and Washington's prestige, what would the document look like? The estimates display a delegation that collectively favored reform but was also sharply divided in some ways. Rather than being a unified delegation, they were a collection of reformers working with allies far less enthusiastic about some of the proposed changes.

Because the Virginia delegation arrived first on the scene (other than the Philadelphia residents, of course), most accounts of the Convention begin with the two delegations planning together in a tavern. Accounts often describe it in much the way Rossiter does.

> Madison had little trouble persuading his fellow Virginians to sit through a series of daily conferences "in order," as Mason put it, "to form a proper correspondence of sentiments." The sentiments were those that Madison had been communicating to his closest friends. . . . Of all the services he rendered to the Constitution, this "consultation among the deputies" of Virginia, which had brought together and then pushed delicately toward the end he had in mind, was the most consequential.
>
> (Rossiter 1966, 261)

This picture of Virginian unity is, no doubt, accurate, at least as an aspiration they shared. However, it was clearly an unfulfilled aspiration, as can be seen in the figures above. On representation, Madison strongly favored reform, as did the center of the delegation—Blair, McClurg, and Washington—with Mason and Randolph more skeptical. Indeed, in some respects they look more like Small-state delegates, although not extremely so. On federalism, the delegation was far more unified, but again Madison is seen as the true nationalist who favored dramatic reform. Finally, on executive power, most of the delegation (including Washington) favored a strong executive, but Mason and Randolph were sharply opposed.

In each figure, one can see that James Madison was at the extreme edge of opinion at the Convention. He was just about as extreme as any delegate, virtually defining a pole of nationalism: proportional representation and a strong central government. Banning (1995) described Madison as a man who believed "lesser changes would not work" (138).

However, Banning found Madison "impossible to place . . . at a single point on any single spectrum of opinion . . . on the matter of . . . responsibilities that should be placed in federal hands, he stood much closer to the middle" (164). Perhaps Banning is thinking of Madison's later career and Republican partisanship, because we can find literally no evidence in the record of the Convention for a moderate Madison opinion. The dimension where he is the closest to his colleagues is on the question of national institutional design, but even there Madison favored a strong executive as much as the core of the delegation did.

His opponents were George Mason and Edmund Randolph. Mason, born in 1725, was one of the oldest members of the Convention. His provincial upbringing in Virginia—indeed, this was the first time in his life that he was away from the state for more than a few days (Beeman 2010, 42)—was offset with a first-rate education and a background in the law. As the author of Virginia's Declaration of Rights, Mason is typically portrayed as most deeply concerned with the protection of his natural rights and placing this consideration above most others at the Convention. Nothing in the model contradicts this, but it also makes clear that Mason was also concerned about the basic structure of the government being put into place. Beeman describes Mason's relationship with Washington as "long and affectionate" (44) but notes that friendship would be tested. The figures clarify why.

One biographer describes him as a man who "feared the power of a solitary official equipped with the power to veto legislation and to appoint federal officeholders. The president could use his patronage to corrupt Congress the way the British monarchy had used a similar power to manipulate the Parliament" (Broadwater 2006, 197). Mason's voting and views led him to prefer a more localist stance. He did, no doubt, favor some centralization of power in the national government but would keep Congress supreme. Mason later wrote against provisions of the Constitution that gave the executive and the Senate "an exclusive power of legislation" (Mason 1787).[25] As Broadwater (2006) puts it "Republicanism, more than states' rights, provided the rationale for Mason's opposition [to the Constitution]" (207).

Edmund Randolph displays a position on the graph similar to Mason, though his explanation of his position was not terribly convincing; he said he might not "oppose the Constitution without doors. He meant only to keep himself free to be governed by his duty as it should be prescribed by his future judgment" (Farrand 1966, vol. II, 641). Since he later supported the document, he was clearly keeping his options open. When he transmitted the document back to Virginia, he claimed that "it is not, therefore, to be concluded that we are opposed to its adoption" (Reardon 1974, 119).[26] Overall, taking into consideration some of the available text evidence and the model, it is best to think of Randolph as somewhat confused in his thinking and positions, though he did obviously provide signs of resistance in his voting record at the Convention.

Finally, we note George Washington's estimated positions. With respect to both representation and federalism, Washington is very near the average of his delegation, but with respect to executive independence, Washington was as in favor of reform as any other delegate at the Convention. Unfortunately, there is no way to know how calculated this position was (since Washington must have known the high likelihood that he might come to hold this office). Perhaps some of Washington's position was driven by his experience in the revolution and the need for a firm executive hand; perhaps some was driven by personal ambition.

It is ironic that the core of the reform coalition is made up of some relatively fractious delegates. Randolph and Mason would not even sign the Constitution, nor would Gerry. Yet it was these delegations that pushed the hardest for changes to their system of government. This irony is a reminder that the rules of voting were crucial. For instance, Randolph's and Mason's votes would have carried more weight at the Convention—or possibly even have been pivotal—if they were not constrained within the strongly pro-reform Virginia delegation.

It is one thing to visually inspect the ideal points and see coalitions. It is another to test the coalition structure more formally. We take that up in the next section.

3.4 The Coalitions

On June 30, in the midst of the debates over the representation compromise, James Madison said

> the states were divided into different interests not by their difference of size, but by other circumstances; the most material of which resulted partly from climate, but principally from the effects of their having or not having slaves. These two causes concurred in forming the great division of interests in the U. States. It did not lie between the large & small States: it lay between the Northern & Southern. And if any defensive power were necessary, it ought to be mutually given to these two interests.
>
> (Farrand 1966, vol. I, 486)

To the best of our knowledge, Madison's statement here was the first example of any scholar attempting to explain the divisions and factions at the Constitutional Convention. Madison would not be the last. Our own entry is the latest in a long line of work that has tried to clarify the number of coalitions that varies between two (Beard 1913) and more than 30 (McDonald 1958). More conventional answers have tended to lie in between (Ulmer 1966; Londregan 1999; Jillson 1988; Slez and Martin 2007; Heckelman and Dougherty 2013). Though the idea of "two" in the sense of nationalists against parochialists remains powerful.[27]

The question of those coalitions—how many? what are they?—is central to an explanation of the deep structure of voting. Our visual inspection of the plots above suggests three coalitions. Is this supported by the data? And how well do they compare to the literature we just cited?

Given the low dimensionality and small number of states, our visual inspection and grouping of delegations should be fairly accurate, but we check our assessments using more formal approaches to classification. In particular, we apply an agglomerative hierarchical clustering to the average positions of the state delegations (Everitt et al. 2011). The approach begins with each state in its own cluster, then recursively combines clusters one at a time according to a distance criterion of closeness (in this application, a comparison of the spatial distance between the largest space between observations in the two compared clusters). This process continues until there is only one cluster left. The entire process is reflected in a tree structure denoted by a dendrogram. The order of these mergers is reflected in the height of the connections between branches (the axis is the distance between clusters; the recursive nature of the merging requires that these distances always increase as the number of clusters decrease). One informal method of selecting the number of clusters to interpret is to inspect the dendrogram and draw a line where there is a "large cut" (Everitt et al. 2011, 95).[28]

Figure 3.5 displays the three coalitions (ignoring individual delegates). The estimated clusters here correspond very well to a simple visual inspection

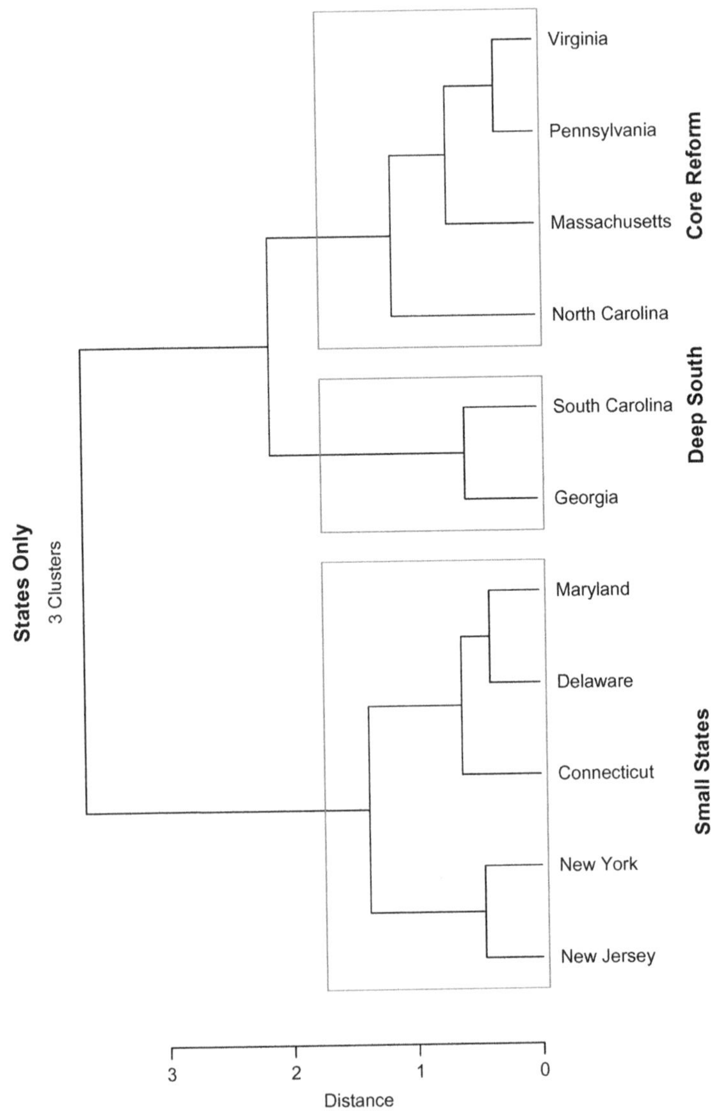

Fig. 3.5. Clusters of State Delegations

of the ideal points. The exception is North Carolina, which clusters slightly better with the core reform states than it does with the rest of the Deep South. Note that this clustering is applied to the mean ideal point positions of the states. Applying this to the entire Markov chain Monte Carlo (MCMC) sample, iteration by iteration, this indeed turns out to be the most likely structure (with a probability of 28.2%). However, our inspected structure that groups North Carolina with the Deep South is the second most likely structure (16.25%). However one classifies North Carolina, it is clear that the delegation was deeply interested in the reform project, as long as it favored slaveholders' interests. Sometimes they voted most closely with the Core Reform states, but other times they looked just like the Deep South, depending on the issue (as will be seen in subsequent chapters).

Figure 3.6 includes the individual delegates and shows a six-cluster model that looks at the individuals alone. We found that, for individuals, the number of clusters was somewhere between four and six. This figure shows the largest number of clusters for the individuals only. It corresponds to our visual inspection of the ideal points reasonably well, confirming our intuitions. The Core Reform states are easily seen in that those delegations tend to cluster together, though there are exceptions, like Washington, who clusters with the mid-Atlantic state delegates.

One very interesting point about this result is that the three delegates who refused to sign the constitution—Elbridge Gerry, Edmund Randolph, and George Mason—all cluster together.[29] It is clear also that the most traditionally "nationalist" delegates—Alexander Hamilton, James Wilson, and James Madison—all cluster together, suggesting that the model is picking up on their behavior well.

States like Maryland and New York that were often divided are separated into different clusters. Similarly, Roger Sherman, who often opposed his colleagues, is separated from them. Finally, Delaware delegates, like Dickinson, who were strongly in favor of a powerful chief executive are separated from the others in their delegation who were less enthusiastic about this plan.

Table 3.1 displays our best estimate of the coalitions and compares them, very briefly, to the literature cited above. There are significant similarities but also differences. Beard's claims are essentially unlike ours. In his original critique of Beard, McDonald describes the complex nature of the coalitions and suggests three coalitions and two lone wolves (Maryland and Connecticut).

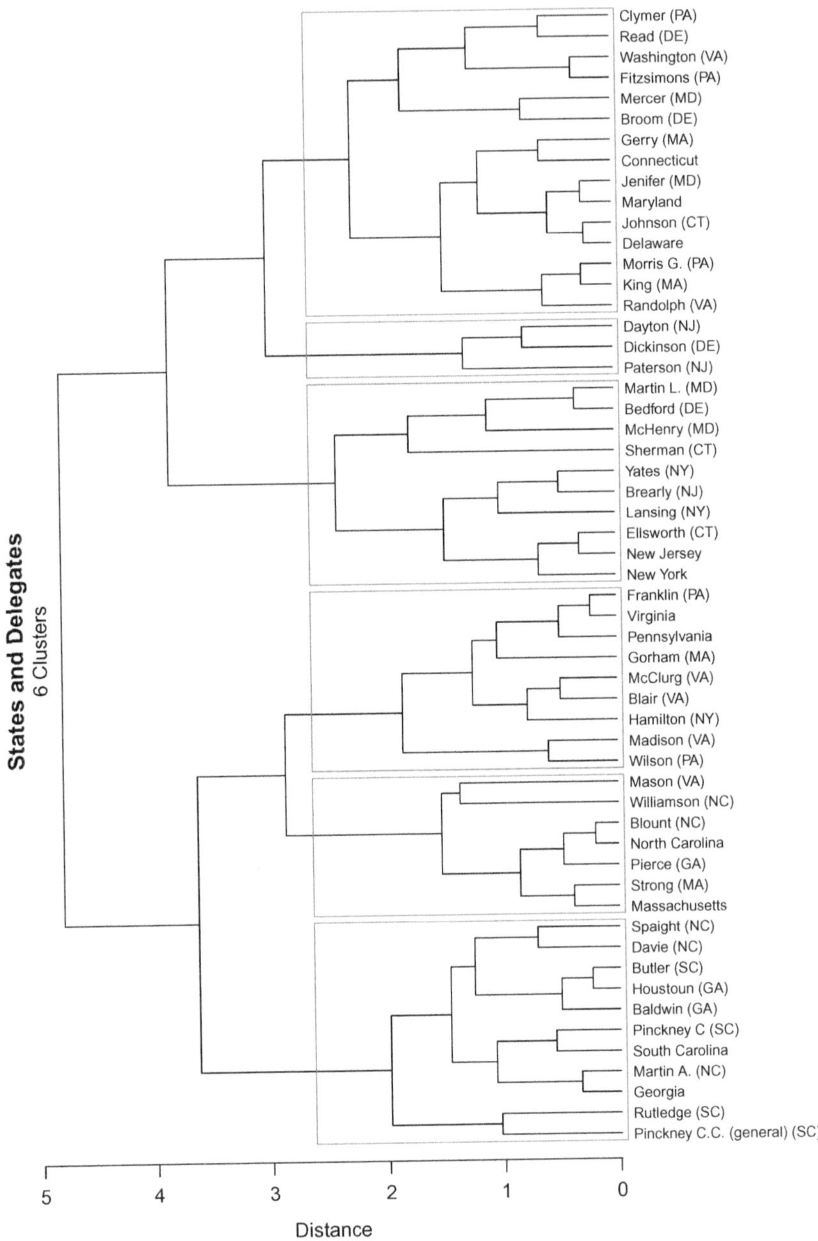

Fig. 3.6. Clusters of Individual Delegates

Table 3.1 Estimated Coalitions Compared to the Key Points in the Literature

Author(s)	Group 1: Small States	Group 2: Core Reform States	Group 3: Deep South States
Pope and Treier	Connecticut Delaware Maryland New Jersey New York	Massachusetts Pennsylvania Virginia	Georgia North Carolina South Carolina
Compared to:			
Beard (1913)	Little commonality with ours or any other suggested coalitions.		
McDonald (1958)	Splits the small states in ways we do not, and MA is, again, separated from PA and VA.		
Ulmer (1966)	Very similar to our estimates, though MA is separated from PA and VA.		
Londregan (1999)	Similar to our estimates, but focuses more on a large- vs. small-state distinction, ignoring other relevant cleavages.		
Jillson (1988)	Similar to our estimates, but GA and MA are placed in their own coalition, and CT is separated from other small states.		
Slez and Martin (2007)	Very distinct from our estimates.		
Heckelman and Dougherty (2013)	Somewhat different from our estimates; based on a single dimension that separates the small states.		

When he looks at individual delegates (as well as ratification), he sees more individuality than actual coalitions. However, McDonald and subsequent critics all realize that the coalition structure is complex. Among historians, the traditional two-class structure prevails, but that is not the norm among most social scientists who write on this subject. It is true (and not surprising) that if we cluster into two categories or focus on a single dimension, we typically see the large state vs. small state dichotomy; however, this result is driven by assuming, like Londregan, either a single dimension of conflict, or assuming that the winning coalition is constant during the Convention.

More recent scholars, like Jillson and Slez and Martin, have critiqued the idea of a constant coalition structure. They have used a model that divides the Convention into several periods, with each period often dealing with a discrete set of issues (although never exclusively so). Consequently, they have found five coalitions.

In comparison, we think the structure is simpler. Their conclusions are driven by the periods of the convention they employ. However, because the Convention delegates talked about all of the issues across multiple months, we think it is more realistic to think about an underlying agenda that may change across periods but does not truly reflect a change in preferences or coalitions. The scholar we come the closest to is Ulmer, whose claims are quite similar to ours, although he separates Massachusetts from what we label the Core Reform states.

In conclusion, we draw the following inferences. First, the Convention structure is not explained well by a single dimension or a pair of clusters. This, by itself, implies that the structure of the voting is not simply based on the fight over representation between the "large" and "small" states. The debate was about more than that; issues such as federalism and the presidency were of significant importance as well. The second implication is that the key interest at the Convention that defined how the Constitution unfolded was slavery. The Core Reform states constantly favored dramatic change, but they could not stitch together a single coalition that was constant. On representation and federalism, they were aligned with the Deep South, but this would never have created the powerful executive that was the end result because Georgia and the Carolinas were interested in maintaining their perceived advantages in the legislature. The key states that helped create a strong president were Delaware and Maryland, which took the place of the small states in the coalition that created that power. That slavery is known to be important is already part of the literature. What is new here is that slavery divided nationalism into two types: southern nationalists favored congressional power, while other nationalists favored a strong executive.

We do not believe that it is surprising that the Constitutional Convention was a complicated affair involving multiple and sometimes cross-cutting coalitions. The implication of that claim is that a simple one- or two-dimensional structure of opposing coalitions is not enough to explain the outcome. Further, seeing the importance of these three overlapping coalitions shows the significance of slavery on specific dimensions. Our aim in the next three chapters is to show how events played out on each of the three dimensions. In the final chapter, we conclude with a discussion of what this means for our beliefs about the Constitutional Convention, the document they produced, and any interpretations we might offer today.

CHAPTER 4

Representation: The Primary Cleavage

Once delegates had finally arrived, George Washington opened the Convention and began the business. The Convention had to start somewhere, and Washington formally opened the agenda by turning to his colleague from Virginia, Governor Edmund Randolph. "Mr. Randolph [then] opened the main business" by introducing a series of resolutions that came to be known as the Virginia Plan (Farrand 1966, vol. I, 18). It may have been Randolph who introduced the plan, but it was James Madison who had authored most of it and was truly setting the agenda at this propitious moment. Madison was about to set off a chain reaction that would end in massive changes to the governing institutions of the young country. Very quickly—and with much less fanfare than we might imagine, given the scope of the changes—Madison's agenda would quickly become a reality. What Madison chose to focus on, as a prerequisite to all other issues, was *representation*.

While he would see initial success on this representation dimension, he would also soon find the limits of that success in that the Convention had deep divisions on the issue; in fact, representation cleavages were the clearest divisions on any dimension. When they first met in Committee of the Whole—a procedural device used to begin the debates—the reformers won victory after victory (with the Deep South in full support of their representation agenda). However, the rules they had created for the Convention, combined with the agenda, and the preferences of all of the delegates, inherently meant there was only so far the reformers could go. Once they secured their initial victories, the alternatives available that would beat the existing plan (win-sets) started to shrink quickly.

Historians have described this agenda-setting moment, where Madison structured the dimensions of debate, in different ways. Clinton Rossiter (1966) titles his chapter on the opening of the Convention "The Nationalist Assault." His impression was that small-state delegates, or opponents of a strong national government, would become the targets of a rhetorical assault. Jack Rakove (1996) similarly describes the introduction of these resolutions as an "ultimatum" (60), implying that the opponents of the plan would be forced either to respond with their own terms or possibly face a breakdown of the Convention. Also emphasizing the theme of conflict, Beeman (2010) describes the introduction of the Randolph resolutions as a "high-stakes" gamble launched by the "co-conspirators" of Virginia and Pennsylvania (87). Note that, in both cases, the focus—and this is true for most accounts of the Convention politics—was on differences over representation. There were other dimensions of conflict, as discussed below, but the key point here was that the specific dimension of representation best described the focus of their conflict.[1]

Despite the deep divisions over representation, they would soon discover, with some exceptions like Robert Yates, a strong desire for change that would yield the U.S. Constitution. The Confederation Congress's authorization said that the Convention met for the "*sole* and *express* purpose of revising the Articles of Confederation" (Farrand 1966, vol. III, 14, emphasis added). Perhaps because of the limited nature of this mandate, some delegates were surprised to hear the tenor and tone of Randolph's resolutions,[2] but others must have realized this was the real business of the Convention, and that the possibility of dramatic change was real.

Yates was among those who was surprised, so he recorded on that day that Randolph's plan was for a "consolidated" union (Farrand 1966, vol. I, 24). No longer would the national government simply be an administrative unit—really a government over other governments—but it was to become a national whole. Thus, even at the outset, both supporters and opponents of reform must have understood that the basis of representation would have to change. Randolph's opening resolution—following the authorization of the Congress—described itself as a plan to make sure the Articles of Confederation would be "corrected & enlarged" (Farrand 1966, vol. I, 20). That description obviously did not fool Yates (nor others, we suspect): "The house then resolved, that they would the next day form themselves into a committee of the whole, to take into consideration *the state of the union*" (Farrand 1966, vol. I, 18, emphasis in original). Given that Yates may have already been learning just how out of step he was with his colleagues, he may have been less than pleased that the Convention was taking up the Randolph resolutions. Nevertheless, perhaps he took some comfort from the fact that they were only beginning in Committee of the Whole.

Committee of the Whole certainly sounds benign, and some authors treat it that way. Van Doren (1948) described it as simply "a parliamentary device . . . for keeping discussions as informal as possible and for leaving certain decisions still subject to review by the Convention" (51–52). The implication of this interpretation is that delegates would merely debate and consider ideas, finally taking up the real debate later, outside of the Committee. Perhaps this is how the Committee began: to discuss and learn about preferences and attitudes so that delegates could form judgments and test ideas in the crucible of debate at the Convention. It left open the possibility that a simple restart of the debates was possible if the Committee was unsuccessful in achieving any kind of unity. Thus, the possibility existed that nothing would come out of this debating society, and the Convention might go nowhere.

Yet, other authors have noted that the Committee of the Whole provided for much more than simply feeling out preferences.[3] The consequences of Committee of the Whole meant that the agenda created in the first few weeks would carry through the entire Convention. It was just a committee, but it was also the means by which to influence the subsequent debates. Agenda-setters, like James Madison, made immediate and impressive progress toward their goal of reforming the government in this setting. Yet, because of the rules (see, section 3.1), Madison and others would find that the decisions of this committee were not truly final. All votes were subject to reconsideration.

Still, Madison's preparations and specific proposals set the agenda in a way that turned out to be remarkably successful on multiple dimensions (not just representation, though that came first). Of course, he could not have known that in advance, and it was possible that Madison's proposal would fall flat if the delegates were unreceptive to his ideas. Finally, there was no guarantee that Madison's (formally Randolph's) proposals would be the blueprint. Indeed, the Committee debated several possible proposals and could have advanced any of them to the floor. It could have simply restarted debates on the floor without any proposals, or it could have selected one particular proposal to serve as the working document of the Convention. Either of the first two possibilities would have meant that the Committee was closer to a debating society, considering ideas about government in the abstract. The reality turned out to be that the Committee served as a relatively smooth transition to the debate on the floor. Instead of simply being a "parliamentary device," with all decisions remaining tentative until later, the Committee produced a clear plan based on Randolph's motions. That plan was never discarded in the way other competing plans were dismissed.

This fact is important to our modeling strategy. If the Committee was merely a debating society, we ought to allow for significant preference changes between periods—modeling delegates and delegations separately for each period. Elsewhere, we have tested for the possibility that preferences changed between periods of the Convention and have found little evidence that this was the case (Pope and Treier 2011). This is because the key movement was the agenda and not the preferences of the delegates. Madison's agenda proposals, combined with the open debate rules, created the conditions for the coalitions that would form.

This chapter explains how the agenda interacted with delegation preferences and created the changed basis of representation: the Core Reform states united with the Deep South states to reform representation. Although this coalition would break down on other conflicts (see chapter 6), it solved the key division at the Convention. Delegates could have chosen many different paths of reform. As the Convention was opening for business, no one could have been certain how far the changes would go. As we saw in the earlier chapters, Madison's preferences—especially with respect to the nature of representation—went very far indeed. But could the delegates to the Convention deliberate their way down a path that would see Madison's goals realized? This question highlights the importance of how they would debate these questions and in what order. The debates tested whether or not proposals were acceptable to the delegates at the Convention. Though Madison's aspirations would win some decisive victories, they were never fully realized because, before the Convention did anything else, they began by reaffirming an old principle that the Convention would have equal state votes.

4.1 Equal State Representation?

Questions about representation had been asked long before this particular meeting in Philadelphia. Thirteen years earlier, in that same city, when the first Continental Congress met in September of 1774,[4] the question had first come up for the states. The delegates from the separate states had assembled to consider what course of action they could unitedly take in the face of the recent Intolerable Acts, which closed the port of Boston and imposed de facto military rule in the city. Though there had been much correspondence between the states in the years leading up to this meeting, an assembly of the 13 colonies was unprecedented.

Consequently, before anything could be done on that day, they had to agree to the rules of their novel chamber. Though they might not have realized it at the time, the most important rule to fix was the rule of voting. Historian Jack Rakove (2010) describes their problem: "[s]hould it be by colony, with each delegation casting a single vote; by 'poll' with each delegate voting as an individual; or by 'interests,' which meant proportioning the vote of each colony to its population, wealth or trade?" (54).

Patrick Henry, of Virginia, forcefully argued for the latter option and delivered one of his famous lines: "I am not a Virginian, but an American."[5] The problem with proportioning the vote on anything other than an equality of the states was information. The Congress lacked it, and delegates pointed out the difficulty in getting it. Today we think of equality as being about individual citizens—one person casting one vote. But in the absence of clear information about how to weight by population, that conversation could not even really begin. In the midst of a revolutionary crisis, they very quickly decided on a very different form of equality. Rather than apportioning votes by population or by letting each state delegation cast several votes (one for each delegate), they decided that each state would have an equal vote in the deliberations. Rakove suggests that the need to make decisions of consensus may have been a consideration beyond the practicalities of arguing over how much more weight should Virginia receive than Delaware. Regardless of the reasons, the decision was consequential because it established a precedent that became the status quo. It was almost certainly a useful precedent for the young nation in that it helped induce participation of self-governing states. But it also meant that equal-state voting would still be the status quo when Madison began planning for the Constitutional Convention, and it would become an issue on which the entire country might have come apart or the Convention could have plausibly foundered.

This key sticking point of the first six weeks—representation in the new legislature—was something that some delegates to the Convention considered contesting in the rules of the Convention. In Madison's papers, he writes a note that includes this description of the early discussions between Pennsylvania and Virginia delegates before the Convention opened.

> Previous to the arrival of a majority of the States, the rule by which they ought to vote *in the Convention* had been made a subject of conversation among the members present [emphasis added]. It was pressed by Gouverneur Morris and favored by Robert Morris and others from Pennsylvania, that the large States should unite in firmly refusing to the small States and equal vote, as unreasonable, and as enabling the small States to negative every good system of Government. . . . The members from Virginia, conceiving that such an attempt might beget fatal altercations between the large & small States, and that it would be easier to prevail on the latter, in the course of the deliberations, to give up their equality for the sake of an effective Government, than on taking the field of discussion to disarm themselves of the right & thereby throw themselves on the mercy of the large States, discountenanced & stifled the project.
>
> (Farrand 1966, vol. I, 11)

At least some delegates—both Gouverneur Morris and Robert Morris from Pennsylvania, and perhaps others—suggested that they should change the rule immediately at the opening of the Convention, a dramatic shift away from the established Articles of Confederation rules (Jillson and Wilson 1994). Others believed it would be easier to persuade their fellow delegates of their views on representation during the course of debate. It must also be noted that convenience suggested waiting until the delegates actually debated the question. Delegations were ad hoc and created without equal numbers; they were meant to represent the states as corporate units—the very question Madison and other reformers wanted to address with reform.

Madison was planning to push on multiple dimensions: a correct rule of representation would obviously be a crucial part of the plan, but the delegates would need to simultaneously discuss other features to convince their colleagues of the advantages of the Virginia Plan. And, in fact, much of the first few days of debate focused on other elements of the new government, like separate branches, a new executive, and national courts. All of these represented significant changes from the status quo of the Articles of Confederation set of institutions. Madison and other likeminded participants seemed to believe that showing how different the national government would need to be on many different dimensions would help reluctant delegates see the need for major changes. All of the issues were considered simultaneously during the first few weeks. For clarity's sake, and because our model illustrates how different issues were across dimensions, we take each dimension one at a time and begin with representation. Jack Rakove's (1996) description of Madison's strategy guides our decision here: "it was Madison's insistence on solving the problem of representation first that set the course of debate" (60), and so we begin there.

The Virginia Resolutions, as introduced by Edmund Randolph, stated (in resolution 2): "Resd. therefore that the rights of suffrage in the National Legislature ought to be proportioned to the Quotas of contribution, or to the number of free inhabitants, as the one or the other rule may seem best in different cases (Farrand 1966, vol. I, 21).[6] They did not actually spend much time debating that specific resolution during the first couple of days of real debate. However, the question hung in the air, and proportional representation would very quickly become the central issue of the first six weeks of the Convention, stretching beyond the Committee of the Whole and well into the second stage of debates on the floor. It was not until this question was settled that anything else could be decided. Figure 4.1 displays, using our model, how the agenda unfolded on the representation dimension.

As each of the agenda figures is quite similar (here and in subsequent chapters), we want to take a moment to explain them to the reader here. Similar to the figures that displayed the positions of delegates in chapter 3, each dot in the figure indicates the estimated position of the proposal for each vote. Note that for simplicity we do not include all votes, merely those that are among the most significant proposals or changes. The bar around the point indicates a 95 percent highest posterior density (HPD) interval.[7] This gives us a sense of the location of each proposal in the space. When the error bar is solid, this means the vote passed the Convention, therefore becoming the new status quo from which the delegates worked. When the bar is dashed, this means that the proposal failed.[8] In some instances, for purposes of identifying the model, we have fixed the location of certain proposals, and there is no error bar. This does not change the underlying estimates; those votes merely provide a structure around which all estimates can be fit cleanly. The figure should be read from the bottom to the top, as the agenda moves forward through the Convention. We do not attempt a full explication of every vote at the Convention. In moments where the action does not lead to major status quo changes, we skip over points that others might consider important, keeping our focus on illustrating which votes changed outcomes at the Convention and moved the debates.

For the sake of clarity, we label each of the votes with a value that corresponds to the vote number in Farrand's notes. Anyone may therefore seek out more particular information about the vote in that vital resource. We also include a short description to help the reader understand the substance of each vote (where necessary). The earliest point—the first entry in figure 4.1—displays the position from before the Convention even began: the Articles of Confederation representation rules. For convenience of fixing the estimates, we have placed it at a value of -1.5 on the scale (with no error bar around it because it is a fixed point in the model). Thus, moves toward reform, or in the direction of proportional representation, are to the right as the agenda progresses up the figure. This orientation is used for each dimension: movement to the right represents movement toward reform and change. Movement to the left signals movement back toward the Articles of Confederation and the status quo.

The first significant proposal on this dimension—Vote 5—came on May 31. The proposal was to elect "the first branch of the national Legislature, by the people" (Farrand 1966, 50). As figure 4.1 shows, this was hardly controversial and did not do much to move the decision point away from the status quo. The vote merely established that the House would be elected by the people rather than by the states. This is a good moment to point out that some changes that might seem to be important departures from the status quo are not necessarily significant when one considers these developments from the perspective of scaling the votes in debate. Bowen, for instance, described the passage of this proposal as "surprising" (48). The model suggests it might not have been perceived that way by the delegates. Of course, this was a clear change from the procedure under the Articles of Confederation in which state legislatures sent representatives—who were sometimes referred to as ambassadors—to the national legislature. So it was a change, but, given the preferences of the delegates, it was not a key modification from the Articles. Perhaps this is because the specific mode of election and the apportionment across states was temporarily left untouched.[9]

Discussion of representation continued, but it was not until June 11 that the major changes on the issue emerged (the Vote 37 Proposal in figure 4.1). King (MA) and Wilson (PA) introduced a proposal that "the right of suffrage in the first branch of the National Legislature ought not to be according to the rule established in the confederation; but according to some equitable ratio of representation" (Farrand 1966, vol. I, 192). Presumably, delegates understood that they were not necessarily endorsing the entire Madisonian plan, but the vote opened serious consideration of Madison's ideas about representation. New York, New Jersey, and Delaware voted against this proposal (with Maryland divided). The vote passed without too much trouble and foreshadowed the unified small-state coalition: Connecticut, New York, New Jersey, Delaware, and Maryland. However, it can clearly be seen in the figure that change was occurring, as the proposed representation rules were very different than what had come before. Movement along these lines must have been encouraging to Madison, though to match his plans, the Convention had far to go.

Almost immediately there was another proposal—Vote 39—pushing slightly more in the direction of proportional representation, but it did not do so directly. Wilson (PA) and Charles Pinckney (SC) moved to add the following description to the clause which clarified that people would be represented "in proportion to the whole number of white & other free Citizens & inhabitants of every age sex & condition including those bound to servitude for a term of years and three-fifths of all other persons not comprehended in the foregoing description, except Indians not

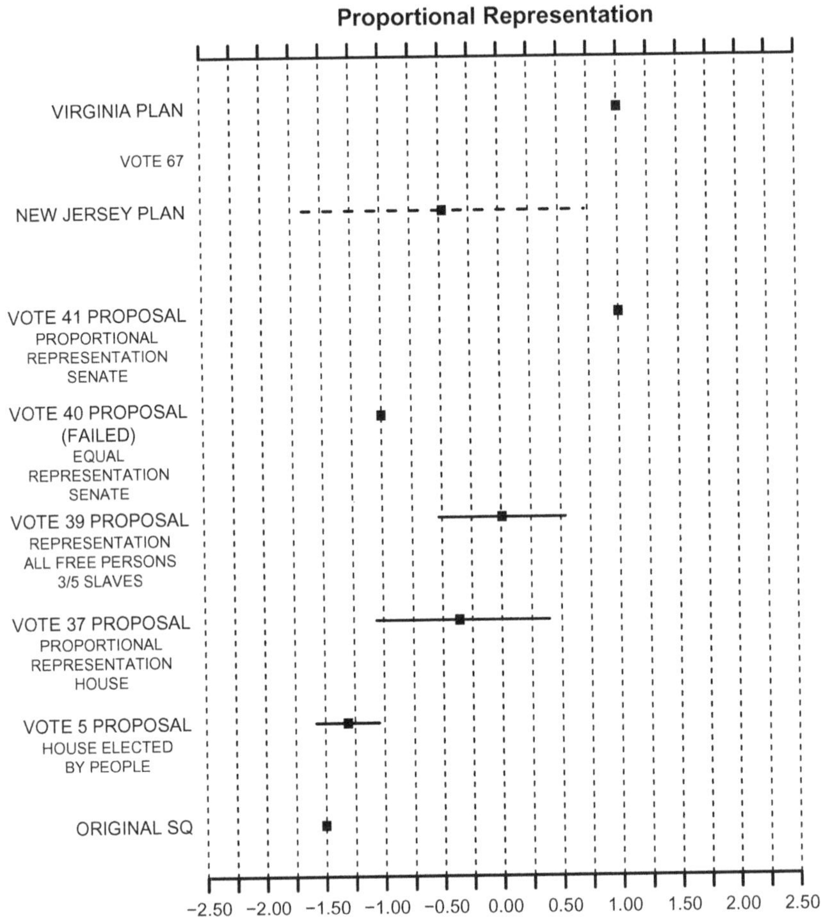

Fig. 4.1. Selected Key Votes in the Early Portion of the Convention's Committee of the Whole (May 25–June 20)

Note: For clarity, Vote 67 is placed in between the two votes, because in this vote, the Virginia Plan and New Jersey Plan were the two options under consideration.

paying taxes, in each State" (201). This moved the proposed rule slightly closer to the position of the southern states that believed they would be the more populous in the future.[10] It was done without explicitly mentioning slavery, known to be a difficult subject. On this vote, which first ties slavery and proportional representation on the agenda, only Delaware and New Jersey can be found in dissent. New York and Maryland were apparently comfortable with the language that would become the basis for the three-fifths compromise, but obviously some delegates disagreed. Elbridge Gerry argued that property should not enter into the rule of representation. "Why then shd. the blacks, who were property in the South, be in the rule of representation more than the cattle & horses of the North?" (192). Despite this provocative question (which would come up again), no one responded to this discordant note. Though we cannot know exactly why, it is instructive that this vote came immediately before two crucial votes on representation: Votes 40 and 41, which proposed equal representation in the upper chamber and proportional representation in the upper chamber, respectively.[11] These two key votes defined the central question: would the people (with the franchise being held only by white males) be represented as equal citizens in the legislature or not? Even before they settled those questions, the desires of the southern states were being considered carefully. After all, the Deep South was already a key part of the coalition.

Until this moment, the delegates had voted on questions that united a fairly broad cross-section of members. The agenda on representation had moved substantially in the direction of Madison, Morris, and others who wished to see representation change. So far, however, the Convention had only danced around the key question about representation of the states. As early as May 30, Madison had been arguing for representation based only on population, and the next day Roger Sherman (of Connecticut) had suggested what would become the Great Compromise by arguing that, in the second branch of the legislature, there should be a single representative from each state selected by the state legislature. The Convention readily approved the principle of selection via state legislatures (see the next chapter on federalism), but put off real discussion of the principle of equality of representation until June 11.

By this point, Sherman was clearly agitated. The Convention was only a few days from closing the Committee of the Whole and moving to the floor. Sherman, no doubt, wanted some resolution of this issue and "moved that a question be taken whether each State shall have {one} vote in the 2d. branch. Everything he said depended on this. The smaller States would never agree to the plan on any other principle" (Farrand 1966, vol. I, 201). The brackets in the quotation are of particular interest. According to Farrand, Madison originally recorded the statement by saying that each state shall have "an equal vote," but at some later point revised it to the word "one." Apparently, such was his hostility to the plan that Madison went back to this page of notes and revised it to remove the word "equal" from the discussion.

Sherman got his wish, as there was no other speech (at least as Madison's record of speeches shows) before there was a vote on equal state representation in the upper chamber. Sherman's motion (see Vote 40 in Farrand), which would have moved the proposal of the Convention substantially back toward the status quo, failed by a vote of 5–6. Massachusetts, Pennsylvania, Virginia, North and South Carolina, and Georgia defeated Connecticut, New York, New Jersey, Delaware, and Maryland. After the proposal failed, it was immediately followed by a motion from James Wilson (Pennsylvania) and Alexander Hamilton (New York) "that the right of suffrage in the 2d. branch be according to the same rule as in the 1st. branch" (202). The exact opposite coalition passed the motion (see Vote 41 in figure 4.1).[12]

This vote, on June 11, completed the movement of the Virginia Plan in a very new direction. Vote 37—taken at the beginning of that day—clarified that a chamber of the new government would be apportioned according to population, but the new vote took things much further. With the victory in Vote 41, the delegates had clearly (in the space of a few minutes, or, at most, a few hours) dramatically altered the character of representation in the government by removing any state corporate representation. It was now clear that the newly proposed government would not represent states as states, but be much closer to representing the people. This would have pleased both those states and delegates favoring proportional representation (the Core Reform states) as well as proponents of slavery and slave-state interests (the Deep South), but it could hardly have gone down well with the Small-state coalition.

They voted on a few other matters that day, but the delegates had already concluded the most important business immediately before them. There is no other recorded discussion of dissent or unhappiness with the vote, though Sherman's words suggest he could not have been remotely satisfied with the outcome. However, he and other Small-state delegates must have understood that this defeat was not final (perhaps because they were in Committee of the Whole). By now, it seems likely to us, they realized that the Committee of the Whole would be reporting some kind of resolution to the floor, rather than the floor simply beginning anew.

From the viewpoint of the Core Reform states, which had hoped to persuade the delegates of the importance of unification in a sufficiently powerful government, this result was probably more than satisfactory. Moreover, it cannot be emphasized enough how powerful Madison's initial victories were. Figure 4.1, in our view, shows the single most dramatic move of the Convention in terms of a victory in Vote 41, and it provoked a response. The Small states would immediately start producing their own plan (discussed in a moment).

Some literature suggests that Madison's influence is overstated, or at least that his opponents require more credit (Robertson 2005). Though readers should be mindful of the fact that Madison would soon lose ground on many issues, figure 4.1 shows the power of his influence; whatever victories Madison would later lose, his influence is never completely erased, but his opponents would try. A victory of this magnitude—moving the projected plan so far on the representation dimension—had to generate a reaction. Small-state delegates began meeting to prepare an alternative to the Virginia Plan. The eventual plan they would settle on—the New Jersey Plan—would have several features that clearly moved away from the Articles of Confederation, but were far less of a change to the status quo than anything contemplated by the Virginia Plan.

4.2 Rejection of the New Jersey Plan

The Committee of the Whole had served its purpose. Delegates had discovered which ideas were acceptable to at least a majority of their colleagues. The Virginia Plan had been revised and was now ready to go to the floor for additional debate. However, there were still competitors for the attention of the Convention. These were the plans that were on the table as the Committee of the Whole ended its deliberations, and they were particularly focused on representation:

- The Virginia Plan: it had occupied the Convention for weeks and was now revised into a new form that was acceptable to a number of delegates (though certainly not all delegates).
- Dickinson's motion: Dickinson made a motion to simply take up the Articles and make revisions.[13]
- The New Jersey Plan: formally a proposal to simply revise the Articles and go not much further; a foil to the Virginia Plan.

- Hamilton's speech: not truly a plan, Hamilton merely sketched out several propositions that would take the Convention much further than it had previously considered going.[14]

This was a key moment of decision, as the Convention could go in any number of directions, even opposite ones. The most logical and obvious agenda was to report the Virginia Plan to the floor (after all, it had the most support), but that was hardly the only option. As indicated by Dickinson's motion and the introduction of the New Jersey Plan, the Small states were dissatisfied. Rakove portrays the New Jersey Plan as essentially the embodiment of dissatisfaction with the Virginia Plan's representation arrangements. Other authors go further. Beeman (2010), for instance, portrays the introduction of the New Jersey Plan as a desire to return to a government that was "part national and part federal, one that mixed federal and state powers in a system of divided sovereignty" (162).

On the surface, this idea that the large-state and small-state delegations were in fairly strong conflict over both representation and national power seems very logical, in part because there is some truth to it. Certainly the Small-state coalition broadly favored far less reform than their colleagues and were unalterably opposed to the question of representation. However, there are exceptions to these broad patterns. Beeman notes that Dickinson was actually a friend to a stronger government, quoting him as saying that they "wish for two branches in the General Legislature, and are friends to a good national government" (162). Indeed, we will return later to this theme of the small states' willingness to make reforms on other dimensions when we note that Dickinson's supposed nationalism had more to do with support for a strong chief executive than the broader set of issues. For now, we focus on representation because that was the crucial cleavage in the debate.

The key difference between the New Jersey and the Virginia Plans was actually on representation (far more than on any of the other dimensions). It must be noted, however, that relative to the Articles of Confederation, both plans were significant departures. As Rakove (1996) put it, the key issue motivating the New Jersey Plan was not federalism or executive power or anything else, but representation. "The supporters of the New Jersey Plan did not bother to defend Paterson's proposals as an adequate solution to the problems of union. Instead they argued that the Virginia Plan was at once illegitimate and impolitic. The Convention had no right even to consider any change in the basic principle of representation under the Confederation" (62).

A straightforward debate would have been to pit the New Jersey Plan against the revised Virginia Plan during discussion. Indeed, there are some speeches made on this point. Consistent with his claim in the notes that he would argue that the Small states should "give up their equality for the sake of an effective government" (Farrand 1966, vol. I, 11), Madison prepared to argue the Confederation's weaknesses and how little the New Jersey Plan did to remedy those ills.

However, before the Committee of the Whole could turn to this discussion, they spent an entire day listening to Alexander Hamilton's beliefs about good government. This day, June 18, is sometimes regarded as a lost day, largely because Alexander Hamilton must have spoken for several hours (historians suggest the speech might have been five or six hours, and it takes up 12 pages of Madison's notes). For instance, Beeman (2010) suggests that "it would have little influence on the subsequent proceedings of the Convention, and, indeed, it no doubt tried the patience of many of the delegates." He goes on to state that Madison would have been frustrated and seen the plan as "at best a diversion from the main issues" (164). Van Doren (1948) dismisses the speech by noting that it was "not even discussed" (94). Some accounts of the Convention even omit a reference to Hamilton's speech. It is ironic that in his work on the Convention, *E Pluribus Unum*, Forrest McDonald—a biographer of Hamilton—does not even discuss the speech.

Bowen (1966), however, may strike nearer the truth when she offers the conjecture that "Hamilton may have anticipated the effect of his words." Rather than seeing the speech as a hopeless effort, she suggests that perhaps "he deliberately outlined to the Convention a system of government so 'national,' so 'consolidated' that it would make the Virginia plan look tame and the New Jersey plan look impossible" (115). Though Bowen is not explicit about the dimensions of the conflict, she leaves open the possibility that Hamilton was trying to influence debate with his proposal. If Hamilton could place his ideas (never formalized as a proposal) in such a way that it framed the New Jersey Plan as being at one extreme and his own plan at a different extreme, with the Virginia Plan in the middle, perhaps he could influence views of Hamilton's own plan.

Rossiter (1966) suggests something very similar but gives the credit not to Hamilton but to "Madison and Wilson [who] had decided to let

Paterson, Sherman, and the others hear the views of a 200 percent nationalist, and thus to make the Virginia Plan appear as a reasonable middle-ground between two positions" (178). However, even he is skeptical of this, as he goes on to suggest that "this is, in truth, to imagine a supremely clever bit of strategy for which the evidence is entirely spectral" (178).

Estimating the locations of the New Jersey and Virginia Plans allows us to consider what Hamilton's plan would have needed to look like to frame the New Jersey Plan at one extreme and the Virginia Plan at the center of debate. This probably cannot conclusively settle the question, but it does

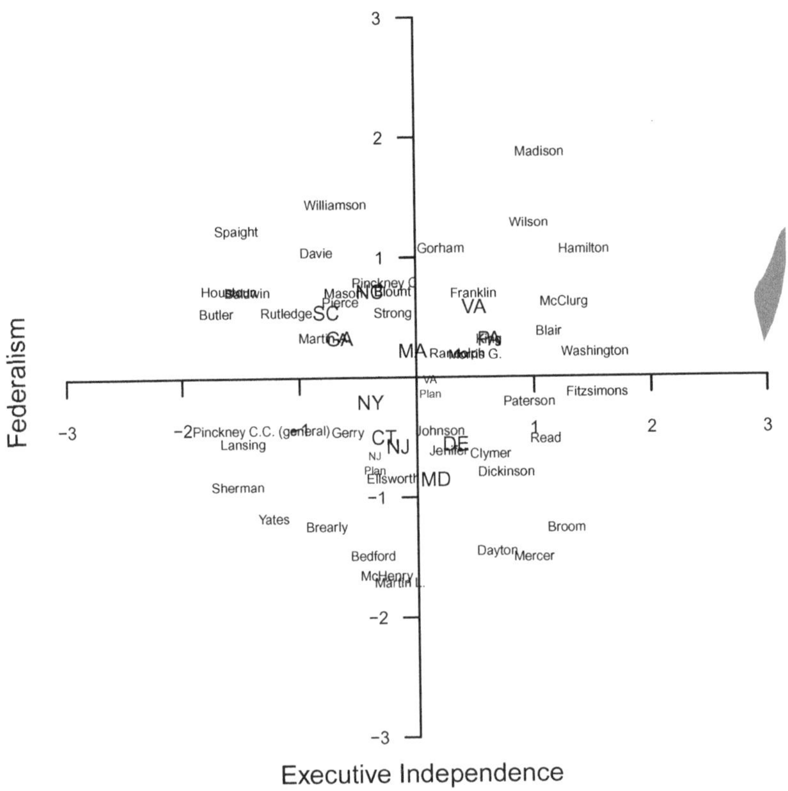

Fig. 4.2.

Note: Ideal points represent the position of delegates on two dimensions—federalism and national institutional design. The shaded area indicates the region where Hamilton could have proposed a plan that would have been unacceptable to any delegate except Hamilton, but that he would have preferred to the Virginia Plan.

go beyond "spectral" evidence to suggest exactly how Hamilton's speech would have needed to be structured to accomplish its purposes.

Figure 4.2 plots the position of the delegates in two dimensions alongside a shaded gray region (in the upper right-hand portion of the graph) that represents every possible Constitutional position on federalism and executive independence that is closer to Hamilton than the Virginia Plan, while also being further away than the Virginia Plan relative to every other delegate at the Convention. We show not the representation dimension here, but the other two dimensions to give a sense of the full scope of what Hamilton was proposing (and because he spent little time talking about representation in his speech). On the question of representation, Hamilton's views on the lower chamber were broadly similar to those held by Madison and other reformers. However, when it came to the rest of the government, Hamilton struck an incredibly strident tone. He proposed an incredibly powerful central government with extraordinary executive power. The figure assumes that Hamilton was not suggesting anything different on the dimension of representation (he does, within the speech, appear to endorse the scheme of representation suggested by the Randolph's resolutions, but only mentions it a couple of times). In general, he emphasizes other points.

The speech opened offering a "comparative examination of the two plans [in order to] prove that there were essential defects in both and point out such changes as might render a national one efficacious" (Farrand 1966, vol. I, 294). Hamilton's plan contained an executive elected for life. He believed such an executive "will therefore be a safer depository of power" because such an executive will be secure in his powers and feel no need to seek greater power than would be granted by the Constitution. In Yates's notes (as cited in Farrand 1966, vol. I, 297), Hamilton argues that there are a "variety of important objects, which must necessarily engage the attention of a national government," implying that the states are incapable of governing. Hamilton's plan would "consist of two branches; and [he] would give them the unlimited power of passing all laws, without exception."

Yates recorded him as saying that the Virginia Plan was "pork still with a little change of the sauce," indisputably a reference to a very moderate Virginia Plan. Perhaps the delegates saw through such claims, but members of the next generation suggested Hamilton went very far on that day. John Quincy Adams recorded in his diary that "[i]f Hamilton were now living, he would not dare, in an assembly of Americans, even with closed doors, to avow the opinions of this speech, or to present such a plan even as a speculation" (Nevins 1951, 477–78).

What is fascinating about figure 4.2 is that Hamilton's proposal is really most different on the points surrounding executive power. It is clearly a plan that emphasizes a more powerful national government, but the extremity of the proposal has to do with what Hamilton was proposing that would change the executive. We surmise that this was what other delegates would have found most distasteful, especially since the alliance of Core Reform states and the Deep South would probably have been willing to go along with much of what he offered on the federalism dimension.

Rossiter says the evidence of Hamilton's role as a "200 percent nationalist" is "spectral," but when you plot the delegate positions it becomes clear just how far Hamilton would have had to go to offer a plan unpalatable to the Convention. Hamilton's plan never gets a vote or even any discussion because it was completely implausible—especially on questions surrounding the executive. Beyond the records of that day, Hamilton's musings were ignored in the published notes. Rakove (1996) suggests that a historian would like to have heard reactions to the speech that evening, as they must have ranged "from outrage to bemusement" (64). Beeman (2010) goes further and says that upon Hamilton's conclusion, "[n]ot a single delegate rose to comment on it, and certainly no one was inclined to second it and accord it as the stature of being brought to a vote. They simply and immediately adjourned for the day. Hamilton's views strayed so far from mainstream republican principles that they appeared not to merit a response" (169–70). William Johnson would say a few days later that Hamilton's plan "was supported by none" (Farrand 1966, vol. I, 363).

But the question is not, was Hamilton's plan popular? Rather, we should ask, what was the effect of his speech? Had Hamilton proposed his ideal point as revealed by the voting, it would have been supported by at least a few delegates of similar mind, like Wilson of Pennsylvania and McClurg of Virginia, among others. Hamilton's speech goes so far that, to suit the condition that only Hamilton would have supported it, requires a point somewhere out in the gray shaded region of figure 4.2. In our view, it is unlikely that Hamilton, a brilliant man, would have been unable to grasp how his extreme proposal would have framed the issue:[15] the Virginia Plan was the truly moderate alternative to Hamilton's ideas. While we cannot prove that this was the effect of the speech, plotting the ideal points and considering Hamilton's positions suggests that he may well have known exactly what he was doing and hoped for at least some effect.

We have established that delegates from the Small states were clearly willing to support shifting power away from the states and toward the new central government. As the delegates learned about everyone else's preferences, this would become clear.[16] Of course Hamilton's "plan" was never a serious contender. Indeed, referring to it as a "plan" is literary license. Its contribution was not to help them select a new path for the agenda, but to frame the real choice that existed: a choice between the New Jersey and the Virginia Plans.

These two plans, after all, were the real alternatives on the table. Typical accounts of the Convention sometimes portray these two plans as competing proposals demanding the attention of the Convention. However, the New Jersey Plan was not really a plan to fully compete with the Randolph resolutions. It was merely a response to them offered to reframe the debate around representation where the real disagreements lay. In this sense, perhaps it was not all that unlike Hamilton's speech. When Paterson introduced it on June 16 he said, "[o]ur object is not such a Governmt. as may be best in itself, but such a one as our Constituents have authorized us to prepare, and as they will approve" (Farrand 1966, vol. I, 250), a claim that clearly nods at the importance of their position on representation.

This statement (and the surrounding text in the original) suggests that pragmatism was guiding Paterson and several other small-state delegates. First, they argued that their constituents would never accept being put on a relatively weaker footing in the new government. In fact, read strictly, Paterson admitted that his plan was perhaps not the best. But it was the only acceptable solution at that point in the game, unless the large-state delegates could bend just enough to satisfy the small states on the question of representation. This was a major move away from reform. Figure 4.1 shows what a move it would have been—back toward the status quo—had it passed. Charles Pinckney of South Carolina took a cynical view of the small-state delegations in a startling phrase given the normal gentility of the debate when he said in response to Paterson, "[t]he whole comes to this . . . . Give N. Jersey an equal vote, and she will dismiss her scruples, and concur in the Natil. system" (Farrand 1966, vol. I, 250). New Jersey was willing to go along with a much stronger national government. The real division was over representation, which was for New Jersey, as we have modeled it here, a separate issue.

If we use the metric of days of attention as a measure of support, the New Jersey Plan received very little backing indeed. It was introduced by William Paterson (NJ) on Friday, June 15 (only four days after the crucial June 11 votes). It was debated on Saturday, June 16, and again during Madison's speech on June 19, after which it immediately went down to defeat. At best, there was a day and a half of debate on the plan, filled with the speeches of its critics. If Hamilton's goal was to push the New Jersey Plan off of the table, he could have hardly seen a better result.

Despite the uncertainty visible in the agenda figures discussed above, the New Jersey Plan was clearly a step backward, from the point of view of the Core Reform states. So, in the final act of the Committee of the Whole, the revised Randolph resolutions were reported from committee. This shows that the floor of the Convention was not going to start over from scratch. Changes to the Randolph resolutions would be the starting point for debate on the floor. Moreover, this action was supported by all states except Delaware, New York, and New Jersey. Maryland was divided, presumably because of Daniel of St. Jenifer, and Connecticut supported voting out the revised Randolph resolutions. The representational nationalists (whether or not they "assaulted," in Rossiter's terms) had won most of the victories. They had proposed policies far from the Articles of Confederation and had clearly won.

By June 19, the delegates clearly felt that the Committee of the Whole had served its purpose, allowing them to move into the second act of the Convention where they would deliberate on the Revised Virginia Plan until July 26, when the proposal would be handed off to the Committee of Detail. The distinction between these two periods—the Committee of the Whole, from May 25 until June 19, and the Convention debating the Revised Virginia Plan until June 26—is an important one for understanding how the Convention proceeded. This division was not simply about timing or plans or debates. The Committee of the Whole existed to discuss and debate initial ideas. Perhaps the original intention was merely to debate and learn preferences, but by June 19 it should have been clear that the delegates had created a new status quo upon which the Convention could deliberate.

Rossiter, in describing this period, emphasizes "pace," noting that the Convention had moved "at a pace neither too fast for Connecticut nor too slow for Virginia, it had taken on a style that was to mark its proceedings to the end" (Rossiter 1966, 178). In the early going, they had moved relatively slowly, feeling their way into the business without making deep, implacable commitments. Still, they were moving in a direction favored by the key actors, including Madison, Morris, and Wilson. Elder statesmen like Washington and Franklin were clearly amenable to this direction—at least they had made no expression against these moves. Sherman's attempt on June 11 to reach a compromise on representation had seemingly failed, though he knew that the proposal was not dead yet. However, the "pace" was about to begin moving more quickly.

Given how much was left to be decided, perhaps spatial movement is a better analogy than is Rossiter's "pace." The question of whether or not the small states could win concessions on representation had not yet been resolved. Jack Rakove (1996) notes that "the real debate over the thrust of the New Jersey Plan thus began only *after* its rejection" (64, emphasis in original). If the New Jersey Plan was solely an effort to get the delegates to pull back from the extreme positions considered at the end of this period of Committee of the Whole, then there was no reason to believe that the small states had yet really lost. Their fate would be decided as the Convention moved away from Committee of the Whole and debated the plan on the floor. These early steps set the stage for a possible compromise, but they had hardly guaranteed it.

4.3 The Great Compromise

William Jackson's notes on June 19 open with the description that the president (George Washington) "left the Chair" and that "Mr Gorham took the Chair of the Committee." Immediately after that the "President resumed the Chair." This dance symbolized a shift in the tone and tempo of the Convention. Gorham was about to report the work of the Committee. He paused to specifically note that the "Committee do not agree to the propositions offered by the honorable Mr Paterson" (Farrand 1966, vol. I, 312), dispensing with the full New Jersey Plan. Despite that action, the core idea of the New Jersey Plan was still on the agenda: equal state representation in at least one chamber of the legislature.

On that same page of Farrand's notes, Robert Jackson wrote that "they again submit the resolutions, formerly reported, to the consideration of the House." Except that this is slightly inaccurate. Read strictly, Jackson implies that the Randolph resolutions were being reported to the floor of the Convention. However, the resolutions had been refined and revised in several crucial ways. When the floor received those proposals, they had been changed substantially. There is no evidence that the Convention wished to revisit all of the issues they had started settling in Committee of the Whole; though they do revisit some of them, this moment was not simply a "reset."

Starting on June 20, the Convention treated the Virginia Plan[17] as the working document of the Convention. This is not to claim that all questions were settled; far from it. Several proposals would be voted on again (sometimes multiple times), and some degree of uncertainty hung over the question of representation. Several delegates—largely from the small states—were trying to convince the large-state delegates that the small states were immovable on the issue of representation. Whether or not they were truly immovable on this question will never be answered by history. For both good and ill, the small-state delegates probed for the weaknesses in the large-state coalition in order to peel off a state or two and cement their proposed "compromise" of equal representation in the upper chamber.

Madison (at this point) probably breathed a sigh of some relief that his principles of proportional representation had prevailed. But, like Sherman and others, he must have known that the plan had not yet been ratified by the Convention on the floor. Figure 4.3 captures the crucial next series of proposals on representation offered from June 19 through the end of July. Essentially every vote taken during this period was about whether or not to conclude, finally, whether representation in both chambers should be according to population or not.

On June 25, the Convention began to take the final steps on representation. The specific first question came in Vote 87. The specific language, as recorded by Madison, was to agree "that the members of 2d. branch be chosen by the indivl. Legislatures" (408). Only Virginia and Pennsylvania protested. Some might argue that this proposition was not truly about representation. This is because, in theory, a state legislature could have simply

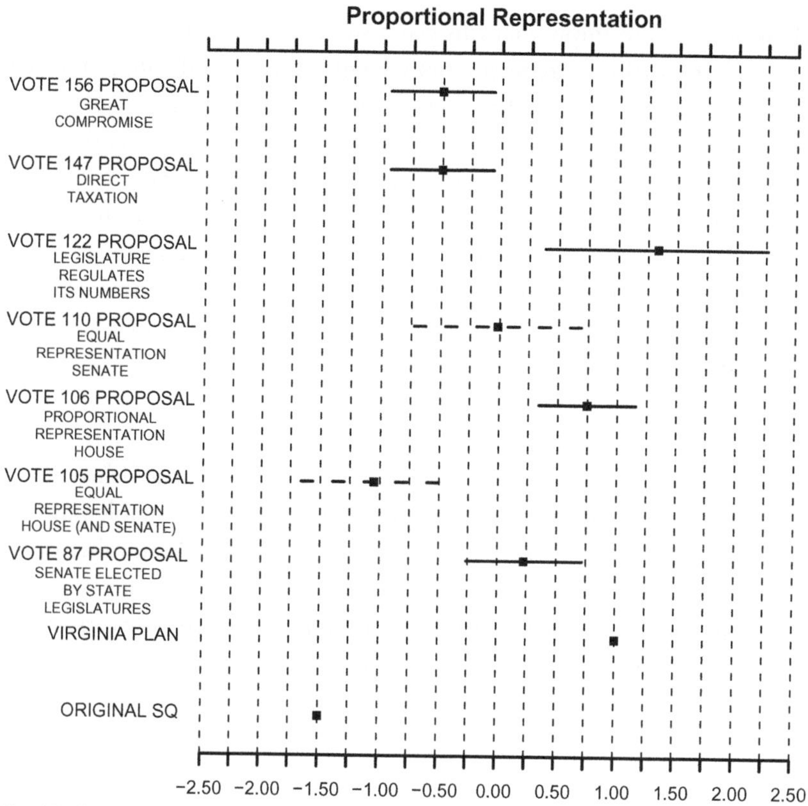

Fig. 4.3. Selected Key Votes on Representation in the Middle Portion of the Convention (June 21–July 28)

elected a delegation that was apportioned to the population of the state. Madison did not see it that way. At some point, probably after taking his original notes, Madison recorded a footnote:

> It must be kept in view that the largest States particularly Pennsylvania & Virginia always considered the choice of the 2d. Branch by the State Legislatures as opposed to a proportional Representation to which they were attached as a fundamental principle of just Government. The smaller States who had opposite views, were reenforced by the members from the large States most axioms to secure the importance of the State Governments.
>
> (Farrand 1966, vol. I, 408)

Madison seems to imply that this was a significant defeat for delegates in favor of proportional representation. Figure 4.3 certainly supports that view: the proposal was the first significant move away from the decisions taken in Committee of the Whole and shows that the Convention was ready to compromise in some way—the New Jersey plan had done its job.[18]

The small-state delegates wanted that proposal (Vote 87) to be merely a way station on the way back to a system of representation more favorable to their interests. Four days after Vote 87, on June 29, they made a new proposal (Vote 105 in Farrand). The seventh resolution that had been reported to the floor read as follows:

> Resd. that the rights of suffrage in the 1st. branch of the National Legislature, ought *not* to be according to the rule established in the articles of confederation but according to some equitable ratio of representation, namely, in proportion to the whole number of white & other free citizens & inhabitants of every age sex and condition, including those bound to servitude for a term of years, & three fifths of all other persons, not comprehended in the foregoing description, except Indians not paying taxes in each State.
>
> (461, emphasis added)

That conjunction, *not*, was the focus of their proposal. Lansing, of New York, moved that the word "not" "be struck out" (468), in order to return them to equal state votes. The vote was defeated along predictable lines: Connecticut, New York, New Jersey, and Delaware voted in favor, with Massachusetts, Pennsylvania, Virginia, the Carolinas, and Georgia voting against the proposal. On this day, for some reason, Maryland was divided. A possible reason is attendance, since some of the delegates, like Jenifer, had been somewhat supportive of proportional representation. We note that even this vote—now considered the compromise position—was dramatically different from the original status quo of the Articles of Confederation. Our model suggests it was different from that position with a probability of 0.92, so things had clearly changed.

Sherman's proposed compromise was proportional representation in the lower branch with equal state representation in the higher branch. However, at least at this point of the Convention, that proposal was not acceptable. Vote 106 ratified the Virginia Plan with proportional representation and appears to move the status quo slightly to the right in the direction of reform, solidifying the changes on this dimension. Though it was simply continuing what had been proposed in Committee of the Whole, now the vote was confirmed on the floor. The delegation votes were exactly the opposite as in Vote 105. Madison and his allies must have been pleased. Vote 87 had threatened to move representation in the direction of state representation. After all, if the states controlled representation in a piece of the legislature, it moved representation in their direction. Madison and his allies would come to learn, however, that any such victory was fleeting. The forces of compromise were already at work. The status quo as it stood on June 29 would not last.

July 2 was an interesting anniversary of the signing of the Declaration of Independence.[19] Vote 110 was a proposal from Ellsworth of Connecticut "[t]hat in the second Branch of the Legislature of the Unitd States each state shall have an equal vote" (Farrand 1966, vol. I, 509). The proposal died five votes to five with Georgia divided, probably because of the absence of a delegate. On the day of the vote, Pierce and Few were absent. Both had pretty clearly favored proportional representation. In their absence, William Houstoun and Abraham Baldwin must have divided on the vote. One interesting feature of the vote is that it is estimated to move back slightly in the direction of the status quo, but not all the way back to Vote 40—no doubt because of Georgia's support of this vote and its influence in the model.[20]

Baldwin is the interesting case. Forrest McDonald puts it that "Abraham Baldwin, born in Connecticut, regressed to his youth and started sitting with and voting the same as the Connecticut delegates" (Beeman 2010). Beeman, Rossiter, and Bowen all confirm this general idea that Baldwin was searching for a compromise and decided to divide Georgia to get there. Beeman goes further and argues that Daniel of St. Thomas Jenifer, though he had spoken out in favor of proportional representation, was absent that day (allowing Luther Martin to cast the Maryland vote with the small states) because he "may have realized that the insistence of the large-state nationalists on proportional representation in both houses might spoil any chance for a successful outcome for the Convention. He may have concluded that his temporary absence would help ease the way toward compromise and thus keep the Convention alive." Collier and Collier (1986) also argue that Jenifer's choice was deliberate:

> Jenifer had an excellent record of attendance at the Convention: he had missed few sessions, if any. Furthermore, the moment the voting was finished, he strolled calmly into the room. There can be no doubt that he stayed away on purpose, and there can be no doubt, either, that he did it to allow Martin to vote Maryland for the small states' side. Although he was from a small state, he believed that proportional representation was just: nonetheless, he would allow his state to vote against it, to save the Convention.
>
> (126)

We have more doubts about this than Collier and Collier, as Jenifer could have been absent for any number of reasons (and, indeed, if their story is correct, then any strategic motive seems problematic, as it permits the state to maintain a sincere position). Motives are always difficult to discern in any legislative setting. However, regardless of motive, the bottom line is that the vote was a tie. The conventional way of interpreting this moment is that "the small states had somehow prevented Madison and his coalition from steamrolling them into submission" (Beeman 2010, 187). Several accounts use the term "deadlock" to describe it. Five votes for the small-state proposal and five votes against (with Georgia divided) gives the veneer of truth to this interpretation, but it is probably incomplete.

A better way of describing this moment of the Convention is not as a deadlock but a small-state defeat—though a temporary one. They had been striving hard to find some kind of compromise that would satisfy the larger states, and it was now clear that this was not likely to happen without additional action. They simply were not going to break the Core Reform state–Deep South alliance without picking off some state delegation. Even with a fortunate set of circumstances where they had more votes than usual, the small-state delegations were unable to defeat the large-state coalition. The voting rules are key: it required a majority vote of the states to change the status quo. The small states were simply not able to move that many votes. Some change in the agenda was necessary to pick off at least one additional large state.

The solution was a committee (or really a series of committees). The ostensible reason for the committee was to develop some kind of compromise. The specific proposer was General Pinckney of South Carolina—a slave state. He argued that "a Committee consisting of a member from each

State should be appointed to devise & report some compromise" (Farrand 1966, vol. I, 511). Some delegates spoke in favor of the Committee (or at least did not oppose the formation of it): Gouverneur Morris, Edmund Randolph, Caleb Strong, Hugh Williamson, and Elbridge Gerry (all from large states, though some were willing to consider equal state representation). The only small-state delegate who spoke for it was John Lansing, and Madison described him as "expecting little advantage from it" (515). Beeman, Rossiter, Rakove, and Bowen all, to some degree, reference the composition of this committee and suggest that it was biased.

Bear in mind that this Committee was not the brainchild of the small states. The story that makes the most sense to us is that the Convention had grown weary of the debate but needed some kind of mechanism to keep the hopes of the small states alive. A committee served both purposes. Discussion of the small-state concerns would be moved off of the floor and onto a committee (for at least a time). If the committee could find some solution, so much the better.

The proposal that emerged from the Committee can be found in figure 4.3: Vote 122 on July 9.[21] Note that this proposal was far from a move back in the direction of the small states.[22] This was a vote about several combined issues. Here is the text of the resolution, as drawn from Jackson's notes:

> But as the present situation of the States may probably alter as well in point of wealth as in the number of their inhabitants that the Legislature be authorised from time to time to augment the number of representatives: and in case any of the States shall hereafter be divided, or any two or more States united, or any new State created within the limits of the United States the Legislature shall possess authority to regulate the number of representatives in any of the foregoing cases upon the principles of their wealth and number of inhabitants.
>
> (558)

Implicitly, the key points were that the legislature would control the number of representatives in the House, including in cases of state division or admission along some principles (not yet finally decided, but possibly including wealth). Our model estimates that this, rather uncertain, proposal moved (very) slightly in the direction of the reformers (including the

Deep South).[23] It was to be the high-water mark on this dimension, as the coming Great Compromise would erode this position. It seems unlikely that the Committee was directing compromises with this particular proposal (which was only opposed by South Carolina and New York).

By July 9, the Convention had created a deep set of reforms that pushed representation as far as any reformer probably could have hoped (including James Madison). There was, however, reason to believe that it had gone too far. Earlier, on June 30, Gunning Bedford from the small state of Delaware had said "Will you crush the smaller states, or must they be left unmolested? Sooner than be ruined, there are foreign powers who will take us by the hand" (501). He was at least threatening to exit the union over representation issues if the Convention persisted in this course, away from the equal state vote of the Articles. The small states had failed to win their desired concessions simply by voting for equal state representation (they had been discussing and proposing this option for several days). They needed to acquire additional votes for their side. In fact, by this point, they needed two additional votes since the New York delegation had left. The logical solution was to find some kind of proposal that would peel off some members of either the Core Reform states or the Deep South. The proposal came in Vote 147. The text of this proposal was as follows:

> Provided always that representation ought to be proportioned according to direct Taxation and in order to ascertain the alteration in the direct Taxation which may be required from time to time by the changes in the relative circumstances of the States—Resolved that a Census be taken within six years from the first meeting of the Legislature of the United States and once within the term of every Ten years afterwards of all the inhabitants of the United States in the manner and according to the ratio recommended by Congress in their resolution of April 18, 1783—and that the Legislature of the U.S. shall proportion the direct Taxation accordingly.
>
> (591)

Superficially, this was a very popular proposal. Only Delaware and New Jersey voted against it (Massachusetts was divided, as was South Carolina). The remaining six states voted for it. The model suggests that this proposal moved substantially back toward the position of the small states (see figure 4.3). Why? Perhaps the main reason is that this laid the groundwork for the final vote in 156 (which is no different, as can be seen). The clause represents a rule about taxation methods that directly, but subtly, incorporated and solidified the three-fifths compromise. This was based in part on Gouverneur Morris's logic that incorporating the three-fifths clause by appealing to a rule for taxation would cause "less umbrage" (595).[24] Note the end of the proposal that clarifies the census would use the three-fifths rule in its administration of taxes. Though the three-fifths compromise had been discussed beforehand, this is the first moment that completely links it with representation as a matter of firm policy. Though many delegates argued against this proposal, it passed and forever links the two famous compromises. In the end, on Vote 156, when Massachusetts divided and North Carolina switched sides—to preserve the slave power in the compromise?—the "Great Compromise" passed (with the three-fifths compromise smuggled in on the earlier vote).

By this moment, Madison had already sensed that the Convention was sliding against him. He gave a very long speech arguing for the retention of proportional representation and made a play to hold the caucus of Core Reform states together with the Deep South—using the appeal to slavery mentioned in chapter 1. He argued that equality of state suffrage would be very bad, particularly for the Deep South, in that it would give the North a veto over their actions in "perpetuity." Alluding to an earlier speech, he now saw that "the real difference of interests lay, not between the large & small but between the N. & Southn. States. The institution of slavery & its consequences formed the line of discrimination. There were 5 States on the South, 8 on the Northn. side of this line. Should a proportl. representation take place it was true, the N. side would still outnumber the other: but not in the same degree, at this time" (vol. II, 9). Madison was desperate. Though he did not have figure 4.3 to help him, Madison was looking for some proposal to hold his coalition together.

This is because the delegates, at this moment, were not simply agreeing to a minor point about tax policy, but were also ratifying the implicit compromise over slavery, by taking away the legislature's power to alter the bargain, perhaps forever. This series of votes on representation (including 147 and 156) had implications for slavery that helped induce slave states, perhaps including North Carolina, to support the compromise.

One has to realize that the proposal about taxation actually originated a few days earlier during the discussion of slavery. In the previous days (beginning with Vote 132 on July 11), the delegates had been arguing over the method of the census and who exactly would be counted. They never directly voted on every piece of this compromise, but they did discuss how taxation would be linked to representation and the counting of the population. The Grand Committee's proposal contained two major parts, a compromise that we know today as the "Great Compromise" and an apportionment of initial representation. From July 11 to July 13, the details were hotly debated, but the substance was never significantly changed. As the northerners continued to bring up objections to the counting method and the proportion of slaves that would be counted, the southern states must have grown more and more nervous. These southern states were voting not only for reform, but also to protect their peculiar institution, and the Small states succeeded in finding a proposal that would induce a state to accept the Great Compromise.

Rakove (1996) describes the action by quoting Morris arguing that it was "better to trust to a future legislative discretion that would surely take the value of slaves into account . . . [r]emarks like these could only prompt southern delegates . . . to favor a rule explicitly linking representation and slavery" (72). James Wilson of Pennsylvania noted that

> [L]ess umbrage would perhaps be taken agst. an admission of the slave into the Rule of representation, if it should be so expressed as to make them indirectly only an ingredient in the rule, by saying that they should enter into the rule of taxation: and as representation was to be according to taxation, the end would be equally attained.
>
> (Farrand 1966, vol. I, 595)

When the delegates agreed that direct taxation should occur by the rule of representation in the first branch (including the three-fifths compromise), they were reforming representation and clearly making representation more fair than it would have been under equal state suffrage, but with the crucial caveat that slavery—a special, protected class of property—would be guaranteed. This powerful precedent for how the national government would treat slavery was reassuring to the southern states, North

Carolina in particular. Even this alteration in the agenda was not quite enough (though it may have persuaded North Carolina). The compromisers needed one additional vote, and it came from Massachusetts. Elsewhere, we have argued that the Massachusetts vote is plausibly linked to a desire to compromise (Pope and Treier 2011; the standard story often told about the Convention). However, North Carolina's vote in particular could have been motivated by desires that may have been rooted in a specific, peculiar interest, an interest in representation that was pro-reform and pro-slavery at the same time.

4.4 Final Details on Representation

With this decision, on July 16, questions of representation had effectively been settled by the Great Compromise. Any delegate who entertained notions of overturning Sherman's proposed compromise had probably long since dismissed them by now. That is not to say, however, that there were not clear attempts to slightly alter the bargain. August 8 was the second full day of debate following a recess, and it was a day devoted largely to questions related to representation. The delegates debated matters of citizenship and the specific apportionment of representatives, and they held some very interesting discussions of slavery. The specific point that touched off the debate was a small substantive change proposed by Hugh Williamson of North Carolina in Vote 252.

On July 26, the Convention had, in the words of Bowen (1966), decided to "appoint a small committee . . . to set aside their resolves, suggestions, amendments and propositions into workable arrangement, or, as Washington phrased it in his diary, to 'draw into method and form the several matters which had been agreed to by the Convention as a Constitution for the United States'" (192). This committee's work was typically, but not always, uncontroversial, and Williamson did not like the line in the report from the Committee of Detail regarding representation. Article IV, section four of the Committee of Detail's plan read that the legislature fixed representation "by the number of inhabitants, according to the provisions herein after made." Dissatisfied with this unclear reference to the compromise over representation and slavery, Williamson moved that it be stricken and substituted with the phrase "according to the rule hereafter

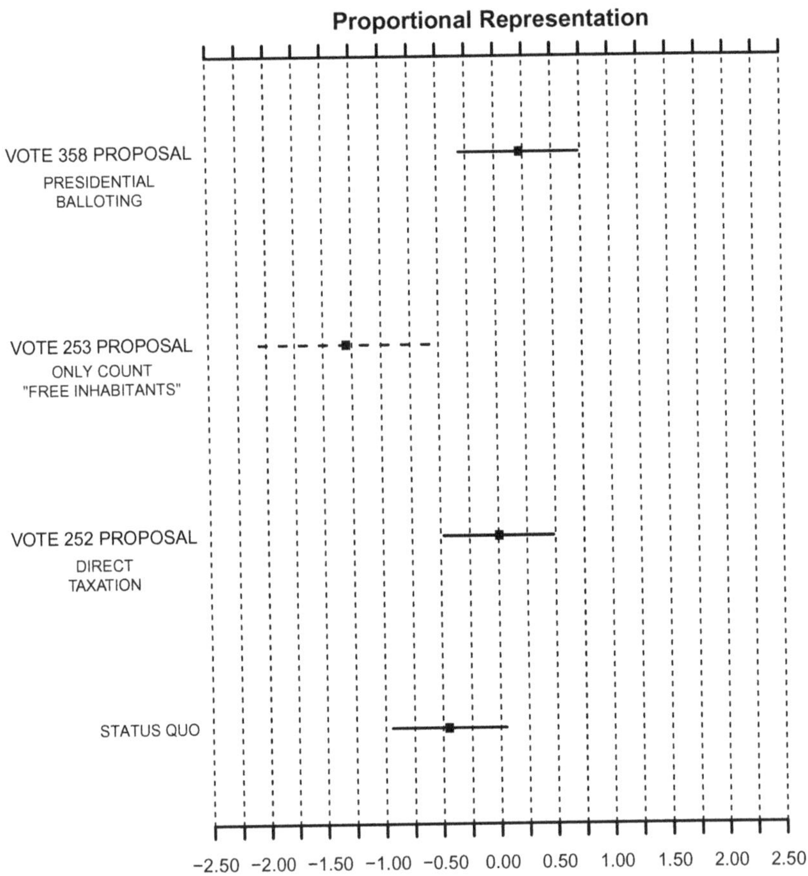

Fig. 4.4. Selected Key Votes on Representation in the Final Portion of the Convention (August 6–September 17)

to be provided for direct taxation" (Farrand 1966, vol. II, 178). Figure 4.4 plots this vote (along with the few other significant representation votes that came up during this period).

As argued above and elsewhere, the question of representation was not simply one that could be resolved by splitting the difference between the New Jersey Plan and Virginia Plan schemes of representation. North Carolina had to be enticed with guarantees over slavery. Williamson's motion had the effect of ratifying the compromise but emphasizing the direct taxation rule for representation. Madison recorded literally no debate on the motion (Vote 252) whatsoever (it passed by nine votes, with only Delaware and New Jersey in opposition). The proposal, as can be seen in the figure, makes some difference, moving slightly in the direction of greater proportional representation.[25]

Despite the lack of debate on that specific language, Williamson's motion touched off a series of arguments on slavery. King began the debate by effectively admitting he was not (at least now) sure "what influence the vote just passed was meant [to][26] have on the succeeding part of the Report, concerning the admission of slaves into the rule of Representation" (Farrand 1966, vol. II, 220). King was clearly uncomfortable with ratifying slavery's part of the compromise and launched into a tirade against the practice. Sherman agreed with his underlying point about the iniquity of slavery (Sherman's term) but did not want to revisit the question of representation after it had been "Settled after much difficulty & deliberation" (221). King had already noted that he had not "made a strenuous opposition" to the compromise before because he had wanted to make concessions in order to produce a national government in which they could have "confidence" (220). He, and others, were apparently willing to revisit the issue now.

King's objections were just the opening act of this little rebellion. Gouverneur Morris quickly moved to insert "free" before the word "inhabitants" which would, frankly, undo the entire delicate compromise, not over the simple question of the rule of representation but over the question of slavery and its counting. Morris eloquently argued against the pernicious effects of the practice.

> Compare the free regions of the Middle States, where a rich & noble cultivation marks the prosperity & happiness of the people, with the misery & poverty which overspread the barren wastes of Va. Maryd. & the other States having slaves.
>
> (222)

But simply describing the practice was not Morris's only tactic. He was also prepared to shred the logic of the compromise.

> Upon what principle is it that the slaves shall be computed in the representation? Are they men? Then make them citizens & let them vote? Are they property? Why then is no other property included? The Houses in this City . . . are worth more than all the wretched

> slaves which cover the rice swamps of South Carolina . . . . the inhabitant of Georgia and S.C. who goes to the Coast of Africa, and in defiance of the most sacred laws of humanity tears away his fellow creatures from their dearest connections & damns them to the most cruel bondages, shall have more votes in a Govt. instituted for protection of the rights of mankind, than the Citizen of Pa or N. Jersey who views with a laudable horror, so nefarious a practice. (222)

The problem, of course, was that reopening the slavery issue would undo the rest of the precarious representation compromise that had opened the way to create this new national government. No one, according to Madison, rose to rebut Morris's speech. Perhaps they knew it was in vain because it went so far, or perhaps Southerners did not want to dignify the argument. The only Southerner who spoke was Mr. Pinckney, who made an almost wholly irrelevant argument about the "burdensome" nature of the fisheries of New England or the problems of the western frontier. However, he admitted that this comparison between New England fisheries or frontier speculation and the slave trade "could" be demonstrated on some other more "proper" occasion (223).

Sherman offered the only real rebuttal to Morris by noting that "It was the freemen of the Southn. States who were in fact to be represented according to the taxes paid by them, and the Negroes are only included in the Estimate of the taxes. This was his idea of the matter" (223). But it was a demonstrably incomplete rendition of the compromise. The question of taxation was offered as a sop to southern states like North Carolina to get them to accept the compromise, but the real import of the question was not just about representation, but also about the ability of the national government to affect the peculiar institution.

Whatever debate took place on that day was mostly prelude to a clearly intact status quo. As can be seen in figure 4.4, Morris's proposal (Vote 253) to count only "free" inhabitants in the enumeration goes down to defeat. It would have moved the agreements over representation far to the left and away from proportional representation and southern interests, but only New Jersey favored Morris's proposal. We cannot know, with certainty, the motives of the delegates at this point in the proceedings. The records of the Convention grow sparser in this period, and we are less able to be sure about their motivations. However, it seems extremely likely that the delegates had accepted the reality of the compromises. Morris's proposal in Vote 253 was simply too extreme to be consistent with the compromises they had already made, and it was discarded. The only final change in representation came on August 24 in Vote 358 and surrounded how the president would be elected. Upon the motion of Mr. Pinckney, of South Carolina, the delegates agreed to limit the election of a president to a "majority of all the votes of all members present" (397). Though this was a question of the presidency, it was also a question of representation in national elections. However, as can be seen in figure 4.4, it made little difference to the outcome.

At this point, they were finished with representation, in large measure because they had created a compromise that could not be substantially changed with respect to the legislature (merely presidential election issues that we will revisit in chapter 6).

4.5 The Shape of the Compromise

What had they accomplished? The Virginia Plan was a clear victory for the reformers, but those goals were eventually scaled back once other delegates found their way into the argument and located the right proposal to pry loose a member of the winning coalition (North Carolina). Despite the gains on this dimension, Madison must have seen this result as something of a loss. In fact, on July 17, reacting to the Great Compromise, he wrote

> On the morning following . . . a number of the members from the larger States, by common agreement met for the purpose of consulting on the proper steps to be taken in consequence of the vote . . . . Several of them supposing that no good Governnt could or would be built on that foundation, and that as a division of the Convention into two opinions was unavoidable it would be better that the side comprising the principle States, and a majority of the people of America, should propose a scheme of Govt. to the States, than that a scheme should be proposed on the other side, would have concurred in a firm opposition to the smaller States.
>
> (Farrand 1966, vol. II, 19)

However, these delegates lacked the power to make a change, as the estimate shows: they had found the middle position on representation, and it was not Madison's. Regrettably, Madison was not specific about which delegates attended this meeting or their specific opinions. This moment reflected a key turning point. Until that moment, as all of our figures show, the tide had been moving toward greater and greater reform. By the end of July, those ideas brushed up against the realities of what could and could not be accomplished, given the limits of the Convention (Robertson 2005). Still, we think that, on balance, this chapter vindicates Madison's efforts. A look back at the figures shows an almost wave-like pattern, as Madison gets very close to everything he wanted, but then falls (somewhat) short. Nevertheless, while Madison's highest aspirations go unfulfilled, his contributions are enormous, and it is only by comparing aspirations that we can see what he accomplished.

Madison aspired to make the government a representative body that was only responsive to a legislature proportioned by population. He managed to create a completely new branch that went halfway toward that goal (and gave the people a veto over any state-originated proposals). In contrast, his opponents, Sherman among others, aspired only to limit Madison's success. Though he might have felt that the compromise was unjustified and lacked merit, generations of Americans who would point to the idea that votes should be equal for people—and not for states—could look to this series of votes as their inspiration. The irony is that Madison was only able to accomplish what he did because of his alliance with the Deep South and their heavy interest in slavery. His downfall came, in part, because of one of those slave states, enticed to vote for a more proportional (and fair) system on the grounds that their slaves would be a protected class of property in this Constitution. That is about as complicated and complex an agenda as one sees in politics.

CHAPTER 5

A *National* Government

If Robert Yates was surprised by the changes to representation, he must have been aghast at what was happening on the decisions around federalism. In journaling May 29, he wrote that Randolph's resolutions "were not intended for a federal government—he means a strong *consolidated* union, in which the ideas of states would be nearly annihilated" (Farrand 1966, vol. I, 24, emphasis in original). This chapter is the story of how that process of creating a stronger national government unfolded. The story about federalism is in one sense quite simple: the delegates immediately decided to make a much more powerful central government. Indeed, on this score, Yates is far out of the mainstream. Large states, small states, pro-reform states, and proslavery states (and so forth) all voted to make the central government larger and more powerful (Connecticut was the only state that voted against it, and New York was divided because Yates and Hamilton split). This consensus held through the early period of the Convention and July; it was only then that the real debate on federalism began because, in some ways, they had to wait until questions on the representation dimension were more settled.

Once the Great Compromise was solidified, the delegates were free to return to the various other issues that animated the Convention's discussions. This is part of why it is so important to be clear about the questions surrounding dimensionality. Accounts of the Convention that explicitly or implicitly see a single dimension of reform (Rossiter's description of an assault of the nationalists, for instance) miss key changes in the debates that are tied to the dimension of discussion. Our model treats baskets of issues, such as representation and federalism, distinctly, so even when the coalitions are similar, we can see change over time on each separate dimension. Certainly, many delegates favored or opposed reform on both dimensions (federalism and representation) simultaneously, but it was often to varying degrees (see figure 3.3). There was a significant difference between a delegate like John Dickinson, who was relatively more open to increasing national government power, and one like Luther Martin, who was unalterably opposed to it.

As an example of this variability, before the Convention, John Dickinson had gained instructions from the Delaware legislature to prevent him from voting for any changes in Delaware's representation. On the surface, this seems consistent with small-state intransigence on creating larger powers for the central government (Beeman 2010). Of course, in some respects this is accurate. However, there were cracks in this small-state position. Not all delegates felt as strongly as did someone like Luther Martin. Some delegates were open to revising the Articles substantially and giving the central government more power. As we will see below, the Convention quickly moved to that position for the new government.

However, that sort of stance left open many major questions that were resolved in the wake of the Great Compromise. How far should they go with those revisions in the new system? Dickinson's instructions may have held him back on proportional representation, but they gave him wide latitude in other ways. On the dimension of federalism—the question of how much power the states would have relative to the national government—he took a relatively moderate stance, as opposed to Luther who rarely, if ever, supported any meaningful changes.[1]

Figure 3.3 also makes clear that the delegate most strongly opposed to state power was James Madison. Like other southern delegates—such as those from Georgia and the Carolinas—the Virginia delegates were all pro-reform on this dimension, but even among that group, Madison stands out. Only a few others like Nathaniel Gorham (MA), James Wilson (PA), and Alexander Hamilton (NY) are in his same range, though Madison was still more extreme on this dimension: the model estimates that he was more extreme than Hamilton, with a probability of 0.84. There is also a range across the small-state delegates. As a group, they certainly all questioned how far power should be moved toward the national government, and none of them was as strongly in favor of centralization as people like Madison or Hamilton. Nevertheless, there are shades of gray as to how they would think about the questions of federal power and, especially, executive power (discussed in the next chapter).

The Articles of Confederation was, essentially, a government of other governments (state ones, that is). The new government—at least for those who wanted reform on this dimension—had to be something completely different. Their first task was to end the agreement to leave sovereignty with the states, but it turned out that this was the easy part. What followed was a difficult argument about just how powerful the new government would be. At the same time, they had to confront the issue of ratification. How would this completely new and national government be put into place?

5.1 Ending State Sovereignty

As Rossiter (1966) puts it, "Madison was proposing . . . the demolition of the Articles of Confederation and the erection in its place of a strong national government on a popular foundation. There was nothing that could be called 'confederate,' and not much that could be called 'federal,' about the Virginia plan" (170–71). As with representation, Madison had strong intentions that were signaled from the outset, and the early votes show a pattern of immediate success.

Figure 5.1—similar to the earlier figures on representation—displays the key votes on federalism that came in the early part of the Convention (essentially the beginning through the end of July) and displays a story that is fairly straightforward, setting the stage for how they would tackle the issue of federalism: the Committee of the Whole immediately took steps to move away from the Articles of Confederation and then had to find an exact position of compromise among all of the delegates—but only once the Great Compromise was finalized. The key point is that this early decision to end complete state sovereignty—and that's exactly what this meant—was never really revoked by the Convention. Certainly, some delegates may have entertained the notion of going back and restoring the power of states, and as the voting unfolded, delegates would need to decide just how powerful that central government would be. However, the early decision to trim state sovereignty would stand. In the end, the broad pattern is that both extremes were consistently defeated in favor of more moderate positions (at least relative to the Convention).

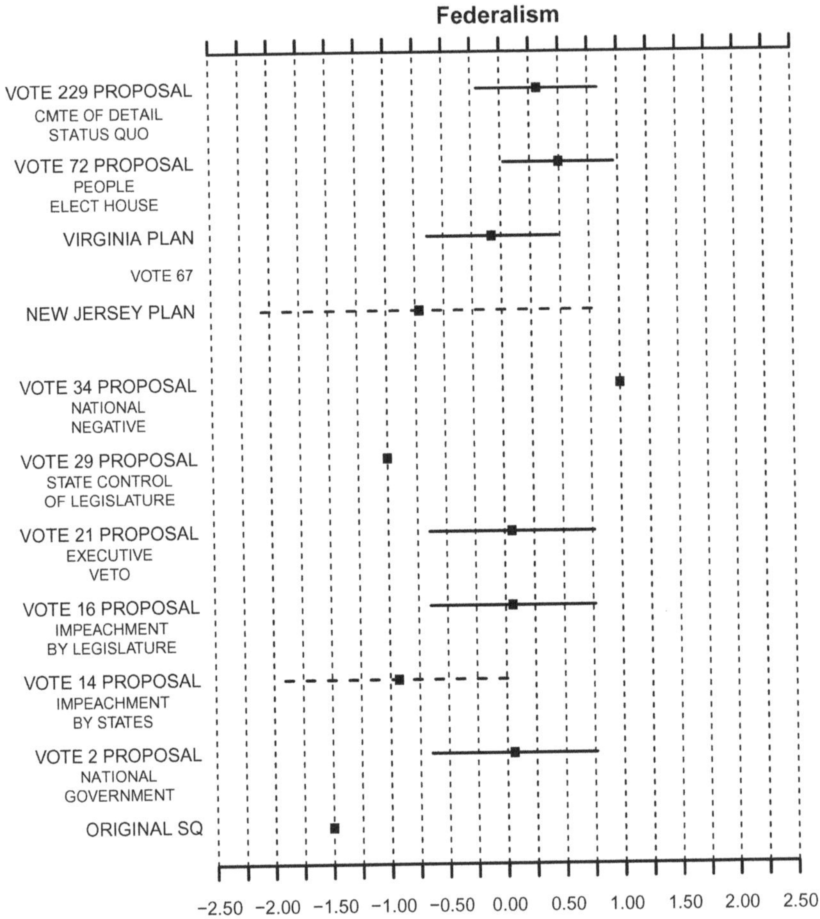

Fig. 5.1. Selected key votes on Federalism in the early period of Committee of the Whole (May 25–July 28), encompassing both the Committee of the Whole period and the mid-Convention period in July

This is an important element of our story. Once the Convention had made an early decision, the number of available options that would be acceptable to the delegates shrank.[2] It was impossible to locate positions that were outside the core of delegates. This meant that all of the major decisions that really changed the structure came early. Later decisions about details were important, but not nearly as substantial because, by that point, there was no longer room for major changes.

The most substantial move—for the entire Convention on the federalism dimension—came in Vote 2, on May 30.[3] The proposal, as recorded by Madison, was that a "national Governt. ought to be established consisting of a supreme Legislative Executive & Judiciary" (Farrand 1966, vol. I, 35). Two states dissented: Connecticut (their vote was clearly negative) and New York (which was divided).[4] The remaining states—Massachusetts, Pennsylvania, Delaware, Virginia, North Carolina, and South Carolina—all supported the proposal. Without very much debate, the delegates agreed to move away from a relationship where the national government was clearly subordinate to the states—in some respects, this is the most revolutionary moment of the Convention. The terms of the debate had shifted following a decade of revolution when the states had agreed upon the Articles of Confederation (drafted by John Dickinson) under which state power was preeminent.

It is important to note that, in general, our method reveals few votes where all three dimensions were deeply affected. There are several reasons for this. First, using three dimensions and coding how votes were keyed to each dimension means that, some of the time, we make a theoretical choice to limit the ability of votes to move. Second, and perhaps most importantly, once the Convention reached a middle ground they were comfortable adjusting (and not overthrowing), it was far less possible for a vote to make a massive change on multiple dimensions and succeed, thus relatively few votes do. There are a few exceptions. Vote 67, to table the New Jersey Plan, is just such an exception in that it impacted both representation and federalism dramatically (and succeeded). Similarly, Vote 2, on federalism, sent a strong signal on all dimensions, but we note that these came early. Though there were a few votes like this in the early part of the Convention, mostly any such votes had trouble succeeding.

It should be noted that this vote was not simply about rhetoric. When the Constitution would later be debated in the Virginia ratification debates, Patrick Henry would implicitly attack this vote (though, to our knowledge, he had never seen a record of it or the debate) when he argued strenuously against a "consolidated" government (Jensen and Kaminski 1976, vol. 9, 1010–28). By Henry's lights—and many other anti-federalists of the time—this initial vote was cause for alarm, perhaps the key cause for alarm. Though Henry's specific concerns were still in the future, this vote could have also caught several delegates off guard. The terms of the debate had already shifted almost before they had begun for future anti-federalists like Yates or Henry. Beeman (2010) describes the vote by saying,

> May 30 [referencing this vote] marked only the beginning, not the fulfillment, of the attempt to bring about a revolution in the American government. But it was a vitally important step, for it put the delegates on a course to abandon—rather than revise—the definition of federalism embodied in the Articles of Confederation. (104)

It was this vote that signaled the scope of the change to come, and this vote clearly unnerved Yates, who recorded the (unattributed) question "whether it was intended to annihilate state governments?" (Farrand 1966, vol. I, 30). The answer that this would be true only insofar as the new government clashed with the states could not have been reassuring to him. What he would shortly discover is that no new proposals went back on the promise of this vote.

Three days later, on June 2, the Convention began the business of fleshing out the promise of Vote 2 in order to balance state and national power. The day opened with a discussion of the presidency. While we will treat this subject in far more detail in the next chapter, it still bears on the question of federalism. James Wilson of Pennsylvania had motioned that the executive be elected by the people (for more on this, see the next section). The argument quickly moved into a debate about how much states could intervene in this election (Farrand 1966, vol. I, 80). Dickinson and Bedford moved that after a president is in office he should be "removable by the national legislature upon request by a majority of the legislatures of the individual States" (78), pushing the power of the states as political entities. Their proposal would have established the precedent of state control over the executive and clearly moved the outcome back toward the confederation status quo, so the opponents offered an amendment to Dickinson's proposal that would strike out everything after "the national legislature," effectively keeping the states out of presidential selection. Dickinson and Bedford's proposal came up in Vote 14 (see figure 5.1). It was clearly a move in the direction of greater state power, but it was soundly defeated (only Delaware supported it). Two votes later—in Vote 16—the Convention passed a proposal from Williamson and Davie that created the beginnings of the impeachment process, making the president removable after "conviction of mal-practice or neglect of duty" (80). This impeachment by the legislature made little difference to the federalism dimension, but we illustrate it to show that there were efforts to bring states back as more powerful entities than the national government. They failed, but this will be far from the last time we see that pattern.

The fourth proposal in the Virginia Plan read that "Resd. that the members of the first branch of the National Legislature ought to be elected by the people of the several states" (20). This provision would be the crucial link between the people and the national government. Under the Confederation, the central government had merely been the agent of the state governments, but now the national government derived its powers directly from the people—and not from the states as mediating political entities. Vote 29 (see figure 4.2) would have been a major change to that idea. In that proposal (offered on June 6 by Charles Pinckney and John Rutledge), it was suggested to change the resolution so that it would read that the first branch of the national legislature would be elected by the "*Legislatures* of the several states" (130, emphasis added). Similar to Vote 14, it would have given state institutions much more control over the national government. It is a testament to just how committed the Convention was to changing the system that only South Carolina, New Jersey, and Connecticut voted for the proposal.

The defeat of state power in Vote 14 and Vote 29 might have suggested more moves in the direction of national power, but it did not mean that the Convention was willing to go as far as some might want. Vote 21 in figure 5.1 shows the status quo on the idea of an executive veto. This is naturally a vote more about the third dimension we will discuss in the next chapter, but the issue area does bear on federalism because of the national negative. Charles Pinckney moved in Vote 34—no doubt with Madison's support—to change the words in the sixth resolution from "to negative all laws passed by the several States contravening, in the opinion of the national legislature, the articles of union; or any treaties subsisting under the authority of the union" to "to negative all laws which to them shall appear improper" (162).[5]

This proposal—Vote 34—would have clearly moved the Convention's plan in a much more nationalist direction. During the debate, Madison argued that "an indefinite power to negative legislative acts of the States [is] absolutely necessary to a perfect system" (164). Yet, most delegates did not agree, and the proposal in Vote 34 went down to defeat quickly, with only the Core Reform states of Massachusetts, Pennsylvania, and Virginia voting for it.[6] While it was the case that many, though not all, delegates wanted to alter the balance of power between the states and the national government, there were clearly limits on how far delegates were willing to go. The delegates, by and large, did not want a national government that was capable of overriding the states. That simply went too far.

Thus, the first few days of discussing federalism produced two clear results. First, the Convention collectively voted for more national power (Vote 2). Second, however, they rejected proposals that moved the plan too far from the moderate position—Votes 14, 29, and 34. There were other proposals offered on this dimension (not pictured here), some that moved the proposed plan in a nationalist direction, like taking national oaths or ratification by state conventions, but in general, the Committee of the Whole agreed upon a clear middle ground and was not yet ready to make major changes to that position.

We reemphasize that the key vote came very early: it was the initial vote to establish a new national government. When the Virginia Plan was reported out of Committee, it was close to the Vote 2 position, and nothing really changed this until after the Committee of Detail met at the beginning of August. By June 21—when they had left Committee of the Whole—the Convention was ready to take up further questions of state power. In Vote 71, they decided against giving members of the lower chamber power of election over the upper chamber of the House. Moments later, in Vote 72 (see figure 5.1), they ratified the idea that the first branch of the legislature would be elected by the people (and not the states), shifting the proposal slightly further in the direction of greater national power. Only Delaware dissented on this vote (though Maryland was divided). There were additional votes on state controls,[7] but these votes tended to alter the status of state power very little. By the end of July (see Vote 229), at the recess, little had changed.

In describing this moment of the Convention, Beeman writes that, at least publicly, there was a "climate of optimism" (259). On the surface, this seems logical. The Convention was about to turn over their work to a Committee of Detail. Agreements seemed to be coming together. But Beeman notes that not everyone felt this way and there were private misgivings. Perhaps this was because—as we shall see in the next section—despite the apparent agreement and stability on the federalism dimension, there remained a large number of outstanding issues and problems that the Convention would take up in August. The Convention had to avoid two problems with respect to federalism. On the one hand, it had to give enough local control to make the specific states feel like they were safeguarded. On the other hand, they had to make sure that this new central government would not be at the mercy of the state governments. The comity of the early debate on federalism would change in this final period.

5.2 Settling on National Powers

There was a ten-day break between the session on Thursday, July 26 and Monday, August 6. Delegates spent the time in different ways. Washington went on a fishing trip; others remained in Philadelphia. Some left for other locales. But when all of them returned, they knew that this was the final stage. They probably hoped that the task ahead of them would be relatively short, but that was not to be. This last phase of the Convention would contain more votes—though less debate—than the previous two periods combined.

A Committee of Detail—chaired by John Rutledge, with Edmund Randolph, Oliver Ellsworth, James Wilson, and Nathaniel Gorham making up the balance—had produced a revision to the Virginia Plan that reflected the compromises, language, and orders of the Floor that had been agreed upon in June and July. Their report, when made, constituted the first draft of the United States Constitution, and much of what was contained in the final document was present in this draft.

The Committee of Detail was obviously acting as the agent of the Floor of the Convention. Some historians suggest that it was a faithful agent. Of the report of the Committee, Rossiter (1966) says that "[t]he other delegates could tell in one careful reading that the reported constitution was a fair if far-ranging projection of their expressed wishes" (207). If Rossiter is right, this reading must have led delegates to hope for a quick resolution (though, to our knowledge, there is no clear statement to that effect in their papers beyond the basic desire to be done and go home). However, Rossiter's claims are hardly the only perception of the Committee Report. Collier and Collier (1986) state that "it was immediately clear to at least some of the northerners that they had been sold out" (169). The specific claim was that the northern delegates had acceded to the requests of the southern delegates in taking away export taxes on rice and indigo, tolerating the slave trade, and instituting the two-thirds majority required for navigation acts, which gave the southern states an effective veto over future trade policy. Somewhere between these two claims lies the truth, and both help illustrate a certainty about the Convention: though the big decisions had been made, there was much left to do, and it was no longer possible to make major changes to positions.

Though there was little if anything left to debate on Representation, Federalism was a different matter, with clearly more room for debate and maneuvering. In the end, however, the Convention found that they had to accept compromises that ended up leaving the Convention's proposal little different from what it had been in July. Instead, we see a pattern of oscillation: extreme proposals were still to be introduced, accepted, changed, voted down, and then finally settled, but always compromised back to a central position on the dimension. The election of the president, in particular, was difficult (see the next chapter). If delegates did, in fact, expect to finish the task quickly, they were disappointed because they were about to find out that settling on the final adjustments was not easy; it would last over a month, from August 7 until September 17. On balance, this period, though it involved the most votes, accomplished the least—in terms of moving the proposal. The big fights were already over, and all that was left to consider were details and to settle on a middle course.

Figure 5.2 displays the key votes on the federalism dimension that came after the recess. The reader's eye will immediately note far less stability and the pattern of oscillation as the delegates tried—and failed—to find positions that would move out from the center of their collective ideal points. Essentially, what we see in figure 5.2 is the model's estimation of a series of discrete proposals to move the position of the proposed Constitution either toward greater national power (on the right), or back toward the status quo of a great deal of state power (on the left). The first major proposal to move power back toward the states came on August 21, approximately two weeks into this final stage of debate. Luther Martin—no friend of the emerging Constitution—offered an addition to the proposals on direct taxation:

> [w]henever the Legislature of the U: S: shall find it necessary that revenue should be raised by direct taxation, having apportioned the same, according to the above rule on the several States, —requisitions

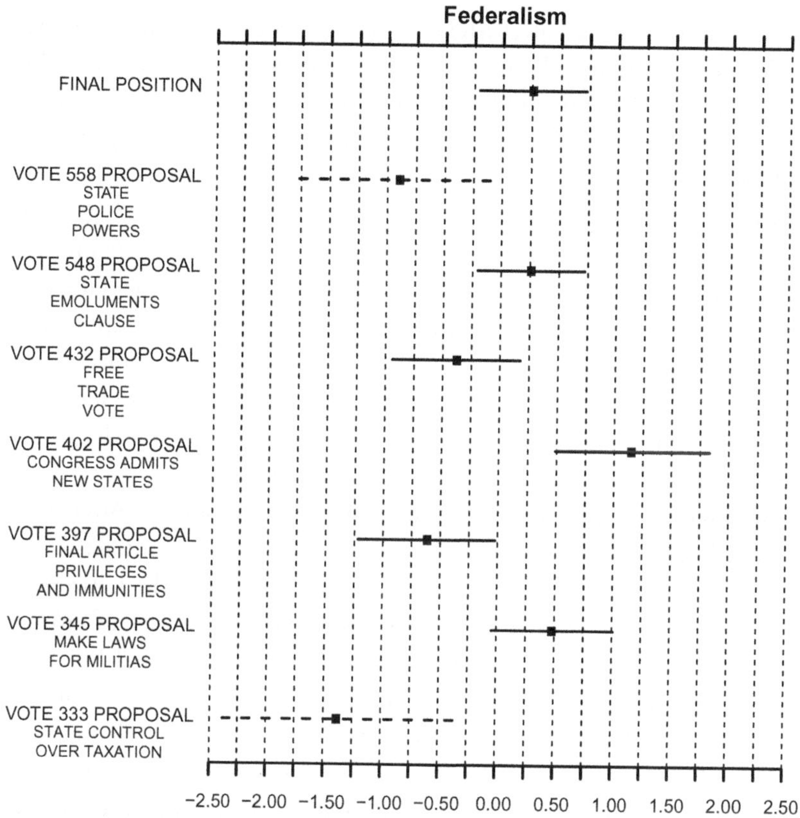

Fig. 5.2. Selected key votes on Federalism in the final portion of the Convention (August 6–September 17)

> shall be made of the respective States to pay into the Continental Treasury their respective quotas within a time in the said requisitions specified; and in the case of any of the States failing to comply with such requisitions, then and then only to devise and pass acts directing the mode, and authorizing the collection of the same.
>
> (Farrand 1966, vol. II, 359)

Martin was proposing to essentially return to the taxation regime of the Articles of Confederation. As can be seen in figure 5.2 it was a drastic move back in the direction of state power. However, by this point in the debates, delegates were tired of pointless motions. This was a proposal deeply in opposition to reform, and it garnered little traction. In fact,

Madison recorded that, after McHenry seconded the motion, "there was no debate" (359), and the question failed with only New Jersey voting for the motion (Martin could not even carry his own state of Maryland). Proposals too far from the center of opinion meant that only adjustments could be made.

Though Vote 333 was a failure, Vote 345 taken on August 23, gave the national government the power to organize, arm, and train state militias. Indeed, they gave the national government power to control the state militias when they were called out at the national level. For a group of men nervous about standing armies, these were the greatest concessions offered on national power—and indeed, the model suggests they were moves in the direction of greater national power. Though there was some discussion about the danger to liberty, the opposition was slight.[8]

By August 28, they had begun discussing judicial powers. After some debate about habeas corpus and state interference in contracts, they decided in Vote 397 to approve the revised article XIV: "The Citizens of Each State shall be entitled to all privileges and immunities of citizens in the several States" (see Farrand 1966, vol. II, 439). General Pinckney thought this did not go far enough—perhaps because it did not clarify the role of slaves?—but his state was the only one to oppose it (Georgia was divided). It was a broadly accepted position, though it did clearly empower states, in their minds, giving citizens of the states the right to wield power against the national government. They had ended up moving the proposed constitution back in the direction of state power, but the next few votes would break that pattern, culminating in Vote 402.

On August 29, the delegates took up questions of contracts across states (the Full Faith and Credit Clause) as well as some initial discussions of trade. This latter point occupied much of this debate (and would continue to do so), but the closest vote came in the final part of the day's debate on whether or not Congress would have the power to admit new states. The proposal under debate said that "If the admission [of new states] be consented to, the new States shall be admitted on the same terms with the original States" (Farrand 1966, vol. II, 454). Gouverneur Morris—an advocate of national power—did not favor that motion and wanted to give the national government the power to authorize different arrangements for different types of states. The implicit argument here was that states entering the union subsequent to the original 13 would be given fewer privileges. This was debated quickly but sharply. George Mason thought this impossible, given growth patterns. Madison did not want to foment arguments over rank and status in the new country. Others, like Langdon and Williamson, were for leaving the legislature free to do as it wished. There was not much support for simply striking out the language cited above (Morris's initial proposal to give the national government *carte blanche* failed), but in Vote 402, Morris succeeded in getting a very narrow coalition to pass his substitute proposal, worded as follows:

> New States may be admitted by the Legislature into this Union: but no new State shall be erected within the limits of any of the present States, without the consent of the Legislature of Such State, as well as of the Genl. Legislature.
>
> (455)

A coalition of the Core Reform states and the Deep South pushed this through in opposition to all of the small states (plus New Hampshire).[9] Why was the vote so close? Some small-state delegates, such as Sherman, argued the provision was unnecessary. Luther Martin argued that this was a point on which some states would dominate the central government, perhaps stopping westward expansion. The arguments on these points were complex, but it seems that the core fight between reformers allied with the slaveholders held up. They wanted legislative control over national expansion and were willing to give the national government this power. The small states, still fearful of this new legislatively dominated national government, were less excited about this position.

The final vote of August[10] approved an amendment prohibiting any regulation to "oblige vessels bound to or from any State to enter clear or pay duties in another" (Farrand 1966, vol. II, 480, Vote 432). To this point, a number of proposals had effectively promoted trade within the young country. Superficially, the text of this vote suggests freer trade. After all, it seems to say that there will be no duties in one state once the vessel has cleared a port in another state. However, it is not quite as simple as that, as the model suggests: the proposal moved dramatically back in the direction of state power.

The debate about the vote makes clear that several states—Pennsylvania, Maryland, and some in New England—were all concerned that the national government would set up a port somewhere that would cut states off from trade and the monetary advantages that would result from it in a state port. Luther Martin in a later claim noted that

> This provision, as well as that which relates to the uniformity of impost duties and excises, was introduced, Sir, by the delegation of this State.—Without such a provision, it would have been in the power of the general government to have compelled all ships sailing into, or out of the Cheseapeak, to clear and enter at Norfolk, or some port in Virginia—a regulation which would be extremely injurious to our commerce, but which would if considered merely as to the interest of the union, perhaps not be thought unreasonable, since it would render the collection of the revenue arising from commerce more certain and less expensive.
>
> (Storing 1981, vol. IV, 63)

Essentially, Martin was arguing that the clause helped make it impossible for the national government to establish a central port (e.g., Norfolk) that would advantage some states over other states—Virginia over Maryland, in the case cited by Martin. Effectively, the passage of this clause (argued for by a number of states) was to make sure that each and every state port became a feasible destination for trade and limited the ability of the national government to prefer one state over another. That is why, as seen in Vote 432, the proposal moved the position of the proposal back toward greater state autonomy. It may seem small to us now, but as Carroll (MD) put it, "this was a tender point in Maryland" (Farrand 1966, vol. II, 481).

The second to last proposal we consider on this dimension that moved the status quo much at all came in Vote 548 on the second to last day of the Convention as the delegates were simply fixing a few final phrases. They agreed that "he [the President] shall not receive, within that period, any other emolument from the U.S. or any of them" (626). This moved the proposal in a slightly more national direction, as it prevented states from influencing the head of the national government (and his agents) via gifts (or emoluments). Matters stayed at that position because there were no more substantive votes on this dimension that could have mattered much at all, with one proposed exception. Vote 558 was the final attempt at moving the proposed Constitution deeply back toward the Articles of Confederation status quo of state sovereignty and final authority. At the end of all of the debate about state powers, Roger Sherman was still not satisfied. Toward the close of debate on September 15 (just two days before the Constitution would be signed), Sherman argued that

> [T]hree fourths of the States might be brought to do things fatal to particular States, as abolishing them altogether or depriving them of their equality in the Senate. He thought it reasonable that the proviso in favor of the States importing slaves should be extended so as to provide that no State should be affected in its internal police, or deprived of its equality in the Senate.
>
> (Farrand 1966, vol. II, 629)

Madison simply replied to Sherman, "[b]egin with these special provisos, and every state will insist on them, for their boundaries, exports &c." (630). Sherman's motion, coming in Vote 558, went down to defeat with only Connecticut, New Jersey, and Delaware supporting it. As can be seen in figure 5.2, the proposal would have moved the position of the proposed constitution dramatically back toward state sovereignty. Moments later, the Convention would agree to equal suffrage in the Senate, which became part of the final Constitution in Article V, although not with the sharp language proposed by Sherman.

This illustrates well the pattern of oscillation at the Convention. Having just negotiated a long series of compromises, fine-tuning all of the bargains over militias, judicial power, ratification, and trade, the delegates were hardly prepared to accept a proposal that would undo the delicate balance. Sometimes scholars describe this as carefully balanced and thoughtful compromises. While not wrong, that description leaves out the chaotic nature of the debates where proposals came and went and the Convention simply accepted what could garner a majority under their rules. In the end, the proposed Constitution clearly did not simply leave state sovereignty intact. In fact, it had changed it dramatically, and Vote 558 could not possibly gain the support necessary to alter those bargains. Debate over how far they would go on state power had ended, largely because there was nothing left that could significantly change the proposal and simultaneously win a durable majority.

5.3 Ratification

In contrast to the rest of the votes about federalism, there is a set of votes that, while they all belong together on this dimension, also can be considered as a particular group: votes about ratification.[11] The first serious debate about ratification at the Convention came on July 23, ironically in a vote that failed. The proposal was to change the mode of ratification, which up until that point had been assumed to be "an assembly or assemblies of representatives recommended by the several Legislatures to be expressly chosen by the People to consider and decide thereon" (Farrand 1966, vol. II, 84). Ellsworth (CT) felt it would be better to simply let the states decide. The vote failed with only Connecticut, Delaware, and Maryland in support, and though there was much discussion during the very next proposal—Vote 204 (see figure 5.3)—in an almost unanimous

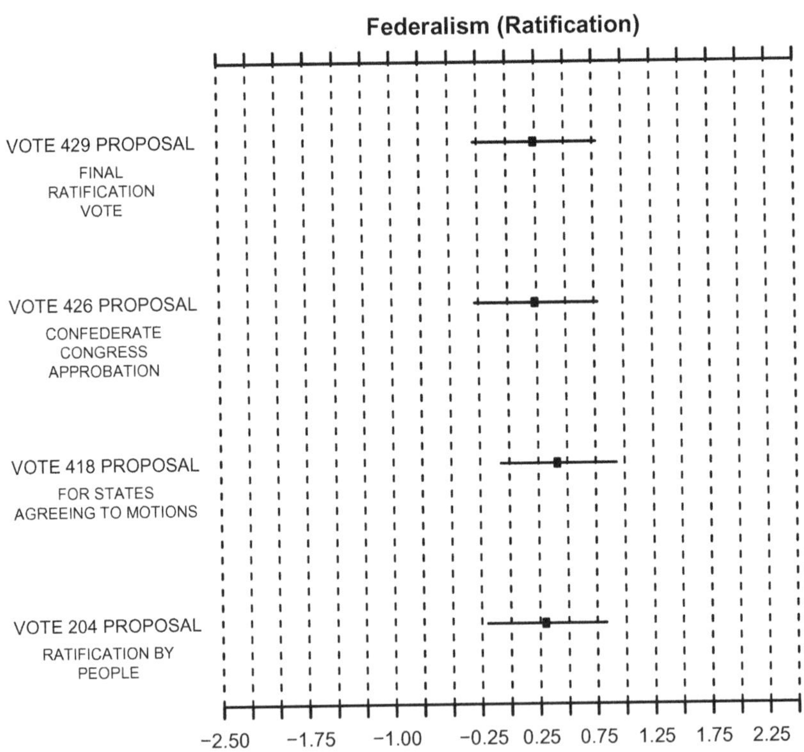

Fig. 5.3. Selected key votes on ratification and federalism in the final portion of the Convention (August 6–September 17)

vote with only Delaware in opposition, the Convention approved the idea of state ratification conventions recommended by the state legislatures, but chosen by the people.

There would be additional debate about this outcome, but there would never be any real movement on the issue of ratification. Simply put, it was never a policy lever that was used to radically change the position of the proposed Constitution. Other issues, as discussed in the previous section, provoked change on the federalism dimension. But on the question of ratification, despite a few proposals to change the specific form ratification would take, there was never any substantial change, and all votes were quite moderate. There is not even the hint of oscillation on these votes.

With a few stray mentions of the topic, they did not return to it until August 31. At this point in the debates, there had been some slight momentum back toward the states, but they had balanced this by allowing the new government to create new states (see Vote 402 above), and the sentiment for strong national power continued to prevail. The first vote of the day was a simple vote to permit ratification only within those states that chose ratification (see Vote 418 in the figure). The effect was to permit states to avoid ratification if they so chose. The Convention could hardly have done otherwise, though it changed the estimate very little.

Shortly after that, in Vote 426, they decided the question of the wording of Article XXII of the Committee of Detail's report. That resolution said that the Constitution would be "laid before the U– S. in Congs. assembled for their approbation" (Farrand 1966, vol. II, 478). Gouverneur Morris (PA) and Pinckney (SC) wanted to strike out the words "for their approbation." This was, admittedly, a consequential step. They were removing the power of the national legislature to hold up ratification, but it passed quickly with only Georgia in opposition. This continued the pattern that, while there was scattered opposition to various proposals about ratification, there was not sustained opposition to the middle-ground plan: hold state conventions. Just three votes later—Vote 429—they approved that exact process.

Jack Rakove (1996) has written about the importance of these decisions, which generate little controversy in the voting and, consequently, our model. He considered the stakes to be very high indeed.

> [T]he framers seized the main chance and then developed procedural and conceptual innovations to give their revolutionary act

> as much legitimacy as they could muster. . . . [T]hey were also attempting to establish new standards of constitutional legality as well as constitutional legitimacy. . . . If most state constitutions and the Confederation itself rested on no authority greater than ordinary acts of legislation, two conclusions of enormous significance followed. First, the lawful decisions taken by the state legislatures to implement the recommendations of the Convention and Congress for ratification conventions could be said to supersede their earlier approval of the Confederation. . . . [I]n the second place, the resort to popular sovereignty in 1787–88 marked the point where the distinction between a constitution and ordinary law became the fundamental doctrine of American political thinking.
>
> (128–30)

Without disputing any of this for understanding the concept of ratification, we note that their debates about ratification were not terribly heated, generated little controversy, and essentially never left the middleground of the Convention. Only Luther Martin seems to have insisted on using the state legislatures. He was opposed in that day's debates by King, of Massachusetts, who said that "the Constitution of Massachusetts was made unalterable till the year 1790, yet this was no difficulty with him. The state must have contemplated a recurrence to first principles before they sent deputies to this Convention" (Farrand 1966, vol. II, 477). Whether or not King is right about that claim, there was little substantive debate about the consequences of this decision. Rakove is, no doubt, correct in his assessment of the crucial nature of this decision, but a glance at figure 5.3 and a bit of knowledge about the debate reveals how little any of the ratification votes affected the process. No one could imagine the Civil War and the role that ratification would fully play in the nation's history, but there was never any serious movement of the proposal on ratification at the debates. It simply was not a point of major contention.

To this point, we have talked only about the dimensions where the alignments were generally clear and consistent. The Core Reform states and the Deep South both wanted to make representation more proportional (though without doing any justice to the slaves) and to make a more powerful centralized government. But while all of these changes were being enacted, there was a separate dimension of conflict where that coalition did not see eye to eye: the presidency. It was a difficult point for the delegates. As they made their way deeper and deeper into that debate, they would change their minds several times. The end result was to create an independent president—not one dependent upon Congress. This incredibly consequential decision was driven by a quite different alignment of the factions: the Core Reform states allied with sympathetic members of the Small states. The story of that decision is told in the next chapter.

CHAPTER 6

An Independent Executive?

The government of governments that was the Articles of Confederation had no executive power (the Presidents of the Congress did not really count, given their very limited powers—they were more like clerks). So, in many ways, the creation of a national executive was the most innovative element of the new Constitution. This is not to say that the idea of executive power was foreign to them. Far from it, given their experience with governors across the states and with the British Crown. However, the very idea of a chief executive carried some controversy, with some colonies avoiding executive power in their state constitutions altogether. The idea of creating a separate branch of the government with its own independent power base was a complete innovation, as far as the national government was concerned.[1] Creating that executive was a slow process; the conception of what that president would look like was a long time coming at the Convention, and the question was not settled completely until the final days. As Beeman (2010) put it, from the moment they began discussing the issue "until the very end of the summer, the form, powers, and mode of selection of the national executive would be a constant source of dispute." He goes on to note that this really needs to be considered a separate dimension from other conflicts at the Convention, writing that "the debate over the executive did not cause sharply defined divisions between whole groups of state delegations . . . there was a greater range of individual opinion among the delegates on the character of the executive branch than on any other issue in the Convention" (124–125).

Our story in this chapter is that the executive represents a massive break with the other aspects of the debate. Chronologically, the story about this dimension certainly overlaps the previous three periods. However, considering the Constitution as we have in this book—by focusing on the deep structure of voting—the agenda and the coalitions change significantly when we turn our attention to the presidency. No longer was there the familiar coherence of Core Reform states allying with the Deep South. Instead, the Core Reform states had to focus on the delegates from the Small states—especially from Maryland and Delaware—who could be won over to their side. This means that this dimension has less consistency than the previous two, but it is still very important—especially in its long-lasting influence over American politics.

The presidency is not the product of the same coalition that created the Congress. Rather, it was a competing, separate coalition that ultimately created the second power structure of the new Constitution: the new executive. This happened without any one individual ever really articulating the design because, according to our model, the coalition that created this innovation was quite different from the one that created the strong national legislature. The Convention's competing coalitions set up these two power centers (Congress and the executive) in ways that they could compete against one another throughout American history. There was no guarantee this would occur. Indeed, for much of the Convention they could only agree on having an executive, not how much power that office would have or from where its power would be obtained. Like the other dimensions, they began with quick agreement that something should change, but after that initial burst of agreement, finding the final solution took much longer.

6.1 Creating an Executive

The first clear decision to rebalance power within the national government came on June 1 with the ninth vote of the Convention (see Vote 9 in figure 6.1). New York, New Jersey, Pennsylvania, Delaware, and Virginia all supported a term of seven years for an executive, in opposition to the Carolinas and Georgia (Massachusetts was divided). To this point, the Randolph Plan had merely suggested that a president would exist for some unspecified term. Vote 9 implied the possibility of much greater executive authority within this new national government, an executive with a lengthy seven-year term.

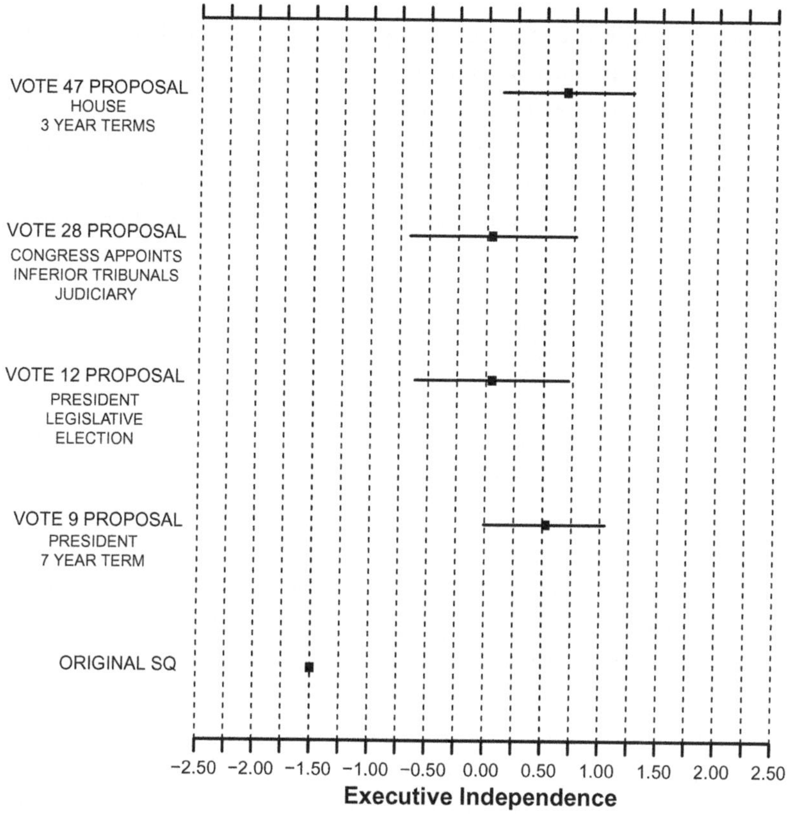

Fig. 6.1. Selected Key Votes on an Independent Executive in the Committee of the Whole Portion of the Convention (May 25–June 20)

In a modern context where the next primary nomination contests can seem just around the corner even after the grueling marathon has just ended, seven years may seem like a very long time indeed. In a world where most state legislatures stood for reelection every single year, it was close to an eternity, and yet it passed with very little trouble. Thus, similar to representation and federalism, the creation of the presidency gets off the ground very quickly. This confirms, yet again, that the Convention moved quickly to establish new parameters for the "revised" government with relatively little fuss, but it is vital to note how the coalitions had changed, and this vote helps to reveal that. Who supported the new president with a long term? The coalition was essentially the Core Reform states (minus divided Massachusetts), allied with key Small-state delegates, against the

Deep South. This is the rough grouping that would create this new executive branch, revolutionary in so many ways.

It was, arguably, too revolutionary because the Convention decided only one day later to make the national legislature the body that elected the president—to have, what we would call in modern terms, a Parliamentary form of government. This took place in Vote 12. Originally, James Wilson proposed electors (of a sort):

> that the Executive Magistracy shall be elected in the following manner: That the States be divided into districts: & that the persons qualified to vote in each district for members of the first branch of the national Legislature elect [blank] members for their respective districts to be electors of the Executive magistracy.[2]
>
> (Farrand 1966, vol. II, 80)

Before the Convention had gone very far, they began disagreeing on the question of who should elect the president. This would be a major sticking point over the course of the Convention, though at this early stage it was resolved very easily. For the time being, they would pair the long presidential term with a strict limit of a single term.[3] What the roll call model reveals is that this was not a dramatic change from the proposal in Vote 9. The coalition pushing for a stronger presidency with greater national authority was apparently content to limit terms, as long as the term was long and the national legislature elected the president. At this early stage, it may have appeared that the coalition fighting for a stronger executive—the Core Reform states and the Small states—were winning significant battles, but the Convention was already striking a balance on this dimension.

On Tuesday, June 5, the Convention debated judges indirectly by focusing on the power to appoint judges. Which elected officials should be entrusted with this significant power? Wilson was against giving it to the legislature because of the "intrigue, partiality, and concealment" which were "necessary consequences" of that route. He was opposed by Rutledge who argued that giving the president such a large amount of power was unwise: "the people will think we are leaning too much toward Monarchy" (119). Ben Franklin, characteristically, somehow wanted to split the difference by finding another way. After a series of votes and speeches, the decisive vote came from a proposal made jointly by Wilson and Madison: "that the National Legislature be empowered to institute inferior tribunals" (125). This had the virtue of establishing the broad precedent that the legislature would have power over this area, but also permitted some debate about fine-grained distinctions in the future. In this case, the Core Reform states were fully united but saw token opposition from both of the other coalitions in the form of a divided New York, with New Jersey and South Carolina voting no (see Vote 28). The compromise position had passed, and the status quo of increased presidential power would remain in place, but with the legislature making nominations.

By Tuesday, June 12, the Convention had revealed that it was not about to move off of the idea of a newly strong president, but it was also equally clear that there was no appetite to make that president stronger. Part of understanding the relationship between the executive and the legislature was deciding how long members of the legislature would sit. Would they be there a long time, able to oppose the executive, or for a shorter period? The Connecticut delegation argued for a single year. Rutledge (SC) argued for every two years. Jenifer (MD) argued that three years was best because "the too great frequency of elections rendered the people indifferent to them, and made the best men unwilling to engage in so precarious a service" (214). The shorter the term of service, the greater the power of the president would be, as he would have consistency and permanency that the Congress would lack. Even three years was less than half of the time they had already previously set for the chief magistrate. Gerry (MA) noted that New England would "never give in on the point of annual elections." He even referenced the septennial elections of Parliament in England, echoing the choice made for the presidency. "He was as much agst. a triennial House as agst. a hereditary Executive" (215). In a vote of seven to four, the Core Reform coalition won, but without Massachusetts, which was joined in voting no by Connecticut, New York, and New Jersey (Maryland and Delaware divided). This is a complicated vote. In some ways it echoes the coalition formation of the large and small states, but there are key differences. Though the small states voted against a long term for House members, the apparent alternative was really only a couple of extra years on the term, not seven as in the case of the president. Southern delegations wanted the national legislature to be powerful and so voted for longer terms, though not nearly as long as in the case of the emerging president.

This is how things stood when they stopped using the Committee of the Whole on a daily basis. The presidency had been clearly created, and this was a major change. However, in many respects, the Convention had decided very little since there was merely a president with undetermined powers. The exact balance of congressional power, as opposed to power distributed to the other branches, was clearly moving away from the Articles, but how far it would go was not yet decided. The debates—particularly the debate over representation discussed earlier—had provoked a reaction from the Small states where the divisions were deepest. Differences over the presidency were simply less stark and less well-formed, but this left a lot of room to create additional powers for both the legislature and the executive.

6.2 Power Centers

As can be seen in the last subsection, relatively less was done on this dimension until representation was resolved by the Great Compromise. However, once that issue had been resolved, the delegates attacked the question of the executive. Rakove (1996) puts it as follows: "On July 17 [they] returned to an issue they had ignored since early June: the executive" (82). He also describes this period as more "pragmatic" (82). Bowen (1966), for her part, argues that after the resolution of July 16, "matters would move more easily; the little states were ready to meet the big, and yield on many questions" (186); the implication here is that the concerns of the small states had been met over representation.

While we agree with this general tone about the changing debate, we note that the discussions were, in at least some respects, even more difficult because they were less clear and the coalitions were fighting about novel issues on which they differed starkly. Some authors find in the notes of the debate "fatigue, impatience and homesickness" (Rakove 1996, 83, is just one example of this refrain). Without disagreeing, we would note that these later debates were about issues that were far less settled and less clearly connected to constituency interests.

Rakove describes this period by saying, "A narrative of this . . . phase of debate cannot take the same form as the one that culminates on July 16" (83). Still, figure 6.2 presents the key issues decided on the executive independence dimension and shows a clear pattern: the delegates were comfortable with a powerful president, but they could not agree on electors (yet) and so ended up deciding on legislative selection of the president.

As the Convention moved away from Committee of the Whole, the focus was initially federalism (discussed in the last chapter), although it is also true that the balance of power between the executive and the legislature was never terribly far away from debates, and there were a few key votes—as illustrated by figure 6.2. The argument over how powerful the states would be relative to the federal government involved balancing how much power state legislatures would have over the national arrangements. On June 23, they debated how much power the national legislature would have with respect to compensation. Part of that discussion was inevitably about how much power the states could indirectly influence legislators by letting them hold offices created by the second branch.

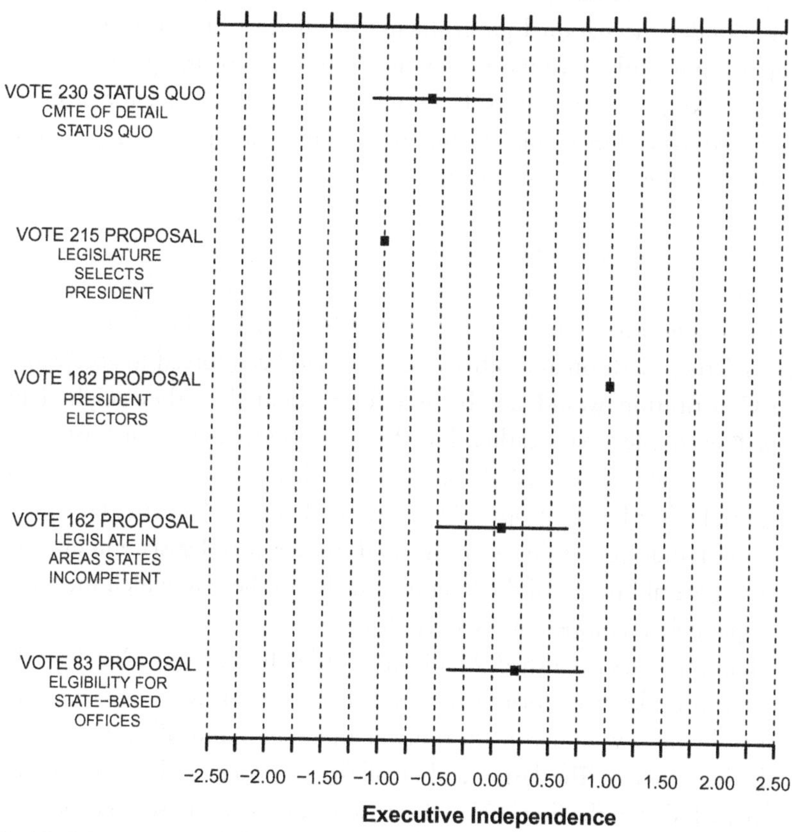

Fig. 6.2. Selected Key Votes on an Independent Executive in the Middle Portion of the Convention (June 21–July 28)

They had already rejected the idea that state legislatures would have power of election over the members of the lower chamber (see the debates of June 21, immediately after ending the broad use of Committee of the Whole). However, a few days later on June 23 (see Vote 83 in the figure) they permitted states to have some power to influence state legislators. In that vote, they accepted Pinckney's motion to make members of the first branch of the legislature eligible for offices "established by a particular state" (Farrand 1966, vol. I, 386). So it was established that there would be some room for states to exert influence over the legislature, even if that was only indirect influence. A striking feature of Vote 83, however, is that it only ratified the amended Randolph clause (see Farrand 1966, vol. II, 235) for offices created under state auspices. The vote left open the possibility, explicitly raised by Randolph's resolution, that legislators could hold office "under the national government" for at least one year. Thus, this proposal implicitly gave the executive additional bargaining chips to use when working with legislators. It did not dramatically change the proposal on the executive independence dimension, but it did move things slightly in the direction of executive power.

Vote 162 was a slightly different move. This came on July 17, one day after they had agreed to finalize what we now call the Great Compromise, and that context is important. By this point in the proceedings, the idea that the legislature would be supreme was beginning to be taken as established. True, Madison and other reformers had been forced to accept that the Constitution would not be as reform-oriented as they might have hoped, even a few days earlier, but the powerful Congress (at least when Congress could act unitedly) was now a reality and part of an accepted bargain. Bedford (DE) proposed what would become Vote 162. He moved that the Randolph resolution read: "and moreover to legislate in all cases for the general interest of the Union, and also in those to which the States are separately incompetent" (vol. II, 26).

Randolph was perturbed. Madison recorded him as immediately replying that this idea was "formidable" and that "it involves the power of violating all the laws and constitutions of the States, and of intermeddling with their police. The last member of the sentence is also superfluous, being included in the first" (26). This is, admittedly, a very strange moment and may show some of the incoherence of Randolph. The original clause actually read that "to legislate in all cases to which the separate States are incompetent; or in which the harmony of the U.S. may be interrupted by the exercise of individual legislation; to negative all laws passed by the several States contravening in the opinion of the National Legislature the articles of Union, or any treaties" (vol. I, 236). So Bedford's opinion was hardly far from what Randolph had originally proposed, and the overall vote on the clause (Vote 162) passed by a relatively wide margin of 8–2, slightly increasing the power of the Congress. It did not obviously diminish the power of the president, though it is the balance that matters.

Over the next couple of days, they made some progress on executive versus legislative power but still could not seem to resolve it. Madison, in company with a relatively nationalist coalition, argued that "it be a fundamental principle of Govt. that the Legislative, Executive & Judiciary powers should be *separately* exercised; it is equally so that they be *independently* exercised" (vol. II, 56, emphasis in original). Many disagreed. Rutledge, for instance, argued that a president "not re-eligible" would be "sufficiently independent" (57). Eventually they had to vote, and the pivotal vote came in Vote 182,[4] when, by a margin of 6–3–1 (the Carolinas and Georgia were opposed, along with Massachusetts being divided) the delegates called for electors to select the president. This proposal moved executive power much further away from Congress, who would not elect the president under those circumstances. The use of electors meant that the president would have an independent base of power, and this is a very pivotal moment at the Convention. Indeed, by our model, the president is never quite as powerful again; much of the later period (after the Committee of Detail meets) is devoted to slowly trimming the president's powers. But the deed was done. By agreeing to this motion, the Convention created two separate electoral power bases—but, as it turned out, this could not hold forever.

On July 24, the Convention reconsidered the motion that the President be appointed by the "Natl. Legislature, instead of Electors appointed by the State Legislatures" (99). Though the delegates had already decided that there would be a recess and a Committee of Detail, they had not made any final decisions on the presidency. As evidence of this, Beeman (2010) notes that they had explicitly excluded the question from the charge to that committee (see 247), so this was clearly a point of significant contention. Elbridge Gerry fought the motion, arguing that the national legislature should not be given the charge to control the executive. If the Convention did go down this path, he posited, they should make the executive ineligible for reelection. Williamson (NC) said that he "did not like Unity in the Executive. He had wished the Executive power to be lodged in three districts into which the states should be divided." He concluded that "there is an essential difference of interests between the N. & S. States" and that "the power will be dangerous, if the Executive is to be taken from part of the Union, to the part from which he is not taken" (vol. II, 100–01). Raising the specter of a King, Williamson's speech stands out as the key point offered against election by electors. When the vote came up (Vote 215 in the figure), the legislature regained control of selection. All of the Deep South voted this way, in opposition to Connecticut, Pennsylvania, Maryland, and Virginia.[5]

This was one of the most dramatic shifts in the Convention. In the space of little more than a week, they had gone from approving a very independent president to rejecting that proposal and picking one that would be the vassal of the Congress. This major reversal to the fortunes of a powerful, independent executive might well have been seen as decisive and as the final shift back in the direction of congressional power. Little would change in the next few votes as they turned the resolutions over to the Committee of Detail. As things stood then, the president would be elected by the Congress. Despite this apparent resolution, they were not nearly as settled as they would appear, and the issue that increased presidential power would turn out not to be election, but the power over nominations.

6.3 Balancing the Powers

The votes that had come to this point were merely a prelude to the flurry of votes that would finish allocating power to the presidency or to the Congress. Some votes would pass, others would fail, and the Convention would, again, settle in at the moderate point of acceptability. It is impossible to read the debates and not get a sense of uncertainty about this key dimension and the set of votes that compose it. The Convention wanted to create a well-designed government but was struggling to choose between two options. The first— the one they had chosen implicitly to this point—was to keep the new government rooted completely in the legislature, with an executive who was beholden to them. In essence, had they chosen this path, but weakly and without any firmness, they would have created a modern parliament. The alternative was an independently elected executive that would set up a competing power center. This final section of this chapter is the story of how they opted for that latter choice and tried to find a way to balance the set of powers held by each center of authority in the new government.

After the Committee of Detail met in early August, the Convention returned and pushed through its largest number of proposals. Figure 6.3 shows the basic story. Initially, there was a set of proposals to move power away from Congress to an independent president. The first of these votes failed, but the proponents of a powerful executive eventually succeeded,

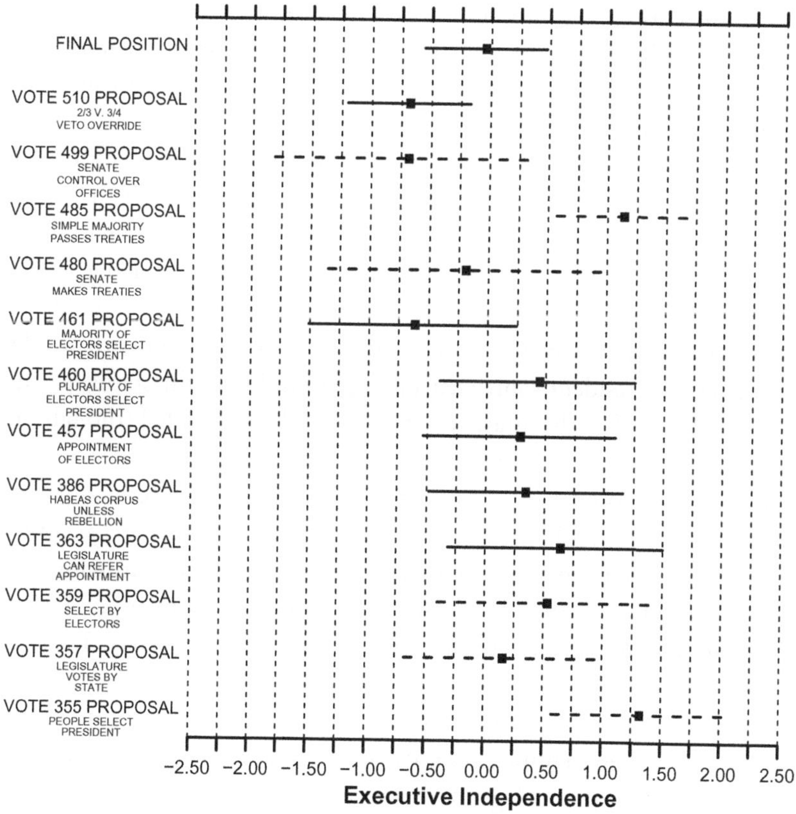

Fig. 6.3. Selected Key Votes on an Independent Executive in the Final Portion of the Convention (August 6–September 17)

though not completely. By Vote 461 in early September, the delegates who favored congressional power gained the upper hand, with a final position that was not quite what either side of this debate had intended.

It was not until August 24 that the delegates really returned to the issue of presidential selection in earnest—one month to the day since they had decided to give the president's election back to the legislature. Despite this status quo, there were still questions about how that election would work. A joint ballot across the House and the Senate? Only the House? In the midst of this debate, Carroll (MD) moved to strike out the legislative election and insert "by the people" (Farrand 1966, vol. II, 402) instead. This proposal would have made a president far more independent of Congress, reflected in the position of the proposal for Vote 355 in figure 6.3. Indeed, one could argue, it was the most revolutionary move of the entire Convention on this dimension (offered not by anyone from the Core Reform states, but from a Small-state delegate sympathetic to presidential power). Only Delaware and Pennsylvania were willing to tolerate such a move.

So, in late August, they were still focused on having the legislature elect the president, and in Vote 357, Dayton (New Jersey) moved that each state should have a single vote in that election. The model estimates this vote as being a move toward independence of the executive relative to the status quo of July, but there is no debate on this specific point to guide us in how they conceived of this motion. It is easy to imagine that it would have made the president somewhat more powerful than the status quo in that he had a smaller electorate to satisfy. Still, the vote failed (though on the narrow margin of five votes to six).

In stepped Gouverneur Morris who "opposed the election of the President by the Legislature. . . . If the Legislature have the Executive dependent on them, they can perpetuate & support their usurpations by the influence of tax-gatherers & other officers, by fleets armies &c. Cabal and corruption are attached to that mode of election" (403–04). To stave off these horrible outcomes, Morris proposed electors "chosen by the people of the several states" (404). The model suggests that this vote (359) was somewhere between the extremity of election via the people (see Vote 355) and the status quo of legislative election, but it also failed. New Jersey, Pennsylvania, Delaware, and Virginia supported Morris, but the other delegations voted against his position. On the last presidential election vote of the day, they considered the first part of Morris's motion: electors "as an abstract question" (404), but this also failed in a vote not pictured on the figure. The pattern was that they could not agree, and that the factional alliance between the Core Reform states and the Deep South was clearly broken on this dimension.

It was at this moment that the logjam began to break. Election was not a point on which they could agree, so John Dickinson (DE) moved to give the president "the power to appoint to all offices established in this Constitution, except in cases herein otherwise provided for, and to all offices, which may be hereafter created by law" (405). This was a revolutionary move and not one that went unremarked. Randolph (VA) immediately called the power of appointments "a formidable one"[6] and raised the possibility that the states should be allowed to have some say over such appointments. However, without any other recorded debate, they held a vote on Dickinson's motion (Vote 363 in the figure), and it passed: Connecticut, New Jersey, Pennsylvania, Maryland, and Virginia voted aye with New Hampshire, Massachusetts, South Carolina, and Delaware voting no.[7] It is ironic that Dickinson's own delegation opposed him, but it shows how the delegates on this question of the presidency were more jumbled than usual. This vote is the high water mark of presidential power in our model, and we do agree with Randolph that, at this moment, the president was given a very formidable power.

On August 28, the Convention turned to Vote 386 and took up the question of habeas corpus. This proposal was not a major shift in any direction, but it did slightly limit the power of the executive to suspend the right of judicial oversight. It was not a solution to the overall design of the presidency, but it did limit its prospective power. On the general question of presidential power, at least so far, the delegates were still clearly undecided. As evidence of this, they created the Brearley Committee, or as Beeman (2010) refers to it, the Committee on Postponed Parts. Rossiter (1966) describes this committee well: "[t]his admirable Committee moved in as a rescue party to make up the Convention's mind" (218). It was tasked with producing a number of proposals that the Convention could test on the floor. On September 4, the Brearley Committee reported on a number of matters, presidential selection being the most important of them. The proposal for selection read as follows:

> Each State shall appoint in such manner as its Legislature may direct, a number of electors equal to the number of Senators and members of the House of Representatives, to which the State may be entitled in the Legislature. The Electors shall meet in their respective States, and vote by ballot for two persons, of whom one at least shall not be an inhabitant of the Same State with themselves. . . . The Person having the greatest number of votes shall be the President, if such number be a majority of that of the electors.
>
> (Farrand 1966, vol. II, 497–98)

If there was no clear majority, the Senate would then select the president.

This proposal was voted on in pieces. In Vote 457 (not pictured), they approved of the idea of electors in proportion to the number of senators and House members in each state (by a vote of 9–2, with only the Carolinas in opposition). In Vote 460, according to Jackson, they approved of a plurality threshold for these electors—the person winning the greatest number of votes would gain the office. These two votes retained the idea of an independent president. However, immediately (and without any debate), they then decided that this election would require a majority of the electors in Vote 461. As seen in figure 6.3 the model records this as a pivotal moment back toward state power.[8] This second proposal about a majority makes a significant difference leading to far less presidential independence, at least in their minds. Presidents who have to garner a clear majority of votes from these electors—selected by state legislatures—are inherently more constrained than presidents who need merely achieve the largest number of votes. They later agreed that if no one gets a majority, the House (with each state having one vote) would select the president (Vote 469, but not pictured as it was of little consequence in the model). What this meant was that Vote 461 ratified—at least in their view—Electoral College election for candidates with overwhelming support and legislative election if that condition did not hold, something they obviously expected would happen often.

By September 7, time was growing short, but Madison—who had clearly been far less active for a time in August—was not done proposing changes, and the changes he offered suggest that he was not as sure about executive power as some of the other reformers. In Vote 480, he proposed that the Senate should be able to conduct a "peace" treaty without consulting the president. As things stood, the proposal allowed the president to make a treaty of peace without recourse to the Senate. With this new offering, the Senate would be permitted to make a treaty in the absence of presidential support. His reasoning was that presidents would "derive so much power and importance from a state of war that he might be tempted, if authorized, to impede a treaty of peace" (Farrand 1966, vol. II, 540). The measure, which was clearly on the side of greater congressional power, failed with only Maryland, South Carolina, and Georgia in support. It is tempting to think about how this proposal, which, after all, does seem grounded in reasonable logic, would have changed the balance of national power. However, it was too much for the Convention to consider. Immediately after this vote, the Convention approved, in Vote 481, the general clause that gave presidents the power to make treaties.

The process continued the next day. Vote 485 was a proposal from Wilson (Pennsylvania) and Dayton (New Jersey) to strike out the concurrence of the Senate entirely. This would have moved power dramatically toward the president (see the figure), but it failed by a wide margin. Rutledge (South Carolina) and Gerry (Massachusetts) then argued, in Vote 486 (not pictured), for an amendment that would require two-thirds of the entire Senate, rather than merely two-thirds of the senators present (as the draft proposal then read). This point was apparently too much of a cut to presidential power for the Convention to approve, although, in practice, it has worked out that this clause effectively meant that all senators are present on such key votes. Then, in Vote 487, they considered a "majority" of senators as the requirement for a treaty; however, this also failed by a vote of five to six. In the end, they let the status quo stand; they were not willing to move power too much toward the president.

After a series of votes hemmed and hawed about presidential power, they were unable to agree on increasing it much. Finally, came the key set of proposals. In Vote 499, Gerry (Massachusetts) proposed to limit presidential appointments only to those offices established by the Constitution, an incremental move away from presidential power. This would necessarily keep power in the hands of Congress because it would mean future presidents could not appoint future agency or department heads without the approval of a congressional law. But this vote also failed, again showing how difficult it was to settle on a final position.

By this point—late September—they were clearly barreling toward a final disposition of the presidency. On September 10, the Committee of Style produced a document that was close to the final set of bargains about the proposed Constitution. This was considered for a couple of days, and then the Convention made a momentous choice in Vote 510 that continued the trend of favoring congressional power over presidential power. Until this late date, the rule had been that three-quarters of each chamber of the legislature could overrule a presidential veto. However, on September 12, Williamson, Gerry, and others proposed that the number be changed to two-thirds of each house. The model notes that this change was significant and moved power back toward Congress and away from an independent, powerful executive, though not by a large amount.

What finally changed? Shortly after Vote 510, the Convention moved into a series of final proposals, all on very seemingly discrete topics of varying importance. On the significant end, for instance, the very next vote (Vote 511) was a unanimous decision to reject a proposal to draw up a bill of rights (unanimous at the state level of voting, a few individual delegates supported it). There were arguments about whether or not states could charge inspection fees on goods coming into the state (though not tariffs beyond that). Madison himself made a proposal that persons in the executive branch tried for impeachment would not be suspended from office to prevent the House of Representatives from merely voting impeachment articles to remove a distasteful official from service. It should be said that our assessments of the agenda are perhaps the least reliable in this portion of the Convention. The notes are far from clear. There are inconsistencies and questions about the record that make us reluctant to place too much weight on any individual vote.

Despite this uncertainty about the agenda, we are confident that the broad pattern of the model reveals what happened. The original proposal to dramatically reform the new government by creating a powerful executive was carried out—but only to an extent. The president was not made the creature of Congress, depending on their whims and changeability. He (at least until the twenty-first century) would also not be powerless. His veto need only carry against two-thirds of the Congress, and his power over nominations to appointments was absolute (if not the power to confirm). Indeed, it is this power of nominations that was the key moment that really advanced presidential power. When the delegates decided to give power over nominations to the executive, it was a powerful move toward a strong presidency, and it can be seen today that fights over nominations remain one of the most contentious parts of a president's actions.

The final position of the presidency was a compromise between two factions, but not the clear factions on the other two dimensions—Core Reform states working with the Deep South. On this dimension, the reforms came because the Core Reform states (occasionally with Massachusetts wavering) allied with key Small states like Delaware and Maryland to create this relatively strong presidency. In many ways, this set of compromises created the conditions for a strong presidency. These conditions would not bear full fruit until the twentieth century, but certainly Washington, Jackson, and Lincoln gave hints of what the presidency could one day become: a power center that would rival the Congress, perhaps unintentionally, as we describe in chapter 7.

6.4 The Final Position

What did they finally and actually accomplish? To see the estimates in context, figure 6.4 shows several key points. AC denotes the status quo of the articles. V1 denotes the position of the status quo after the initial vote. Vote 230 plots the point at the end of July, going into the Committee of Detail. GC plots the point at which they agreed to the Great Compromise, while the NJ and VA plans are also labeled. Finally, the point labelled "final" shows the end position of all of their debates. Compared with Vote 230 (where the Constitution stood at the end of July), the changes in this final period are not major. The agenda moved slightly in the direction of more proportional representation and toward more independent executive power. However, on the federalism dimension, little had substantially changed. All of this is consistent with the stories we have already told above.

A glance at figure 6.4 on the federalism dimension shows just how small the changes were in the final period. In chapter 5 we noted that Madison's successes all came in the earliest phase, and this graph certainly confirms that. A few major changes were contemplated but never really gained any traction. Essentially, after the Convention decided to finalize the Great Compromise and settled the major points, it was difficult to find

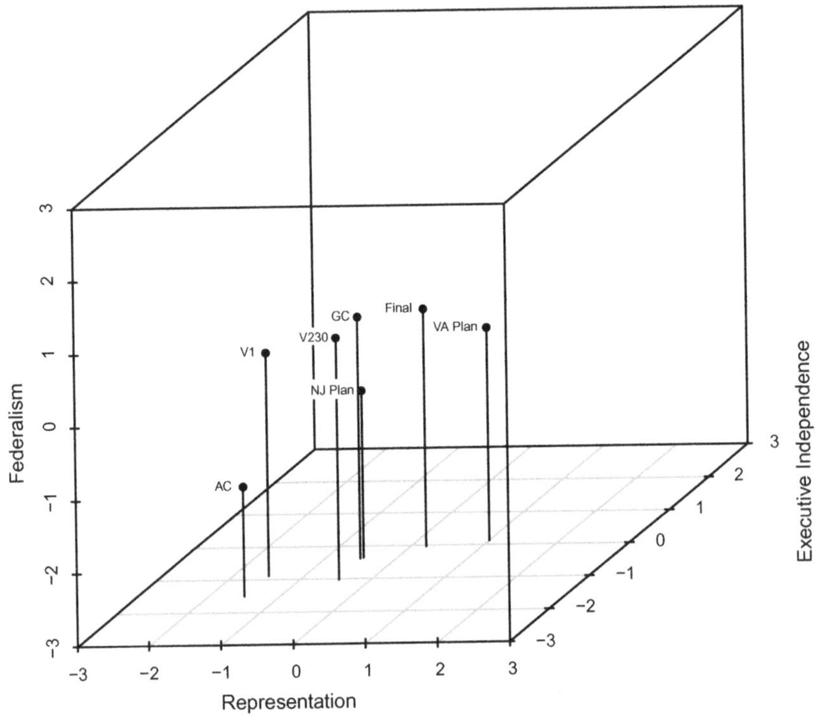

Fig. 6.4. The Final Positions

any new gains on any particular dimension. Though scholars may mine the final few weeks of the debates for nuggets of intention or hopes for the new regime, the major decisions were all made early.

A question that repeatedly comes up when discussing the Constitution was just how much did Madison gain at the Convention? Robertson (2005) argues that Roger Sherman played the pivotal role in "spoiling Madison's agenda and altering his substantive plans for Constitutional design" (225).[9] He notes all of the ways in which Sherman forced compromises on Madison and others with similar viewpoints. In many respects, figure 6.4 validates his point of view. It certainly shows how the final position was not as extreme as the Virginia Plan, but not quite the New Jersey Plan either. It reflects a central position near the center of the delegations that attended the Convention. However, when we compare the final position of the Constitution with the first vote at the beginning of the Convention and the status quo before that—the Articles of Confederation— the picture that emerges is one of significant change.

Unquestionably, the Constitution has moved relatively far away from the Articles of Confederation, especially on questions of representation and federalism, as well as executive independence.

Madison's success came early at the Convention. Most of the movement away from the Articles of Confederation came relatively early, and this can be seen in the estimated position of the very first vote (V1), which shows how quickly they were willing to move into a dramatically different space of policy. Once the major questions had been settled, the final period saw the delegates focus on minor adjustments, but even in that period, the movement is generally toward Madison's estimated position. It was only around the time of the Great Compromise that Madison's aspirations were really denied. At most other moments of the Convention, Madison appears to have won a great deal of success, if not, perhaps, everything he might have wanted. If he failed in some respects, it is only because he aspired to so much.

The Constitution has often been described as a bundle of compromises. This is certainly true in the sense that it was a process that did not reflect any single view. The eventual product that emerged was at the center of the delegates' many different preferences. However, this tour through the voting on the Constitution should convince any observer that a significant number of the products of the Convention are not thoughtful, designed compromises accepted by a group in concurrence, but the outcome of a deliberative process that was occasionally given to accidental outcomes, something not intended by anyone. Certainly, the presidency reflected that pattern, as did the fact that the Convention ultimately decided to create two competing power centers in the national government.

The process of finding a balanced set of compromises, a proposed constitution that satisfied everyone as much as possible, was difficult. Finding that key middle ground on each of these dimensions left everyone dissatisfied. Franklin summed it up well on the last day of the Convention:

> I confess that there are several parts of this constitution which I do not at present approve, but I am not sure I shall never approve them: For having lived long, I have experienced many instances of being obliged by better information, or fuller consideration, to change opinions even on important subjects, which I once thought right, but found to be otherwise. It is therefore that the older I grow, the more apt I am to doubt my own judgment, and to pay more

> respect to the judgment of others. Most men indeed as well as most sects in Religion, think themselves in possession of all truth, and that wherever others differ from them it is so far error. Steele a Protestant in a Dedication tells the Pope, that the only difference between our Churches in their opinions of the certainty of their doctrines is, the Church of Rome is infallible and the Church of England is never in the wrong. But though many private persons think almost as highly of their own infallibility as of that of their sect, few express it so naturally as a certain french lady, who in a dispute with her sister, said "I don't know how it happens, Sister but I meet with no body but myself, that's always in the right."

An emergent agenda, where each delegate was given equal authority to offer proposals and test ideas, allowed them to find the true middle ground on each of these major dimensions. By definition, this meant that everyone was a little dissatisfied. The Constitution was the product not only of many minds but also of many proposals. What are we, reading the document hundreds of years later, supposed to take from that event?

CHAPTER 7

Factional Design

In the end, which states got what they wanted the most? No delegation or delegate won everything, and there is a substantial amount of uncertainty remaining, but we close our analysis of the deep structure of voting with a table and a figure that helps answer these questions. Table 7.1 shows—by the three dimensions—the order of the ideological positions of the states compared to the final position of the Constitution. Figure 7.1 is complementary and includes a line at the status quo of the Articles of Confederation to show the positions (including the new Constitution) relative to that point. While we do not wish to place too much emphasis on any rank ordering (there is limited data to estimate all of this, after all), we do want to comment on a few basic patterns.

On representation (see the top third of the table and the left-most panel in the graph), the states closest to the final outcome are, ironically, the Deep South and Core Reform states. They were forced to compromise on representation, but they still managed to make dramatic moves away from the Articles of Confederation. According to the model, New York and New Jersey were fine with the status quo of one vote per state. It was only the slaveholders allied with the reformers who managed to make the changes to representation on that dimension. The story is broadly similar for federalism. The Core Reform states got what they wanted, as did those in the Deep South. The Small-state coalition simply lost.

Nevertheless, the deep structure of voting does also implicate the presidency, and it is here that the coalition structure changed. While the Core Reform states got much of what they wanted, they were joined by Delaware and Maryland from the Small-state faction, and the Deep

Table 7.1

	State	Percent Rank	Percent Closest	Percent Support
Representation	South Carolina	83.2%	0.03%	100%
	Georgia	81.0%	0.52%	100%
	North Carolina	77.6%	12.2%	100%
	Virginia	47.2%	21.3%	99.98%
	Pennsylvania	43.1%	26.7%	100%
	Massachusetts	57.8%	26.5%	99.95%
	Maryland	46.3%	7.3%	91.4%
	Connecticut	36.7%	3.9%	83.9%
	Delaware	55.9%	1.5%	67.4%
	New York	57.5%	0.00%	1.8%
	New Jersey	58.8%	0.08%	4.3%
Federalism	North Carolina	56.4%	5.4%	100%
	South Carolina	28.5%	10.4%	100%
	Virginia	25.9%	9.1%	100%
	Pennsylvania	24.2%	20.1%	100%
	Georgia	27.0%	20.2%	100%
	Massachusetts	43.2%	22.3%	100%
	New York	58.7%	9.5%	90.2%
	Connecticut	38.0%	1.5%	74.3%
	Delaware	31.2%	0.82%	63.0%
	New Jersey	31.7%	0.65%	58.7%
	Maryland	76.3%	0.03%	12.2%
Executive Independence	Pennsylvania	75.9%	1.3%	100%
	Virginia	62.0%	3.6%	100%
	Delaware	68.8%	10.6%	100%
	Maryland	71.4%	18.8%	100%
	Massachusetts	60.0%	20.9%	100%
	New Jersey	44.5%	14.8%	99.99%
	Connecticut	36.7%	10.5%	99.7%
	North Carolina	36.6%	7.6%	98.6%
	New York	28.9%	8.1%	91.7%
	Georgia	56.2%	2.4%	74.1%
	South Carolina	68.7%	1.4%	51.9%

Note: The table illustrates the probability, on each dimension, for each state's rank position, proximity to Constitution, and support of the final document.

South was largely on the losing end of the argument. The presidency came from a very different coalition. On the whole, we think this is quite close to the picture we promised in table 1.1 at the beginning of the book.

Finally, we note that the position of the final Constitution (by dimension) is placed in each of the panels of figure 7.1. It is, appropriately, near

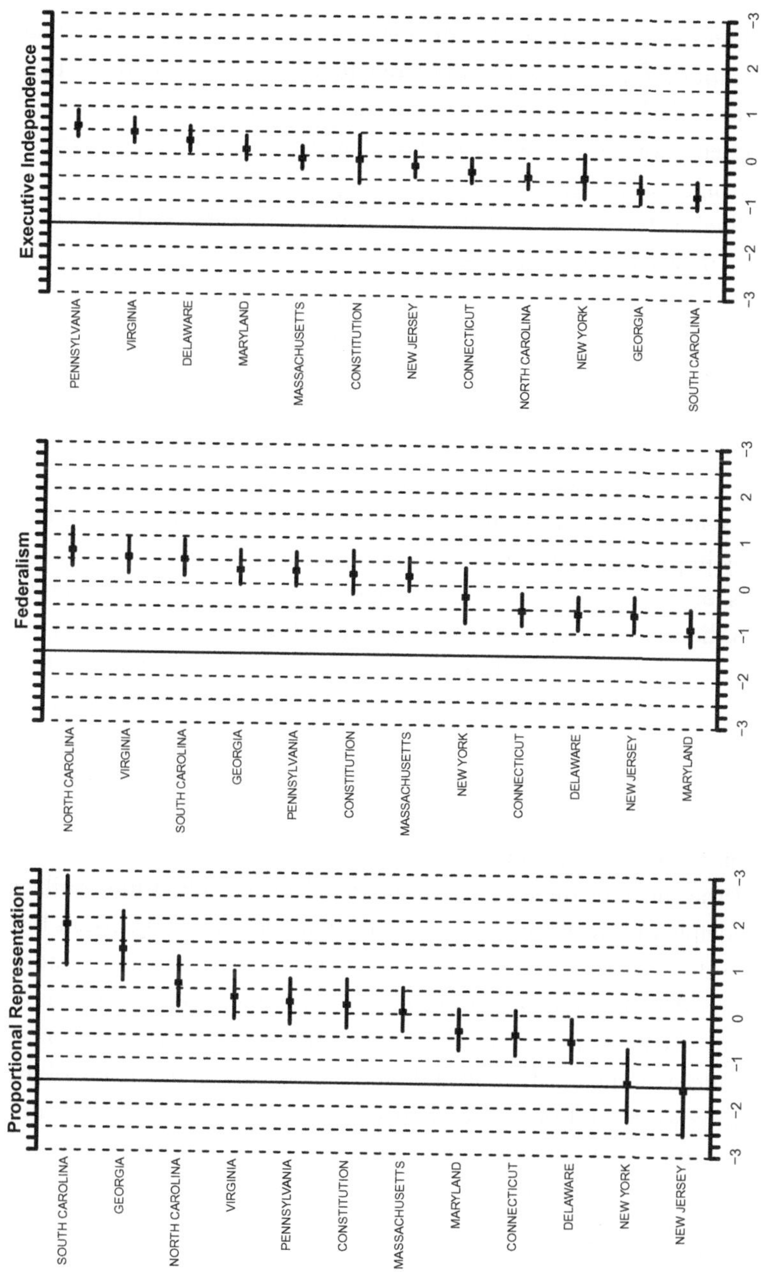

Fig. 7.1.

Note: The figure orders, by mean, the ideological positions of the states, along with the final position of the Constitution. The drawn line is a reference to the initial status quo position of the Articles of Confederation.

the midpoint of each group. In this sense, you can see those states that wanted more reform (generally the Core Reform states) and those that wanted less. With the notable exceptions of New York and New Jersey on the representation dimension, it is clear that the Convention collectively preferred significant changes to the governing structure.

The final picture is one of significant change, tempered by the inherent difficulty of navigating the three key factions—the Core Reform states, the Deep South, and the Small states. With this full picture of the deep structure of voting at the Constitutional Convention in hand, what have we learned? Perhaps the key lesson is that the original design of the Constitution—while not exactly a mistake or an accident—was a competition between two broadly competing factional alignments: the Core Reform states allied with the Deep South on the one hand, and the Core Reform states allied with the sympathetic Small-state delegates on the other. We believe this fact has many implications, which we discuss in this final chapter.

It has long been understood that the drafters in the Convention—not to mention the wider set of people who debated ratification—simply disagreed about quite a bit (Main 1961; Ohline 1971; Elazar 1972; Collier and Collier 1986; Matson and Onuf 1990; Rakove 1996; McGuire 2003; Robertson 2005; Slez and Martin 2007; Heckelman and Dougherty 2011, 2013).[1] What this facile truth obscures is that specific key parts of the Constitution can be traced to the deep structure of voting in Philadelphia. Our aim in this book has been to demonstrate the true underlying set of factions that debated the different dimensions of conflict. Understanding the conflicts in Philadelphia from this perspective casts many debates of American history in a different light. While there probably are a wide range of historical debates that should consider our findings, we think these are the most important: the development of states' rights, the nature of representation, a better understanding of Madison's role at the Convention, the nature of the newly empowered and highly centralized government, and how all of this plays into any type of originalist understanding of the Constitution.

The purpose of this book has been to provide a new understanding of how the original design was created. This does not mean that we fully understand that design, or that we have fully explained it. It just means that to fully understand the voting and the design, we have to think about its origins and what those origins mean for the history of the Constitution. It was a factional design that emerged out of the dance of the different coalitions.

7.1 The Rights of States

Returning to Madison's Memo on the Vices of the States, a very significant reason for the Convention was the nature of the states in the Union of the 1780s. The power, the rights, and the limitations of those states were at issue during the creation of this new nation. Madison knew this, and it was a signal reason for his efforts.

Historically, "states' rights" is a cry associated with the South. Tied to slavery and, later, to Jim Crow laws,[2] the cause of strong states is generally understood as something that helped slave owners protect their peculiar interest; indeed, the nineteenth century is difficult to understand from any other perspective. However, from the standpoint of the Convention, this conception of states' rights is doubly backwards. First, the idea that states should be represented equally was a residue of the Articles of Confederation and was a principle upheld far more by northern and mid-Atlantic states like Maryland and Delaware, who were much less dependent on slavery, than by the states of the Deep South. Oddly, this means that the states that voted most often for the Federalists in the elections of the early years of the republic—1796, 1800, and 1804, for instance—tended to be northern and oriented toward merchants and trade in a way that the South was not (beyond a desire to export cotton and a few other agricultural products). There were relatively few slaves in these northern states (and no evidence that slavery was a major consideration for these delegates beyond a point on which to be compromised). What this means is that, when the Convention almost foundered over the question of state representation, the side pushing the power of states as corporate entities was largely drawn from the northern and relatively non-slaveholding states. The literature on "nationalists" at the Convention is certainly consistent with that description. What is novel in our book, however, is that we show that when the dimensions are separated out by different nationalist projects, the claim is still true for both representation and federalism.[3]

This pattern of voting also means that a key moment of institutional creativity—perhaps the key moment of such creativity in American history—that created a stronger national government came from an alliance only made possible by slaveholders working with pivotal reformers. Perhaps this was simply part and parcel of their beliefs about how the new legislature would protect their interests. Or it may be the case that the Deep South had particular ideas rooted in their own conception of good government. Whatever the cause, at key junctures, delegates from the Deep South were pivotal members of the coalition that was most likely to favor a stronger national government (see, in particular, figure 3.3). Madison's proposed changes to the type of government would have never gone anywhere without the support of the Deep South. As can be seen in chapters 4 and 5, this was not an unswerving preference. They did believe in many limitations on government. They were unwilling, for instance, to accept a national veto over state legislation. However, in the broad brush-strokes, they favored increased national power.

One of the great ironies of this moment in politics is that, despite the fact that the Small states stood in opposition to the project of reform—especially on the dimensions of representation and the size and scope of government—in a few short years, the states they represented became the bedrock of the Federalist Party. This meant that the states with relatively more anti-federalist sentiments would join the Republican Party and provide the margin of victory for that group. Slez and Martin (2007) believe this came about because, through the Convention, the agenda shifted toward an alignment that fostered the growth of the new party system. Whatever the reason, the political alignments of the future were not at all like the alignments of the Convention.

This is a tribute to the power of the Constitution. It reorganized politics in dramatic ways that are difficult to see given how much the institutions changed. Before the Constitution, the national government was really just a government of other governments. Afterwards, it was a government of the people, but people organized into states—a feature that would never really go away.

7.2 Representing People

The new national government was, after ratification, a government of the people—though not all people. And one of the key lessons of this book simply must be the importance of slavery to that eventual government. Waldstreicher (2009) shows how specific clauses protected the institution, but our results go further. Slavery was deeply important to the South, but its impact was felt more broadly than simply adding discrete clauses about three-fifths of a person, counting rules, or trade restrictions. Slavery was the interest that changed representation and made the Constitution possible. At the time of the founding, those pressing the case for one person, one vote[4] were more likely to be slaveholders. This fact should not invalidate the moral calculus of the concept of equality, but it gives the historical context for how the country moved substantially closer to that principle with the Constitution. Any original understanding or interpretation of the Constitution needs to take this into consideration, though we acknowledge that it is an ironic story.

As of this writing, arguments about the unfairness of the Senate and the way in which it over-represents certain states are growing in strength. California gets just as many Senators as does Wyoming, and this would have been the outcome for the entirety of the legislature had the Small states obtained the votes. It was only the slaveholding Deep South that provided the margin for the creation of the House of Representatives—the body that, ironically, pays respect to the one person, one vote principle.

Jack Rakove (1996) put this better than we can in his description of the three-fifths compromise and an implicit comparison to the other "great" compromise:

> it was a compromise in the . . . unhappy sense: a sacrifice of moral principle to attain a tangible political end. But a case can be made that this bargain turned out to have fewer costs than the other deal the framers had to strike to complete their task. It was not, after all, the three-fifths clause that gave the southern states the leverage they needed to keep the Union safe for slavery, but rather the Senate, where the later Compromises of 1829–30 and 1850 did more to preserve the political equilibrium Madison sought.

For Rakove, even after the Civil War, it was the "Senate that continued to embody a vicious principle of representation, giving states with vastly disparate concentrations of population equal weight" (93).

Our key difference from Rakove is to note that the two compromises are far more connected than most authors realize (see chapter 4). We see the two compromises as being linked in order to get North Carolina's vote. That does not justify either the Senate compromise or the three-fifths compromise, but it does mean that we cannot see those in isolation, labeling one as "great" and the other as implicitly "bad." They were part of the same set of bargains.

While the slaveholders' specific demand for changes in representation may have had positive effects, we are not ever likely to feel their motivations were justified. Neither can we deny the fact that it was the slave-state position that carried the day for proportional representation—an abstract stance broadly seen as more just by many scholars and observers. Without the fact of this coalition, there is no reform on representation, no matter how unpleasant that may seem to modern ears. It was slavery that helped remake what had been a government of governments into a government of the people.

7.3 James Madison's Efforts

No one is as well identified with the story of that government reform than James Madison. He is, rightly, called the Father of the Constitution, and his influence stands out here, especially at the beginning of the Convention. Consider figures 4.1, 5.1, and 6.1. In each of these graphics there was an immediate and unambiguous shift in the direction of reform. In some cases, the shift came on the first day of debate; in others, it came in the first few weeks, but it always came at this early point in the Convention.[5] Though this is a poor substitute for a monument on the mall, these institutional changes are Madison's chief legacy.

Madison—and the other key reformers—had the political acumen to realize that the assembly in Philadelphia was eager for change. Men like Patrick Henry of Virginia, who decided not to attend, or Robert Yates, who attended for a time but gave up by early July, ended up playing very little role in the creation of the document (ratification is another matter, obviously) because they were overwhelmed by the fact that the Convention immediately took up the cause of reform. By June 10, it was already clear that there would be no simple return to the Articles of Confederation. Too many votes had already shown that was not possible. Most of our graphics illustrate immediate and early changes followed by periods of debates about how far to go, but rarely are there changes in the proposed document that return to the provisions of the Articles of Confederation. While we agree with Robertson (2005) that "Madison's Convention opponents . . . helped make federalism a lasting political weapon used to win substantive policy outcomes" (225), a review of our graphic depictions of the model also show that the initial moves away from the Articles of Confederation status quo are larger than any corrections in the direction against reform. Madison won a great deal. The success of any of Madison's opponents must be judged in light of his early wins and his ability to utterly change the terms of the debate.

True, Madison's influence came very early, and most of it seems to have occurred in setting the agenda during the first few weeks of the Convention. In later months, Madison appeared to grow disinterested in some ways (Bilder 2015), and his ability to win votes waned as compromises were made and decisions were locked into place. But that should not blind us to the raw achievement of Madison's work.

In another sense, difficult to show with our graphs, the very existence of our model and its key dimensions is a monument to Madison—and not just because Madison influenced Beard, who helped explain what they were debating. Madison forced the issue of representation and turned it into the very first and immediate dimension of conflict. Without that decision, it is impossible to even speculate about how the Constitution might look. Beard (1913), in writing about Madison, described Madison's ideas as "the underlying political science of the Constitution" (156) and laid out the dimensions that are highly influential on our own work. However, we note that he believed he was just following Madison's lead. We tend to agree. If anything, the results in the figures and the overall pattern of findings suggests that Madison's influence on the Constitution is understated. Not only did he gain great victories on the dimensions of change, but he seems also to have picked those dimensions himself. No one else can say anything like that about their proposed reforms. No one even came close.

7.4 Big Government in Two Centers

Despite Madison's success, there is the matter of the uncontrolled, ambiguous agenda. Robertson (2005) puts this very well: "The original Constitution's design is not the product of a systematic philosophical plan, but the by-product of a path-dependent sequence of political compromises" (240). After Madison's initial efforts to frame and channel the debate, the Convention essentially took up whatever proposals were on the table. We believe, in some ways, this contributes to the pattern seen in the graphs of initial movement in a reform direction, followed by nibbling around the margins and relatively less change. More importantly, Madison's design is not really enacted. His proposed upper chamber, selected by the lower chamber, does not come to pass. His one-term executive, elected by the legislature, is nowhere to be found in the Constitution. There is no national negative. Instead, Madison is forced to accept a compromised legislature and an independent executive with a qualified veto.

It is certainly true that this design created a much larger central government. This is a point sometimes obscured with the identification of conservatism and the founding (West 2001). Certainly, it must be understood that the delegates wanted a limited government and that they cared about how that government would be designed. But relative to the status quo, they moved dramatically in the direction of more centralized government. The New Deal may have enlarged the powers of the executive and created a lot of bureaucracy. It did not, however, create two new branches of government and embed them in the founding document. Keith Dougherty (2001) makes this point by contrasting the policies of the new Constitution with some proposed amendments introduced under the Articles of Confederation:

> The Constitution was a much more complex document than any of the amendments proposed by Congress in the 1780s. It would improve the efficiency of the government over the Articles of Confederation, but it also implied tradeoffs in state sovereignty. [It] created a national government that could act directly upon the people, could raise armies and revenues independent of the states, and would reign supreme in interstate commerce. . . . With such an assault on the interest of state governments, it is no surprise that those who pushed for a national republic wanted their proposal ratified without requiring the consent of every state government.
>
> (152–53)

The new Constitution went much further than any official body had previously dreamed of going in terms of centralization and national power. Despite the identification with the founders and small government, this part of the story is well known. What is less well understood but is a deeply important fact about the new government is highlighted by our model: that this new powerful government would have two competing centers of power with independent power bases—one legislative in nature and one executive in nature—and that two separate coalitions helped create these competing centers. Our argument is not that the legislative and executive are co-equal[6] but that the two branches of government are separate in their sources of authority by virtue of being independently elected. Judges are not similar because their appointments are at the mercy of the president and half of the Congress. But presidents and legislators have independent sources of authority (in contradiction to Madison's original ideas).

The two branches are different in other ways, the legislative, though more powerful in the abstract, is consistently hampered by the fact that there are many officeholders. The president has a very large staff—if one includes the bureaucracy, he has an enormous staff—but he has no other competitors for instructions inside the executive branch. The Congress sets the agenda for the bureaucracy, but the president controls it on a daily basis and can use it to great effect (Howell, 2003). While it has long been known that the Convention created a much larger government, what is sometimes less appreciated is that it created one with competing centers of power. Consider for a moment the events in American history that have turned on competing views of presidential or congressional power: Washington declaring neutrality without congressional input; Lincoln's use of war powers and violations of habeas corpus; Johnson's impeachment over the Tenure of Office Act; Teddy Roosevelt's arguments over who should control trustbusting; FDR's bureaucratic innovations and massive government expansion; Nixon's claims of executive privilege in the face of the Watergate investigation; Bill Clinton's impeachment drama; and Donald Trump's arguments with the Congress over who controls COVID-19 relief, are just a few examples. A much longer list could be made simply about presidential powers over war and military action. To this day, debates about the legality of both past (Vietnam) and ongoing (Afghanistan) conflicts rage in Washington, DC. For as long as we debate the presidency relative to the Congress there will be argument over how to balance these two branches (Howell and Moe 2016).

This highlights the importance of Richard Neustadt's (1960) observation that the American government is made up of "separated institutions sharing power" (42). However, we would amend that to say that if we understand the Convention clearly, we see that *competing factions* created a Constitution with separated, independent institutions competing for power. Each side has its own set of advantages in this competition. Presidents and their administrations have a unity that Congress will inevitably lack, but Congress has explicit authority within the Constitution that makes it the more potentially powerful entity in the long run. Skowronek (1997) attributes many of our current conflicts over executive power, in part, to presidential time and opportunities that presidents get. In our view, the seeds for this pattern exist in the Constitutional text, and all later developments lie in this shadow.

What a review of chapter 6 reveals is that the presidency was made potentially powerful for two reasons. First, when they finally decided, in Vote 363, that presidents would gain appointment nomination powers (subject to Senate approval) and that the president would be elected by an independent body (but that a majority of the electors would be required, see Vote 461), the president's new position of power (but not extreme power) was finally solidified. It took the Convention the longest amount of time to reach this compromise. And it was obviously a delicate one, drawing on the Great Compromise principles and the arguments of many previous days of debate. But the fact that it came so late in the process (they would adjourn within a few days) meant that they never revisited the basic grant of executive power offered in the document. Combined with the nominations power, the only effective check on the president ended up being the electoral process and the necessity of Senate consent on appointments. Other than that, presidents face few formal, textual limitations. Those who argue for such limitations tend to fall back on a vision of limited government that, while attractive and plausible, is not specifically stated in the text. In writing about the presidency and prospects for change and reform, Skowronek describes today's presidency as "relentlessly disruptive, and thoroughly politicized" (443). Once one gives the president independent nomination powers and control over the bureaucracy with authority that is only fettered by a unified Congress or electoral defeat, all of the seeds for such a presidency as Skowronek describes are already sown.

In essence, once the Congress passes a law, it shifts power from the limited Congress to the only vaguely checked president. Our account of the Convention shows that no one intended this result, and no clear majority sought both this result and a powerful Congress. Rather, it is the culmination of the unplanned design of the Constitution and the implicit difficulty of getting Congress organized and unified. Moreover, we note that there was no unified group of delegates that believed in this approach as opposed to giving power to the Congress. The Core Reform states tended to believe that power should rest in both bodies in some way. The Deep South states favored legislative power, and it was the Small states that provided the margin for the resulting state of affairs. What are we to make of the original plan for this jury-rigged design?

7.5 Deep Structure and Originalism

Originalism purports to explain how the meaning of the words was understood at the time of the founding—sometimes at the Convention, sometimes during the ratification period, and sometimes just in the period, generally. There is certainly a use for this kind of analysis. Understanding how they used the words will help us to comprehend their arguments and debates. Our work here is not meant to be a comprehensive critique of any particular form of originalism. However, the deep structure of voting is important for any originalist project because it helps us to understand the origin of the document by clarifying the coalitions that helped pass specific clauses and that formed the basic divides over key baskets of issues. The central finding here—that one alliance created the Congress and a stronger national government while another alliance created the independent executive—suggests that, as early as this period of drafting, different people had very different understandings of what was to come.

But is one group paramount? We must deal with the fact that the Core Reform states—Massachusetts, Pennsylvania, and Virginia—were a key part of both coalitions. Does this mean that they are the states that decided what the Constitution means? Given their centrality in the deep structure of voting at the Convention, are they not the key to understanding everything? Superficially, the answer to this is yes, they are. Indeed, Madison, at the heart of this coalition, set the agenda. And it was the agenda of delegates from these states—with Madison standing above all others—that helped create the Constitution. However, they were just three states. In the scheme of voting at the Convention, they had no power to enact their program. They were required to find allies. For good or ill (and probably both), they found different allies for different parts of the new government.

How do we think about originalism with this picture of the Convention? Again, Rakove (1996) is helpful. He divides originalism into three types.

- **Original Intent**: the intentions of the delegates in the room, or possibly those ratifying the document, for what the new government would look like and produce.
- **Original Meaning**: the underlying meaning of the document's text—probably the most difficult, nebulous concept to discern of the three faces of originalism.
- **Original Understanding**: the common meaning of the words in the document and what they implied for the government.

What does the deep structure of voting tell us about how the Constitution was created and these different versions of originalism?

Original intention is deeply complicated by the presence of multiple coalitions at the Convention. It is quite clear that one alliance intended to establish relatively greater legislative power, and another alliance was more comfortable with a newly empowered executive. For any discussion of intentions, this creates a problem akin to when there is a Supreme Court decision with relatively few justices (potentially only one justice) in the controlling opinion. If four liberal justices oppose four conservative justices, and one moderate justice agrees in part with both sides, that moderate justice becomes the decision maker, even though she only represents a small fraction of opinion on this issue. The case of the deep structure of voting is similar. Massachusetts, Pennsylvania, and Virginia represent the group that (broadly speaking) acceded to both of the key structures invented by the Convention: the strong legislature and the independent presidency. But they are a minority. No one majority consented to both innovations. This means that if we look to an "intention" of the delegates, we are only going to be able to find a minority.

It is vital to understand that this grouping of states was hardly moderate; they were the extremists on virtually every dimension. Return to the table and figure at the beginning of this chapter and note the positions of these three states. Virginia and Pennsylvania are always more pro-reform than the Constitution ever became (Massachusetts is always close to the final position). In this sense, though the Constitution is in the middle of Convention opinions, it is the product of the extremists who favored reform. They wanted the most possible reform and the most possible change on each dimension, but they sought out different allies to get it; moreover, they could not have accomplished this without a complicated set of coalitions that could not have been planned or designed. This makes any debate about original intentions of competing factions and alliances highly problematic.

How do the other versions of originalism fare? Better, but still with complications. Both meaning and understanding imply usage and how readers would have taken the specific clauses and texts of the Constitution. The fact that different coalitions favored different competing elements of the Constitution remains a problem for these versions of originalism. Consider Madison and Hamilton as an example. United in their pursuit of ratification, it turned out that they had deeply different understandings of the document and what it implied for the young Republic. Madison favored legislative power and was slightly more ambivalent about executive power (at least in how they turned out on the issue in the 1790s).[7] Hamilton was the opposite. He drastically favored executive independence and the ability of a leader to execute strong, centralized energetic plans.[8] Who was right? Well, once we understand the deep structure of voting at the Convention, it becomes clear that Madison and Hamilton were both right, just about different centers of power. The James Madison of the 1790s and 1800s could point to the clauses on legislative supremacy and the coalition that formed those positions. Alexander Hamilton could quote some of the same for his side, but he was, essentially, pointing to a different group of people who created a conflicting, competing set of institutions. There is no clear solution to this problem, and it afflicts both the meaning and understanding versions of originalism.

Indeed, the Constitutional Convention should be seen as a seminal moment in American politics, especially when we consider this deep structure of voting and the factions that created the structure. Consider that, according to Jillson and Wilson (1994), the period of the Articles of Confederation Congress that followed the close of the war led to a highly regionalized set of coalitions: New England fought the South, with the mid-Atlantic states in between them. In large measure, this was the factional arrangement of the early nineteenth century–with the partisan overlay of Federalists (New England) against Republicans (the South). But the Convention was clearly not that. It was a much more complex set of events that led to the two-party politics that came afterward but did not really mirror that period. Later politicians were able to argue about the original meaning of the Constitution because the coalitions at the Convention had largely settled debates about institutions (at least for a time). Those who came after argued in their shadow.

Today's debates are, in many respects, similar to the period (including in tone). Though the issues have changed and though the passage of time means that the presidency is not what it once was, we still argue from inside of two broad camps trying to gain control of an unwieldy government. If someone in that contest favors executive power, there are clauses, majorities, factions, alliances, and agreements to cite. If one favors legislative power, there are no fewer sets of such sources to point to. Is there a solution? By our lights, no, there is not. By the logic of majoritarian systems, while it is true that the process produced a document that was preferred to the status quo of the Articles of Confederation, the specific proposals that one cites in these debates were created by different alliances and coalitions. The deep structure of voting is of little help for understanding any version of originalism. It merely complicates that understanding.

One last point on originalism. It is common in these legal debates, for good reasons, for lawyers to focus on specific clauses and phrases. While, in principle, we have no objection to this, it does limit one's view of the big picture, focusing attention on the trees rather than the abundant forest. The entire project of evaluating the deep structure of voting requires us to think of the Constitution as a whole. True, there are different dimensions to that whole, but it is the completed system that they were creating, not just specific and isolated clauses or pieces. In the end, what the three factions decided to do was accept competing institutions as the form of government they offered the country. Different coalitions embedded in that structure institutions that could be used by future political actors to advance their political goals. Ratification did not settle any of these fights. In fact, it blessed the future fights by leaving the competing institutions in place. The original design of the Constitution invites a political fight between factions, possibly capturing different institutions, not just an argument over the text of the Constitution. Indeed, with the competing institutions, the original design suggests there are fights we can never settle with an appeal to the text.

7.6 Original Design

Despite the fact that our analysis creates hurdles for any originalist theory of the Constitution, we do not want to be read as being uninterested in these ideas. The Constitution, and how it was created, is of paramount importance. Indeed, we believe that our efforts here pay due deference to the need to gain a better understanding of the original design and the factions that led to that design. The factions that founded the country were not simply wise men who worked together to find solutions (though that description is not a bad place to begin). They were identifiable interests—sometimes reprehensible ones by our standards—that created an unplanned, complicated design for politics that we still inhabit. These interests did not consciously create a fully coherent design, instead it is more of a factional design.

Our work invites a renewed attention to that original design.[9] In principle, we believe this means a kind of attention to the document that comes from a citizen's perspective on the process rather than from a legal perspective. The Constitution is a people's document where the whole—complicated and contradictory though it might be—is greater than the sum of any set of parts. This form of "citizen originalism" would, in truth, be vastly more complicated than any kind of textual originalism that could be dreamed up by any legal minds. There is nothing so complicated as the ambiguity and complexity of social science historical work on the product of many minds and the reactions of millions to those ideas.

Focusing on the original design that emerged from this factional fight, rather than the original meaning or another concept, returns us to a point that is deeply useful for citizens—though perhaps, we admit, not for lawyers interpreting discrete clauses. The concept of original design is distinct from understanding or meaning or intention because it focuses on the system as a whole and what we might learn from that system and the factions and coalitions that created it. One of the first things we have to learn is that there were disagreements about what that system was and would become.

The pattern seen in the graphs above is that the delegates tried to minimize differences over the proposed document. Once Madison's proposals were put in place as a working framework, the product never moved in dramatic directions toward greater and greater reform or back to the status quo of the Articles of Confederation. On those occasions when they did make significant changes to the document, they always pulled back slightly to better reflect the common consensus. The delegates themselves recognized that there were many individual objections. Historians of the Convention often point to the last day when Franklin—in a bid to get recalcitrant delegates like George Mason and Edmund Randolph to sign the document—made a speech trying to convince delegates that they should join in this enterprise whatever their misgivings. As eloquent as that speech was, we note that there was one other contribution to that day. It was less eloquent, but it probably carried more weight in the room.

> When the President [George Washington] rose, for the purpose of putting the question [a proposal from Gorham (MA) to change the ration of representation from one representative per 40,000 persons to one representative per 30,000 persons] he said that although his situation had hitherto restrained him from offering his sentiments on question pending in the House, and it might be thought, ought now to impose silence on him, yet he could not forbear expressing his wish that the alteration proposed might take place. *It was much to be desired that the objections to the plan recommended might be made as few as possible.*
>
> (Farrand 1966, vol. II, 644, emphasis added)

Washington implicitly admitted here that there were substantial objections. No matter how much Dr. Franklin might want to paper over those protestations with a call for unity, Washington recognized that the objections existed. It was late in the game, and he must have been aware that there was little hope of changing the minds of the remaining holdouts, but he wanted to personally make clear both that it was paramount that they agree if they could, and that they make this document as good as it possibly could be given the messy process that had produced it. Unsurprisingly, Washington's support of the motion carried the day (unanimously).[10]

The lesson here was not just a narrow one about apportionment of representatives,[11] but a larger one that this plan needed to be as acceptable "as possible." Washington applied no models (that we know of) to the voting, but he saw it up close and knew that everyone had different reservations. No argument or appeal would change that because the document itself invited misgivings by creating such a complicated, competitive set of institutions. His personal knowledge of the Constitution no doubt suggested that, from many quarters, there were doubts about the parts of the document that individual delegates did not favor. Indeed, all but a few delegates opposed substantial portions (and all delegates must have opposed something). But their goal had been to make a document that had as few objections "as possible," and he clearly thought they had succeeded. That was at least part of his signal on that final day.

The task of all citizens and students of the Constitution is not to avoid objections to the document or to create coherence where it does not exist. It is to better understand the original design and what it implied and created: a Constitution of competing institutions built by competing factional alliances. That does not make the document perfect or imperfect, merely political, but in the best sense. Perhaps they did end up with a document that had as few objections "as possible"; indeed, our models make that seem like a good description, as they slowly found the key points of agreement that could serve as the final compromise. And perhaps the complicated original design was a reflection of the best that they could do. But whether it was the best they could do, or not, we will never understand the document as well as we need to if we do not embrace the complexity of that original design and the factions that created it.

CHAPTER 8

Supporting Appendix

8.1 Estimation Details

In this section, we describe the details of the model beginning with the math behind it and then turning to the data sources. The body of the text is designed to be readable without these details, but they are important for scholars of the period and such models. Persons wishing to skip this section will lose little of the thread of our conclusions and arguments.

8.2 Ideal Point Models

The tools of spatial analysis have advanced substantially in recent years, permitting us to offer a model of delegates and delegations. This flows out of the work of Poole (2005), among others (Clinton, Jackman, and Rivers 2004; Clinton and Meirowitz 2004). The basic idea is to build a model of ideology based on a series of indicators—in this case, the roll call votes of the Convention. This modeled ideology can be thought of as the delegation's "ideology" on a given dimension. Thus, such models produce an "ideal point" that is our best estimate of the position of the delegation on that dimension. Aggregating the points reveals the ideal point across all dimensions.

Spatial models are made of three basic components: legislators, bills, and votes. For most legislatures, legislators are individuals elected to represent some particular group. In the case of the Convention, we will need a model that allows for delegations casting votes but also considers the fact that individual delegates are voting within each delegation (and that we have some information about each of these votes). Bills are simply the proposals on which the delegates are voting, and votes are the individual positions on each bill. All of this takes place on three dimensions, in this case.

In typical spatial models, the legislator i considers two positions, the "Yea" (bill proposal) position $\boldsymbol{\omega}_j$ and the "Nay" (status quo) position $\mathbf{q}_j$, for $j = 1, \ldots, m$ roll calls. $\mathbf{q}_j$ reflects the positions of current policies (on d dimensions) in the ideological space when bill j is proposed. The proposal $\boldsymbol{\omega}_j$ indicates the positions, if passed, of the new policies in d dimensions. The legislator votes "Yea" if $U_i(\boldsymbol{\omega}_j) > Ui(\mathbf{q}_j)$. Following Clinton, Jackman, and Rivers (2004) and Martin and Quinn (2002), the utilities include a random component and are specified as a quadratic loss function:

$$u_i\left(\mathbf{q}_j\right) = -\|\mathbf{x}_i - \mathbf{q}_j\|^2 + \upsilon_{ij} \qquad (8.1)$$

$$u_i\left(\omega_j\right) = -\|\mathbf{x}_i - \omega_j\|^2 + \eta_{ij}. \qquad (8.2)$$

where η_{ij} and υ_{ij} are error terms, which we assume are Type-I extreme value (for logit links), and $\mathbf{x}_i$ is a vector of ideological positions in a d dimensional space. The distance between the ideal points and status quo (bill) positions are measured by the square of the Euclidean norm $\|\cdot\|$. The observed decision of a vote, y_{ij}, which equals either 1 ("Yea") or 0 ("Nay") is governed by the unobserved (but modeled) difference between the utilities:

$$y^*_{ij} = u_i\left(\omega_j\right) - u_i\left(\mathbf{q}_j\right) + \left(\eta_{ij} - \upsilon_{ij}\right) \qquad (8.3)$$

In this basic model of legislative decision making, equation 8.3 can be simplified to

$$y^*_{ij} = \mathbf{x}\beta_j - \alpha_j + \varepsilon_{ij} \qquad (8.4)$$

where $\boldsymbol{\beta}_j = 2(\boldsymbol{\omega}_j - \mathbf{q}_j)$ and $\alpha_j = \boldsymbol{\omega}'_j\,\boldsymbol{\omega}_j - \mathbf{q}'_j\,\mathbf{q}_j$. Thus, this model reduces to a regression model, analogous to a logit or probit model, depending on the distributional assumption for ε_{ij}, with the ideal points coordinates as the (unobserved) independent variables on votes, $\boldsymbol{\beta}_j$ the slope coefficients, and α_j the intercept.

8.3 Incorporating the Agenda

The vote parameters are amalgamations of the proposal and status quo positions, which typically cannot be separately identified if there are two or more dimensions. We can only represent in these models the threshold for deciding "Yea" vs. "Nay". These are represented as cut-points (in 1D), cutting lines (in 2D), cutting planes (3D), or hyper-planes (more than three dimensions). Clinton and Meirowitz (2001, 2004) extend this model by incorporating changes (or lack of changes) in the status quo directly into the estimation, thereby accounting for the evolution of the agenda. If proposal $\boldsymbol{\omega}_j$ passes, then the new status quo point equals this proposal: $\mathbf{q}_{j+1} = \boldsymbol{\omega}_j$. If $\boldsymbol{\omega}_j$ fails, then the status quo remains unchanged: $\mathbf{q}_{j+1} = \mathbf{q}_j$. That is, a vote that passes establishes a new current policy, and a vote that fails retains the current policy to the next vote. Second, if a proposal does not concern dimension *d*, even if $\boldsymbol{\omega}_j$ passes, the coordinates of the status quo for irrelevant dimensions will remain unchanged: $q_{j+1,d} = q_{j,d}$ tracking the course of the policy debate. By imposing these constraints, one can directly estimate the status quo points and proposals and effectively see the unfolding agenda. The parameters $\mathbf{q}_j$ and $\boldsymbol{\omega}_j$ are represented as $\boldsymbol{\theta}$, indexed by $y(j)$ and $n(j)$, where $\mathbf{q}_j = \boldsymbol{\theta}_{n(j)}$ and $\boldsymbol{\omega}_j = \boldsymbol{\theta}_{y(j)}$. The estimated model, in utility differences, is

$$y^*_{ij} = ||\mathbf{x}_i - \boldsymbol{\theta}_{n(j)}||^2 - ||\mathbf{x}_i - \boldsymbol{\theta}_{y(j)}||^2 + \varepsilon_{ij} \qquad (8.5)$$

Because of the additional parameterization, where the same parameter $\boldsymbol{\theta}$ may appear as the proposal at least once and as the status quo for possibly multiple other votes, the utility difference does not simplify to the regression in 8.4.

8.4 Bayesian Estimation

Standard classical statistics involves finding the model parameters $\boldsymbol{\theta}$ that maximize this probability of the observed data $\mathbf{y}$ occurring. The classical expression $L(\boldsymbol{\theta}|\mathbf{y}) \propto f(\mathbf{y}|\boldsymbol{\theta})$, or that the "likelihood is proportional to the data-generating process," illustrates the focus on the parameters of the model, but because it does not constitute a proper probability distribution for the model parameters $\boldsymbol{\theta}$, it does not allow us to describe the probability of parameter values themselves. Our expressions of uncertainty and "margin of error" require additional assumptions about how new data would be generated.

The Bayesian approach subsumes the classical model of the data into a complete probability model for the model parameters, given the data, following Bayes Rule:

$$f(\theta|\mathbf{y}) = \frac{f(\mathbf{y}|\theta)f(\theta)}{f(\mathbf{y})} \quad (8.6)$$

$$\text{Posterior} = \frac{\text{Likelihood} \times \text{Prior}}{\text{Marginal Likelihood}} \quad (8.7)$$

$$\text{Posterior} \propto \text{Likelihood} \times \text{Prior} \quad (8.8)$$

$$f(\boldsymbol{\theta}|\mathbf{y}) \propto f(\mathbf{y}|\boldsymbol{\theta})f(\boldsymbol{\theta}) \quad (8.9)$$

The additional assumptions required are the "priors" for the parameters, i.e., probability statements of the model parameters without information from new data. Those prior beliefs are updated with the data and model specification of the likelihood, with the marginal likelihood serving as the constant that ensures that the entire expression, labeled the posterior distribution, is a proper probability distribution. The advantage of this approach is that inference about the parameters involves probabilistic statements; i.e., a statement that "the probability that legislature A's ideal point is greater than 0 is 0.54" is sensible. We apply these types of calculations throughout the book when comparing delegates or states to each other, or to specific proposals during the Convention.

In addition to a superior conceptual foundation, Bayesian modeling also presents many computational advantages. While the ideal point model is too complex to infer directly from the posterior distribution, we can approximate the posterior distribution by simulating the parameters using Markov-Chain Monte Carlo (MCMC) methods. MCMC methods allow one to draw iterative, non-independent samples from complex distributions with multitudes of parameters and produce a sample that accurately approximates the posterior distribution. Detailed explanations (accessible to social scientists) can be found in Bolstad (2010) and Jackman (2009, ch. 5).

These methods are much simpler than maximizing the likelihood, and even easier is the characterization of uncertainty of the estimates or complicated transformations of them. These advantages are discussed in Clinton, Jackman, and Rivers (2004) and Jackman (2009), and the advantages of Bayesian versions of ideal point models versus the non-Bayesian NOMINATE variants are debated extensively in Carroll et al. (2009) and Clinton and Jackman (2009). An overview of the basics, applications, and extensions of the Bayesian ideal point model is in Treier (2020). In particular, there are two key practical advantages. The first is that creating a summary of the model parameters involves simple calculations of summary statistics. In the models for this book, we produce a sample of 6,000 draws that approximate the posterior distribution of the parameters. To summarize any one parameter (say, Alexander Hamilton's ideal point positions), we simply take the mean of the 6,000 draws. Uncertainty is similarly calculated, either as a 95% central probability interval (which is just the range of the 2.5% and 97.5% percentiles of the 6,000 samples) or a slightly more involved calculation of a 95% highest posterior density (HPD) interval.[1] Second, more complicated calculations, such as the distance between a state and the final outcome of the Convention, or whether Alexander Hamilton favored more power to the national government than Edmund Randolph, can be summarized in the same way (means and measures of uncertainty on the distances, or the number of times Hamilton had a higher value on the Federalism dimension than Randolph). Such calculations are either extremely complex to derive using maximum likelihood methods, or simply inappropriate.

8.5 The Data

The data on votes are all taken from Farrand's notes where all of the delegation votes are available. A few individual delegate votes are known with near certainty because they are recorded in the notes. To supplement this information, we carefully went through the notes of the Convention to discern as many individual votes as possible and assign dimensional content (i.e., was this a vote about representation, the presidency, or was it unclear?). The model, as described above, is fully Bayesian and therefore lets us model delegation and delegate positions despite the large amounts of missing data. We follow a process similar to previous scholars (McDonald 1958; McGuire 2003) who coded individual votes. First, we note the few instances when Madison personally recorded the votes of individual delegates. One particular case is the vote on July 16 to approve the Great Compromise (Farrand 1913). This source of information does generate a handful of votes, but it is only a beginning.

Second, we examine the notes on the debates for any indication that a delegate supported or opposed a proposal, coding their positions to the specific roll call for the proposal (Farrand 1913). The most common form of approval or disapproval was to make a motion or second a motion on a question. For instance, in Farrand's vote 35, we see that Mr. Read motioned (with a second from Mr. C.C. Pinckney) to amend one of Randolph's proposals about the form of government. Such motions and indications are scattered throughout the notes. In other cases, delegates made a speech that clearly indicated support or opposition to a proposal. For instance, in Farrand's vote 214, we read that Ellsworth favored a three-year term for representatives. He did not make the motion or second it, but he spoke in favor of it. Again, this is similar to the process that McDonald (1958) and Heckelman and Dougherty (2013) use.

However, even this small amount of data on each delegate's position can be combined with other knowledge about attendance to yield even more information. For instance, several delegations (such as Massachusetts) were relatively small and conveniently made up of an even number of delegates. In such cases, we are occasionally able to calculate a delegate vote by knowing both attendance and some other votes. If we know that Massachusetts' vote was divided, and that two delegates made a motion or spoke in favor of a particular question, we can assume the other two

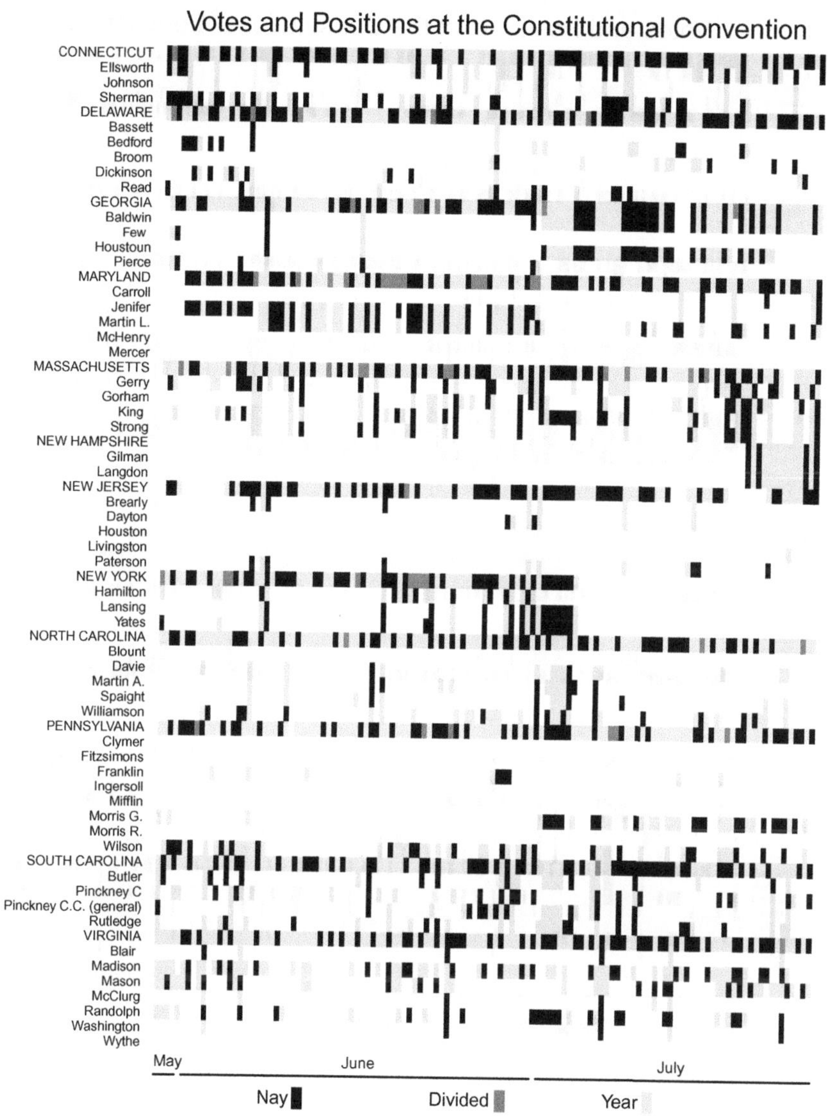

Fig. A1. Delegation and Delegate Inferred Positions for all Votes at the Convention, Grouped by State

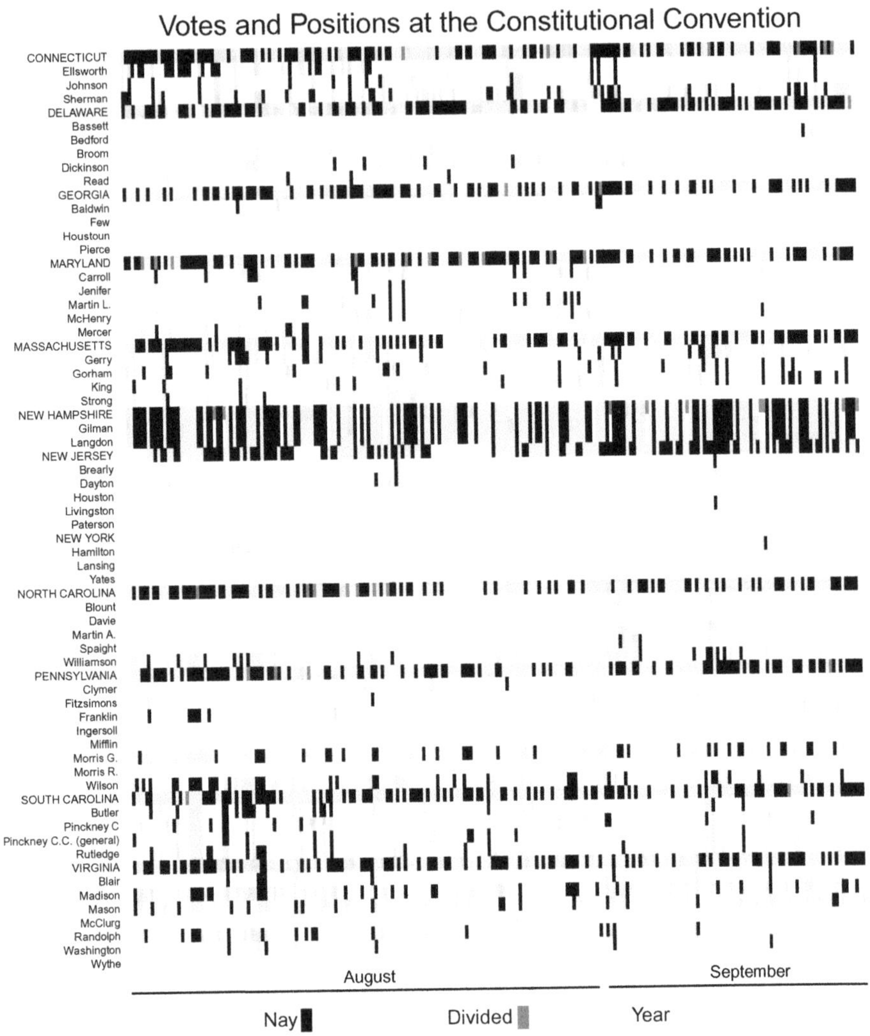

Fig. A1. *Continued*

delegates must have voted against the motion to produce the divided vote. Similar logical rules were employed throughout the process to analyze the positions of delegates. Figure A1 displays the amount of data we have available for each delegate. Obviously, it is an imperfect sample. Some delegates, like Madison, Wilson, and Luther Martin, among others have a great deal of additional information, while, for some delegates, the information is sparse.

8.6 Combining States and Delegates

Aggregation is a complication and requires caution when discussing the "ideal point" of state k. An estimate of $\mathbf{x}_k$ with a low score on representation and federalism reflects a state delegation that supported equal voting among states and a limited national government.[2] We consider the recovered position as simply the reflection of a representative (and artificial) individual actor with a position consistent with the voting record of the state. Our minimum requirement in connecting this position with the individual delegates is that if the delegates of the state have identical preferences, then this common preference will be represented in the estimated position of this representative actor. This holds, and is the equilibrium position, since we assume identical (quadratic) utility functions for all delegates, and also assume this artificial actor perceives the votes the same way as individual delegates; i.e., that the vote parameters $\boldsymbol{\omega}$ and $\mathbf{q}$ are constant across individuals and states. The latter assumption implies that the definition of the issue space is the same for states and individuals, consistent with research by historians, who do not often distinguish the two levels of voting. The assumption would fail if the vote by a delegation did not reflect the majority opinion. That would occur if delegates strategically misrepresented their preferences. In our context though, we assume (quite reasonably, and typical of all ideal point estimation) sincere voting, and in any case, members of a delegation on a particular vote cannot manipulate an agenda determined separately by the entire convention.

It is also possible for states to become deadlocked on any particular vote. How should these votes be addressed? If divided votes are treated as missing, as in all previous analyses, one loses important information about the states' revealed positions. Following the approach in Pope and Treier (2011), we express the stalemate as the delegation split evenly between "Yea" and "Nay" positions. The resulting behavior produces a revealed position close to the cutline, the closeness measured by parameter δ. Since some states are more likely to be divided than others, we estimate separate δ_k for each state. One obvious factor was whether the delegation was small or large, odd or even. Also, some delegations had several opposing state political factions represented, whereas others were more homogenous. Consequently, if two states have the same x_k, the state with the larger δ_k will be more likely to vote "Divided." The approach incorporates the model of Sanders (1998, 2001) within the quadratic utility measurement model, with a decision rule

$$y_{kj} = \begin{cases} \text{"Yea"} & \text{if } u_{kj}(\omega_j) - u_{kj}(\mathbf{q}_j) > \delta_k \\ \text{"Nay"} & \text{if } u_{kj}(\omega_j) - u_{kj}(\mathbf{q}_j) < -\delta_k \\ \text{"Divided"} & \text{if } -\delta_k \leq u_{kj}(\omega_j) - u_{kj}(\mathbf{q}_j) \leq \delta_k \end{cases}$$

This is equivalent to an ordered model with state specific thresholds $\boldsymbol{\tau}$ that are common across votes, with the restriction that $\tau_1 = -\tau_2$. As long as the state has been divided on a roll call at least once, δ_k is estimable. The utility representations for the states in this model are

$$u_k(\mathbf{q}_j) = -\|\mathbf{x}_k - \boldsymbol{\theta}_{n(j)}\|^2 + v_{kj}$$
$$u_k(\boldsymbol{\omega}_j) = -\|\mathbf{x}_k - \boldsymbol{\theta}_{y(j)}\|^2 + \eta_{kj}.$$

where $\boldsymbol{\theta}$ are the unique set of proposals that are either status quo and/or proposal positions in the Convention agenda.

We will estimate ideal points of individual delegates, using inferred votes, jointly with the state position model. The estimated model, in utility differences, is

$$y^*_{ikj} = \|\mathbf{d}_{ik} - \boldsymbol{\theta}_{n(j)}\|^2 - \|\mathbf{d}_{ik} - \boldsymbol{\theta}_{y(j)}\|^2 + \varepsilon_{ikj} \qquad (8.10)$$

where $\mathbf{d}_{ik}$ is a matrix of ideological positions in a d dimensional space. The model is a straightforward representation of the binary-choice Clinton–Meirowitz model. We connect the individual model to the state model in the following manner. First, the vote parameters $\boldsymbol{\omega}$ and $\mathbf{q}$ are constant across individuals and states. Second, the individual delegate ideal points are connected to the state positions hierarchically; the position of the state delegation $\mathbf{x}_k$ is the prior mean for delegate ideal point $\mathbf{d}_{ik}$: $\mathbf{d}_{ik} \sim N(\mathbf{x}_k, 1)$, with $\mathbf{x}_k \sim N(0, 1)$. The model is a special case of the one presented in Pope and Treier (2015). Without any additional information, our prior belief is that the individual delegate is the same as the representation of the state. If the delegate's votes are in complete congruence with the state, then the delegate will have approximately the same position as the state. If the delegate contradicts the vote of the state frequently, then the delegate's ideal point will deviate substantially from the state position—an approach identical to a formulation where individual estimates are simply deviations from a state component. This hierarchical model substantially reduces problems with missing individual votes. In absence of contrary voting behavior by the delegate, we expect the delegate's position to be related to the state. Nevertheless, we still allow for these positions to deviate substantially from the state position. The posterior distribution for this model is

$$f(\mathbf{x},\mathbf{d},\theta,\delta|\mathbf{Y}) = \prod_k f(\mathbf{y}_k \mid \theta,\delta_k,\mathbf{x}_k) f(\mathbf{x}_k) \times \left(\prod_{i=1}^{n_k} f(\mathbf{y}_{ik} \mid \theta,\mathbf{d}_{ik}) f(\mathbf{d}_{ik} \mid \mathbf{x}_k) \right) f(\theta) f(\delta)$$

The model is estimated in WinBUGS 1.4.3 (Lunn et al. 2000). Given that there is no reduction in equation 8.10, the vote parameters $\boldsymbol{\theta}$ and the state delegation and individual delegate positions $\mathbf{x}$ and $\mathbf{d}$ are estimated through separate random walk Metropolis sampling from normal proposal densities, and the divided vote parameters $\boldsymbol{\delta}$ from slice sampling.

Notes

Preface

1. As of this writing, only men have had the honor of becoming president, and only men have had the ignominy of being impeached, though we anticipate that this will change in the near future.

Understanding a Secretive Convention

1. In a modern legislature, such votes are typically called "roll calls" and are common for individual legislators, but in this context the only comparable event was the collective state vote, as only their group decisions were recorded consistently.

2. Though we will capitalize on it through this book, it is important to recognize that delegates were not sure that this convention would become anything of lasting importance. At times, they worried that it would accomplish nothing. It is only with hindsight that we see the meetings meriting the capitalization of the Convention.

3. It is evident that Madison was losing interest in taking careful notes, as this speech is not clearly rendered. We have generally preserved the spelling and punctuation of the notes in the quotations taken directly from Farrand.

4. See our discussion of win-sets below on page 47.

The Dimensions of Conflict

1. Bilder (2015) argues that the memo may have been written at a different time, though the ideas certainly seem consonant with Madison's early Convention speeches and work.

2. See, particularly, chapter 3.

3. The term is a play on Pocock's 1975 book, *The Machiavellian Moment*.

4. Madison to Thomas Jefferson, March 19, 1787; Madison to Edmund Randolph, April 8, 1787; and Madison to George Washington, April 16, 1787.

5. Indeed, as we read him, it appears that Beard believed that the economic upper class would take the pro-reform position on every single dimension.

6. Though we have done our best to be faithful to the language of the authors, in several cases it was necessary to simplify their discussion into a word or a phrase for purposes of comparison within the table. This injustice to the complexity of their thinking is simply necessary for tractability.

7. For more in this vein, see Holton (2007).

8. Granted, Wood sees this as more about the developing culture than the specific debates and compromises, but it should affect both of those arenas.

9. Though people sometimes forget it, Beard was actually president of the American Political Science Association before he was president of the American History Association—a time when the two disciplines were much closer together.

10. In both cases, these authors infer two dimensional models by period. Jillson focuses on specific dimensions (seen in table 2.2) by examining the voting coalitions of the state delegations (not directly estimating the location of votes), while Slez and Martin examined vote divisions.

11. An explanation of ideal points can be found in the appendix.

12. Table 2 in that article compares the model fit of various possibilities.

13. Indeed, below we will argue that it probably deserves even more attention than it has been given in the literature because how it relates to the coalitions is not well understood.

14. Beard was essentially concerned with the balance of power between the executive and the Congress, but since a powerful Congress was a given, we believe the best label is about the power of the executive. Still, the reader should not forget that the question is really about the relative balance of power.

15. Arguably, Slez and Martin also emphasized it, as one can see from their article, though the titles of their dimensions do not convey this emphasis.

Delegations and Delegates

1. Additional estimation details can be found in the appendix and in the replication files available at https://dataverse.harvard.edu/dataverse/satreier. We also note that, while we follow the numbered votes found in Farrand, others have documented several non-numbered votes (for more on this, see Dougherty and Heckelman 2008; Heckelman and Dougherty 2013).

2. We should make clear, however, that these voting rules were not exactly the same. The practice of recording was better under the Articles, votes were often public in that setting, and, most importantly, the question about divisions was not relevant under the Articles.

3. chapter 4 offers a longer discussion of this precedent.

4. An alternative interpretation of these passages is a debate over how quickly to bring up the question of altering representation; however, because such a plan never came to fruition, this is quite speculative.

5. Note that this entry comes after George Washington was selected, by delegation vote, as president of the Convention, meaning that the precedent of voting by state had already been established.

6. Note that the second rule is implicit, but still important.

7. Alexander Hamilton (NY), Charles Pinckney (SC), and George Wythe (VA) were appointed on May 25 and drew up the original rule proposal.

8. It is notable that the two objections came from among states most committed to overall reform, though it seems doubtful this was part of any strategy.

9, This assumption—that votes are sincere—is a key assumption of the roll call model used here.

10. A cycle is when a legislature discovers that proposal A defeats proposal B, proposal B defeats proposal C, but it is also true that proposal C defeats proposal A. Without some particular mechanism to end the cycle, the legislature could vote forever without arriving at a solution.

11. Or, the "framers"; we use the two terms interchangeably.

12. The mechanics of the model are described in the appendix for readers interested in technical details.

13. New Hampshire estimates are complicated and difficult to deal with, in part because we have no basis for differentiation among the two New Hampshire delegates who never obviously divided. At best, we can only estimate the position of the state and not the delegates. In general, we find that New Hampshire is most similar to Massachusetts, perhaps suggesting they fit with the reformers, but we do not formally classify them that way here because they missed so many early key votes.

14. To streamline this chapter, we have included all details of estimation and data in the appendix. Readers uninterested in some of the more detailed math can skip that section without too much trouble.

15. It is more difficult to tell with New Hampshire given their participation patterns, though this is the conventional wisdom.

16. Though each figure includes individual delegates, for now we simply focus on the state delegations.

17. In each of the dimensions, our maps are oriented so that preferring the status quo is on the left, while preferring reform is on the right. In a sense, this violates the modern practice of placing conservatism on the right and liberalism on the left, but that is merely a convention, and we do not want the reader to think in terms of modern divisions of left and right. Rather, we want the reader to think in terms of the dimensions that would have divided the delegates: proportional representation, federalism, and executive independence.

18. New York and New Jersey are the two states that were consistently in favor of the status quo. Inherent uncertainty in the estimates means that the state delegations were centered almost exactly on -1.5. Indeed, New Jersey's probability of being positioned at a point less than -1.5 on the dimension is 0.48, essentially a coin flip. For New York, the comparable probability is 0.61, a slightly weighted coin. In both cases they essentially take the position of the status quo.

19. However, it should be noted that there is some evidence Sherman was more moderate on representation (see figure 3.2).

20. McHenry did not abandon the Convention lightly—his brother and business partner was extremely ill—and would return in August for the remainder of the Convention.

21. Presumably Houstoun, the only other Georgia delegate in attendance that day, voted against the proposal.

22. Another problem with the interpretation that Baldwin saved the Convention is that Baldwin's vote was not pivotal, as far as the agenda goes. It is true that the vote deadlocked at five to five, but this did not change the state of affairs at the Convention, as we will see below.

23. Without Massachusetts' voting "divided" on that question, there would have been no agreement.

24. Gorham makes many speeches, though not normally of major consequence. Perhaps Gorham's greatest contribution was to serve as chairman of the Committee of the Whole that helped shepherd the Virginia Plan.

25. This document was a memorandum Mason wrote on the back of one of the reports from the Committee of Style. It was copied and circulated widely during the ratification debates.

26. Apparently Randolph claimed to be speaking for Mason, though there is no way to be sure how true that was. The model indicates they had some correspondence of sentiments, but that is hardly dispositive for the claim in the letter cited by Reardon.

27. This remains true even if essentially all modern scholars reject large portions of Beard's explanation of the Convention.

28. Note, there are many informal and formal approaches to determining the number of clusters, but no conclusive method of selection. In our instance, that cut occurs between the grouping of three coalitions of states and four coalitions, leading to a conclusion of three coalitions among states.

29. We note that this is not driven by a roll call position because the final refusal to sign was not included in the analysis. This is based solely on their overall Convention behavior.

Representation: The Primary Cleavage

1. Of course, there was also a conflict over federalism that broke down along similar lines, but we postpone that discussion until the next chapter, where we will also discuss the overlap in coalitions.

2. Bowen (1966) estimates that he spoke for between three and four hours introducing these plans (39).

3. Bowen (1966) connects the Committee of the Whole to the ancient practice of removing the Mace from the table set before the speaker in the House of Commons (40–41), which symbolized the absence of royal authority to compel or foreclose debate. The delegates had a similar goal: allow as much free debate as possible.

4. They originally met in the first floor of Carpenters' Hall, rather than in what has come to be known as Independence Hall.

5. This is an ironic line in light of his later career. He would not even attend the Constitutional Convention 13 years later, supposedly because he "smelt a rat."

6. This resolution is preceded only by the mild claim in resolution 1 that the Articles of Confederation should be "corrected" to better accomplish the objects of a national government.

7. The HPD interval is a measure of coverage in Bayesian inference that constitutes the smallest range of values for which there exists a 95 percent probability of falling within the range. It has the property that all values outside of the range are less likely to occur than are those within it. It is not defined with respect to the mean value (i.e., it is not necessarily symmetric) and can even be discontinuous in some specifications.

8. Because these unsuccessful votes were often of less importance in the agenda, and because their location is more difficult to estimate, we will discuss them only rarely. However, in some cases, they are of significant importance, as is true in figure 4.1.

9. Later that day, the delegates rejected the proposal to elect the Senate by ballot in the first branch—a peculiarly eighteenth century idea that speaks to the difficulty of creating a second branch similar to the House of Lords in England (Wirls and Wirls 2004, discuss this problem in much greater detail).

10. For more on such beliefs, see McDonald (1985, 218–219) and Swift (1996, 33).

11. Note that we have identified this dimension with Vote 41, so it is fixed in the model. This does not affect the relative positioning of the votes, though it does prohibit the estimation of error around that vote.

12. This estimate was also fixed at 1.0 on the representation dimension for convenience of estimation.

13. Because this vote was procedural, it is not part of our dataset; however, we list it here for the sake of completeness and to note that such a course of action was a possibility.

14. There was one additional plan that could be listed here: Charles Pinckney's Plan. Introduced on the first day of real debate, this plan was apparently all but discarded by this point. Furthermore, it is virtually impossible to discuss given our research design. It was never voted on and never given any significant discussion time, despite what its author might have claimed or wished. While we cannot rule out here the possibility that it was indirectly influential, we have no way of proving that case either. Though Pinckney would later talk about how his plan had great influence, there was virtually no discussion of the plan after its introduction. At this stage of the game, it was clearly less relevant than even Hamilton's speech.

15. Though, we hasten to add that we are in no way claiming that Hamilton's plan was disingenuous, merely that it was convenient for his own views to be offered at this moment.

16. Perhaps one of the reasons Yates and Lansing left was that they saw how difficult it would be for their own positions to prevail at the Convention.

17. The reader can consult p. 233 of Farrand (1966, vol. I) to see the revised proposals.

18. However, we emphasize that this was nowhere near the position taken by the Small states in Vote 40, which is completely different from this position on Vote 87.

19. The Declaration was announced, but not signed, on July 4.

20. This vote is unrestricted in the model.

21. Specifically, the delegates were voting on the controversial second clause that had emerged from a serial committee process.
22. In fact, our model estimates that it was more positive (or in favor of reform) than the Virginia Plan, with a probability of 0.76.
23. The two votes are not meaningfully distinguished by the model, though this one is estimated to be slightly different.
24. Robertson (2013) strikingly describes this linking of the two compromises as a "subterfuge" (182).
25. The model estimates that Vote 252 is more positive than the status quo, with a probability of 0.97.
26. Madison omits this article from his notes, but it seems implied.

A *National* Government

1. Dickinson's position on who should wield national power would become clearer as the field shifted to a discussion of the executive, which we will take up in chapter 6.
2. See our earlier discussion of win-sets in chapter 3.
3. Farrand discusses the uncertainty and issues of recording votes. We direct the interested reader there, simply noting, again, that we follow the convention of Farrand's vote numbering.
4. Madison recorded that the predictable division was Hamilton, favoring the proposal, with Yates in opposition.
5. To identify the model, this vote was also fixed, so it lacks any estimation uncertainty.
6. Delaware was divided, illustrating how some small-state delegates were in some ways open to increased federal power—just not on proportional representation.
7. See, for instance, Vote 81 and Vote 83 (and the entire clause is ratified in Vote 87) where the delegates accepted General Pinckney's motion to make members of the first branch of the legislature eligible for offices "established by a particular state" (Farrand 1966, vol. I, 386). They were willing for states to exert influence, even if only indirectly.
8. It is worth noting that on the militias issue, they later reconsidered the question of national control over the militias when Sherman, in Vote 374, successfully amended the proposal to read that the executive shall have command "and of the Militia of the several States, *when called into the actual service of the U— S—*" (Farrand 1966, vol. II, 426, emphasis added). Constant control of the militias (effectively the military of the day) was too much for the delegates. They were more comfortable approving control under limited circumstances.
9. New Hampshire is only plausibly classified as a small state (though they fit the pattern here) because of their location and size. The delegation arrived so late (July 21) that they never participated in the arguments over representation.
10. Probably, since Jackson is far from clear.
11. We emphasize: this is not meant to be a separate dimension (there are not enough votes here to justify that). It is just that these are all of the key votes on ratification on the federalism dimension.

An Independent Executive?

1. It is worth commenting here that the judiciary, given the outline of the Constitution, does not really fit this description, despite the power that courts wield today. Judges were to be nominated by one branch (the president) and confirmed by part of another that was indirectly elected by state legislatures (the Senate), so there is no independent base of power for that branch—though there was a very long tenure of office, a practice that was less usual in the nineteenth century (Crowe and Karpowitz 2007).
2. Note that this quotation omits a large number of Madison's brackets to indicate the time of the note-taking and revising.
3. See the debates on June 2.
4. Because of the pivotal nature of this vote, it was set to 1 in the model as a reference.
5. New Hampshire, Massachusetts, and Delaware also voted aye.
6. Formidable is clearly one of Randolph's favorite descriptions.
7. North Carolina appears to have been absent, and there is a point of some confusion in the notes. Georgia was initially listed by Madison as voting "no" but was changed at a later date to having voted "aye." If Georgia had voted against the proposal, that would have killed it, and one cannot help but wonder if this vote was somewhat more controversial than the lack of debate suggests.
8. And leaves us somewhat sad that the vote did not include more discussion, given its evident importance.
9. But see also the rejoinder by Dougherty and Heckelman (2006).

Factional Design

1. This list of citations is representative but hardly exhaustive.
2. Though eventually the cause gets taken up by any state that wishes to do something novel and different like legalizing marijuana.
3. This is obviously not true for the third leg of reform: the presidency.
4. This holds constant the cramped franchise restrictions of the eighteenth century.
5. The presidency is a partial exception to this pattern in that there are moments where they dithered, but even on this dimension, Madison won early victories for reform and was, in the end, able to see a massive change. After all, he helped create a completely new branch of government.
6. For a comparison of the power of the two branches see Brams (1989).
7. Figure 3.4 displays their positions and denotes that they were broadly similar in their stances on executive independence at the Convention, though Madison is slightly more ambiguous in his support.
8. The probability that Hamilton was more extreme on the executive independence dimension is estimated to be 0.72.
9. Of course, recognizing that the design is not set in stone but has changed both formally and sometimes informally over time (Gienapp, 2018).

10. This also puts it beyond the analysis of the ideal point model used in this project.

11. However, we take Washington at his word that this was an important issue.

Supporting Appendix

1. In a modern legislature, such votes are typically called "roll calls" and are common for individual legislators, but in this context the only comparable event was the state voting.

2. See our discussion of win-sets on page 47.

References

Bailyn, Bernard. 1967. *The Ideological Origins of the American Revolution*. Cambridge, MA: Harvard University Press.

Banning, Lance. 1995. *The Sacred Fire of Liberty: James Madison and the Founding of the Federal Republic*. Ithaca, New York: Cornell University Press.

Beard, Charles A. 1913. *An Economic Interpretation of the Constitution of the United States*. New York: Macmillan.

Beck, Van. 1972. *Politics without Parties: Massachusetts 1780–1781*. Pittsburgh: University of Pittsburgh Press.

Beeman, Richard. 2010. *Plain, Honest Men: The Making of the American Constitution*. New York: Random House.

Bilder, Sarah. 2015. *Madison's Hand: Revising the Constitutional Convention*. Cambridge, MA: Harvard University Press.

Bolstad, William M. 2010. *Understanding Computational Bayesian Statistics*. West Sussex, UK: John Wiley & Sons.

Bowen, Catherine Drinker. 1966. *Miracle at Philadelphia: The Story of the Constitutional Convention May to September 1787*. New York: Back Bay Books.

Brams, Steven J. 1989. "Are the Two Houses of Congress Really Coequal?" In *The Federalist Papers and the New Institutionalism*, edited by Bernard Grofman and Donald Wittman, 125–41. New York: Agathon Press.

Broadwater, Jeff. 2006. *George Mason: Forgotten Founder*. Chapel Hill: University of North Carolina Press.

Carroll, Royce, Jeffrey B. Lewis, James Lo, Keith T. Poole, and Howard Rosenthal. 2009. "Comparing NOMINATE and IDEAL: Points of Difference and Monte Carlo Tests." Legislative Studies Quarterly 34(4): 555–91.

Clarkson, Paul S., and R. Samuel Jett. 1970. *Luther Martin of Maryland*. Baltimore: Johns Hopkins University Press.

Clinton, Joshua D., and Simon Jackman. 2009. "To Simulate or NOMINATE?" *Legislative Studies Quarterly* 34(4): 593–621.

Clinton, Joshua D., Simon Jackman, and Douglas Rivers. 2004. "The Statistical Analysis of Roll Call Data." *American Political Science Review* 98(2): 355–70.

Clinton, Joshua D., and Adam Meirowitz. 2001. "Agenda Constrained Legislator Ideal Points and the Spatial Voting Model." *Political Analysis* 9(3): 242–59.

Clinton, Joshua D., and Adam Meirowitz. 2004. "Testing Explanations of Strategic Voting in Legislatures : A Reexamination of the Compromise of 1790." *American Journal of Political Science* 48(4): 675–89.

Collier, James Lincoln, and Christopher Collier. 1986. *Decision in Philadelphia.* New York: Random House.

Coulter, E. Merton. 1987. *Abraham Baldwin: Patriot, Educator, and Founding Father.* Washington, DC: Vandamere Press.

Cox, Gary W., and Mathew McCubbins. 2004. *Setting the Agenda.* New York: Cambridge University Press.

Crowe, Justine, and Christopher F. Karpowitz. 2007. "Where Have You Gone, Sherman Minton? The Decline of the Short-Term Supreme Court Justice." *Perspectives on Politics* 5(3): 425–45.

Dougherty, Keith. 2001. *Collective Action under the Articles of Confederation.* Cambridge: Cambridge University Press.

Dougherty, Keith, and Jac Heckelman. 2006. "A Pivotal Voter from a Pivotal State: Roger Sherman at the Constitutional Convention." *American Political Science Review* 100(2): 297–302.

Dougherty, Keith, and Jac Heckelman. 2008. "Voting on Slavery at the Constitutional Convention." *Public Choice* 136: 293–313.

Elazar, Daniel. 1972. *American Federalism: A View from the States.* New York: Thomas Y. Crowell Press.

Everitt, Brian, Sabine Landau, Morven Leese, and Daniel Stahl. 2011. *Cluster Analysis.* 5th ed. West Sussex, UK: John Wiley and Sons.

Farrand, Max. 1913. *The Framing of the Constitution of the United States.* New Haven, CT: Yale University Press.

Farrand, Max. 1966. *The Records of the Federal Convention of 1787.* New Haven, CT: Yale University Press.

Garver, Frank Harmon. 1944. "The Constitutional Convention as a Deliberative Assembly." *The Pacific Historical Review* 13(4): 412–24.

Gibson, Alan. 2010. *Understanding the Founding: The Crucial Questions.* 2nd ed. Lawrence: University of Kansas Press.

Gienapp, Jonathan. 2018. *The Second Creation: Fixing the American Constitution in the Founding Era.* Cambridge, MA: Harvard University Press.

Hall, Van Beck. 1972. Politics without Parties : Massachusetts 1780–1781. Pittsburgh: University of Pittsburgh Press.

Heckelman, Jac C., and Keith L. Dougherty. 2011. "What Influenced Delegate Voting at the Constitutional Convention." *Working Paper.*

Heckelman, Jac C., and Keith L. Dougherty. 2013. "A Spatial analysis of Delegate Voting at the Constitutional *Convention." Journal of Economic History* 73(2): 407–44.

Holton, Woody. 2007. *Unruly Americans and the Origins of the Constitution.* New York: Farrar, Strauss and Giroux.

Howell, William G. 2003. *Power Without Persuasion : The Politics of Direct Presidential Action.* Princeton, NJ: Princeton University Press.

Howell, William G., and Terry M. Moe. 2016. *Relic : How Our Constitution Undermines Effective Government—and Why We Need a More Powerful Presidency.* New York: Basic Books.

Hutson, James H. 1987. *Supplement to Max Farrand's The Records of the Federal Convention of 1787*. New Haven, CT: Yale University Press.

Jackman, Simon. 2009. *Bayesian Analysis for the Social Sciences*. West Sussex, UK: John Wiley & Sons.

Jensen, Merrill, and John Kaminski, eds. 1976. *The Documentary History of the Ratification of the Constitution*. Madison: University of Wisconsin Press.

Jillson, Calvin C. 1988. *Constitution Making: Conflict and Consensus in the Federal Convention of 1787*. New York: Agathon Press.

Jillson, Calvin C., and Rick K. Wilson. 1994. *Congressional Dynamics: Structure, Coordination, and Choice in the First American Congress, 1774–1789*. Palo Alto, CA: Stanford University Press.

Knott, Stephen F. 2002. *Alexander Hamilton & The Persistence of Myth*. Lawrence: University Press of Kansas.

Larson, Edward J., and Michael Winship. 2005. *The Constitutional Convention: A Narrative History from the Notes of James Madison*. New York: The Modern Library.

Londregan, John. 1999a. "Deliberation and Voting at the Federal Convention of 1787.".

Lunn, David J., Andrew Thomas, Nicky Best, and David Spiegelhalter. 2000. "WinBUGS – A Bayesian Modelling Framework: Concepts, Structure, and Extensibility." *Statistics and Computing* 10: 325–37.

Lynd, Staughton. 1962. *Anti-Federalism in Duchess County, New York: A Study of Democracy and Class Conflict in the Revolutionary Era*. Chicago: Loyola University Press.

Lynd, Staughton. 1966. "The Compromise of 1787." *Political Science Quarterly* 81(2): 225–50.

Maier, Pauline. 2010. *Ratification: The People Debate the Constitution, 1787–1788*. New York: Simon and Schuster.

Main, Jackson Turner. 1961. *The Antifederalists: Critics of the Constitution, 1781–1788*. Chapel Hill: University of North Carolina.

Main, Jackson Turner. 1965. *The Social Structure of Revolutionary America*. Princeton, NJ: Princeton University Press.

Martin, Andrew D., and Kevin M. Quinn. 2002. "Dynamic Ideal Point Estimation via Markov Chain Monte Carlo for the U.S. Supreme Court, 1953–1999." 10(2): 134–53.

Mason, George. 1787. *Objections to this Constitution of Government*. https://www.archives.gov/files/legislative/resources/education/bill-of-rights/images/mason.pdf.

Matson, Cathy D., and Peter S. Onuf. 1990. *A Union of Interests: Political and Economic Thought in Revolutionary America*. Lawrence: University Press of Kansas.

McDonald, Forrest. 1958. *We the People*. Chicago: University of Chicago Press.

McDonald, Forrest. 1965. *E Pluribus Unum: The Formation of the American Republic, 1776–1790*. New York: Houghton Mifflin.

McDonald, Forrest. 1985. *Novus Ordo Seclorum: The Intellectual Origins of the Constitution*. Lawrence: University of Kansas Press.

McGuire, Robert A. 2003. *To Form a More Perfect Union: A New Economic Interpretation of the United States Constitution*. New York: Oxford University Press.

Morton, Joseph C. 2006. *Shapers of the Great Debate at the Constitutional Convention of 1787: A Biographical Dictionary*. Westport, CT: Greenwood Press.

Neustadt, Richard E. 1960. *Presidential Power and the Modern Presidents: The Politics of Leadership*. New York: Free Press.

Nevins, Allan, ed. 1951. *The Diary of John Quincy Adams, 1794–1845*. New York: Charles Scribner's Sons.

Ohline, Howard A. 1971. "Republicanism and Slavery: Origins of the Three-Fifths Clause in the United States Constitution." *The William and Mary Quarterly* 28(4): 563–84.

Peters, William. 1987. *A More Perfect Union*. New York: Crown Publishers.

Pocock, J.G.A. 1975. *The Machiavellian Moment: Florentine Political Thought and the Atlantic Republican Tradition*. Princeton, NJ: Princeton University Press.

Poole, Keith T. 2005. *Spatial Models of Parliamentary Voting*. New York: Cambridge University Press.

Pope, Jeremy C., and Shawn A. Treier. 2011. "Reconsidering the Great Compromise at the Federal Convention of 1787: Deliberation and Agenda Effects on the Senate and Slavery." *The American Journal of Political Science* 55(2): 289–306.

Pope, Jeremy C., and Shawn A. Treier. 2012. "Mapping Dimensions of Conflict at the Federal Convention of 1787." *Legislative Studies Quarterly* 37: 145–74.

Pope, Jeremy C., and Shawn A. Treier. 2015. "Voting for a Founding: Testing the Effect of Economic Interests at the Federal Convention of 1787." *The Journal of Politics* 2(April): 519–34. doi: 10.1086/680208

Rakove, Jack N. 1996. *Original Meanings: Politics and Ideas in the Making of the Constitution*. New York: Random House.

Rakove, Jack N. 1999. *Madison : Writings*. Boone, IA: The Library of America.

Rakove, Jack N. 2010. *Revolutionaries: A New History of the Invention of America*. New York: Mariner Books.

Reardon, John J. 1974. *Edmund Randolph: A Biography*. New York: MacMillan Publishing.

Riker, William H. 1986. *The Art of Political Manipulation*. New Haven, CT: Yale University Press.

Rivers, Douglas. 2003. "Identification of Multidimensional Spatial Voting Models." Unpublished Manuscript.

Robertson, David Brian. 2005. "Madison's Opponents and Constitutional Design." *American Political Science Review* 99(2): 225–43.

Robertson, David Brian. 2013. *The Original Compromise: What the Constitution's Framers Were Really Thinking*. New York: Oxford University Press.

Roche, John 1961. "The Founding Fathers: A Reform Caucus in Action." *The American Political Science Review* 55(4): 799–816.

Rossiter, Clinton. 1966. *The Grand Convention*. New York: New American Library.

Sanders, Mitchell S. 1998. "Unified Models of Turnout and Vote Choice for Two-Candidate and Three-Candidate Elections." *Political Analysis* 7: 89–115.

Sanders, Mitchell S. 2001. "Uncertainty and Turnout." *Political Analysis* 9(1): 45–57.

Sheehan, Colleen A. 2004. "Madison v. Hamilton: The Battle over Republicanism and the Role of Public Opinion." *The American Political Science Review* 98(3): 405–24.

Skowronek, Stephen. 1997. *The Politics Presidents Make: Leadership from John Adams to Bill Clinton*. Cambridge, MA: Belknap Press.

Slez, Adam, and John Levi Martin. 2007. "Political Action and Party Formation in the United States Constitutional Convention." *American Sociological Review* 72(February):42–67.

Smith, Charles Page. 1956. *James Wilson: Founding Father, 1742–1798*. Chapel Hill: University of North Carolina Press.

Steiner, Bernard C. 1907. *The Life and Correspondence of James McHenry: Secretary of War Under Washington and Adams*. Cleveland: The Burrows Brothers Company.

Storing, Herbert J., ed. 1981. The Complete Anti-Federalist. 7 vols. Chicago: University of Chicago Press.

Swift, Elaine K. 1996. *The Making of an American Senate: Reconstructive Change in Congress, 1787–1841*. Ann Arbor, MI: University of Michigan Press.

Treier, Shawn. 2020. Bayesian Ideal Point Estimation. In *The SAGE Handbook of Research Methods in Political Science and International Relations*, vol. 1, edited by Luigi Curini and Robert Franzese, ch. 48, 910–27. Thousand Oaks, CA: SAGE Publications Inc.

Ulmer, Sidney. 1966. "Sub-Group Formation in the Constitutional Convention." *Midwest Journal of Political Science* 10(3): 288–303.

Van Doren, Carl. 1948. *The Great Rehearsal: The Story of the Making and Ratifying of the Constitution of the United States*. London: Penguin Books.

Waldstreicher, David. 2009. *Slavery's Constitution: From Revolution to Ratification*. New York: Hill and Wang Press.

Washington, George. 1787. "Letter from George Washington to Marie Joseph Paul Yves Roch Gilbert du Motier, Marquis de Lafayette." https://founders.archives.gov/documents/Washington/99-01-02-05092.

West, Thomas. 2001. *Vindicating the Founders: Race, Sex, Class, and Justice in the Origins of America*. New York: Rowman and Littlefield Publishers.

Wirls, Daniel, and Stephen Wirls. 2004. *The Invention of the United States Senate*. Baltimore: Johns Hopkins University Press.

Wood, Gordon S. 1969. *The Creation of the American Republic, 1776–1787*. New York: W.W. Norton.

Index

Printed and bound by CPI Group (UK) Ltd, Croydon, CR0 4YY
16/09/2026
14963491-0004